Warfare and Agriculture in Classical Greece

ALSO BY VICTOR DAVIS HANSON

The Western Way of War: Infantry Battle in Classical Greece (1989)

Hoplites: The Ancient Greek Battle Experience (editor, 1991)

The Other Greeks: The Agrarian Roots of Western Civilization (1995)

Fields Without Dreams: Defending the Agrarian Idea (1996)

Who Killed Homer? The Decline of Classical Education and the Recovery of Greek Wisdom (with John Heath, 1998)

Warfare and Agriculture in Classical Greece

Victor Davis Hanson

UNIVERSITY OF CALIFORNIA PRESS

Berkeley   Los Angeles   London

University of California Press
Berkeley and Los Angeles, California

University of California Press, Ltd.
London, England

© 1998 by
The Regents of the University of California

Library of Congress Cataloging-in-Publication Data

Hanson, Victor Davis.
    Warfare and agriculture in classical Greece / Victor
Hanson Davis.—[Rev. ed.]

        p.   cm.—(Biblioteca di studi antichi ; 40)
    Includes bibliographical references (p.   ) and index.
    ISBN 0-520-21025-5 (cloth : alk. paper).—
    ISBN 0-520-21596-6 (pbk. : alk. paper)
    1. Agriculture—Defense measures—Greece—History.
2. War damage, Industrial—Greece—History.   3. Attikē
(Greece)—History.   4. Greece—History—Peloponnesian
War, 431–404 B.C.   I. Title.   II. Series.
UA929.95.A35H27   1999
338.1′4—dc21
                                         97-52207
                                            CIP

Printed in the United States of America

9 8 7 6 5 4 3 2 1

This book is printed on acid-free paper.

To the Memory of
Rees Davis and Frank Hanson

CONTENTS

Preface to the Second Edition

ix

Preface to the First Edition

xvii

Introduction

1

PART ONE: THE ATTACK ON AGRICULTURE

17

1. Military Organization

19

2. The Methods of Agricultural Destruction

42

PART TWO: THE DEFENSE OF AGRICULTURE

77

3. Fortification

79

4. Evacuation
103

5. Sorties
122

PART THREE: THE EFFECTIVENESS
OF AGRICULTURAL DEVASTATION
129

6. The Devastation of Attica
during the Peloponnesian War
131

Conclusion
174

Appendix: The Vocabulary of Agricultural Devastation
185

Select Bibliography
195

Updated Commentary and Bibliography
201

General Index
253

Index Locorum
269

PREFACE TO THE SECOND EDITION

Warfare and Agriculture in Classical Greece was first published in 1983 in the monograph series *Biblioteca di Studi Antichi* (edited by Graziano Arrighetti and Emilio Gabba, with Franco Montanari, and published by Giardini of Pisa, Italy). The book was, for the most part, favorably reviewed, occasionally cited, and went quickly out of print. At the time of its publication, I was a full-time viticulturist with no plans either to reenter academic life or to pursue serious research about the ancient Greek world again. Except when the occasional letter of encouragement from a classical scholar arrived, I too forgot about this thesis and went on with the business of trying to preserve our small family tree- and vine-farm during the agricultural recessions of the 1980s. I recalled that a fellow graduate student at Stanford University had remarked to me in January 1980, when I was finishing my dissertation, that few scholars had any interest in ancient warfare, much less Greek farming. Worried over that dual warning, I learned from an informal look at library card catalogues of published works in classics that no English-language book or monograph about the ancient Greek world had appeared with the word "agriculture" in its title or subtitle in the sixty years since W. E. Heitland's engaging study *Agricola: A Study of Agriculture and Rustic Life in the Greco-Roman World from the Point of View of Labor* (Cambridge,

1921). So I was not surprised that by 1985 *Warfare and Agriculture* was found only in a few libraries and was little known; indeed I had long ago given away all but one of my complimentary books to scholars kind enough to write me on the farm expressing interest in finding a copy.

Little did I know that as I was farming in Selma, California, in the early and mid-1980s classical scholars were well in the process of reinventing the entire field of ancient Greek warfare and agriculture. Ongoing field surveys of the Greek countryside were exploring ancient population densities, settlement patterns, and the interplay between habitation and climatic and soil conditions. The completion of the *Thesaurus Linguae Graecae* made possible a comprehensive rather than haphazard study of the ancient Greek vocabulary of farming and fighting. Further excavations of farmhouses in southern Attica, the Crimea, and Italy were coming to light. In England, gifted Cambridge students of Anthony Snodgrass and M. I. Finley were applying various interdisciplinary approaches to ancient agrarianism, often employing theoretical models from the social sciences to reconstruct past agrarian economies and ideologies.

By the late 1980s and early 1990s first-generation summaries of these specialized philological, archaeological, and historical studies were beginning to appear, including M.-C. Amouretti's *Le pain et l'huile dans la Grèce* (Besançon, 1986), Robin Osborne's *Classical Landscapes with Figures* (London, 1987), T. W. Gallant's *Risk and Survival: Reconstructing the Rural Domestic Economy* (Stanford, 1991), Robert Sallares's *The Ecology of the Ancient Greek World* (Ithaca, N.Y., 1991), B. Wells's (ed.) *Agriculture in Ancient Greece* (Stockholm, 1992), A. Burford's *Land and Labor in Ancient Greece* (Baltimore, 1993), and S. Isager and J. E. Skydsgaard's *Ancient Greek Agriculture: An Introduction* (London, 1993). I have had the privilege to review in print all but one of the above books; they are uniformly excellent, and many of their ideas have saved me from more errors and misconceptions than I can recount.

At the same time, largely due to the selfless, two-decade effort of W. K. Pritchett (*The Greek State at War*, 5 vols. [Berkeley, 1971–1991]), the study of Greek warfare was turning from its traditional emphasis on strategy, tactics, logistics, and recruitment to include comprehensive study of economy and social policy. The work of Y. Garlan (*Guerre et économie en Gréce ancienne* [Paris, 1989]), P. Ducrey (*Warfare in Ancient Greece* [New York, 1989]), and J. Rich and G. Shipley (editors of *War and Society in the Greek World* [London, 1993]) ensured that we saw hoplites as citizens of the polis—for so long mostly farmers who represented the property-owning infantry class—and not merely anonymous warriors of the phalanx.

Warfare and agriculture have become fertile areas of contemporary research in ancient Greek history, topics at the heart of the discovery of the true nature of the Greek polis. Consequently, reissue of an updated, accessible, and corrected edition of *Warfare and Agriculture* perhaps makes even more sense now than its original publication did sixteen years ago.

In the present book, I have made some changes from the edition of 1983—corrections of misprints and errors of fact; clarification of arguments; reformation of the entire text; relegation of some material to an appendix; reduction in the amount of quoted Greek and avoidance altogether of Greek script—all in the interest of providing wider accessibility to readers outside the world of classical scholarship. In a few places in the original text and in the updated commentary, I have also inserted the results of some more recent firsthand experience with crop devastation. In the years since I wrote my doctoral dissertation, I returned to farm trees and vines in central California and was sometimes curious whether orchard and vineyard destruction was as difficult as it had once seemed to me in our ancient sources. Thus on numerous occasions I took lengthy notes when it was time to uproot, dig out, burn, or cut down various fruit trees and vines on the farm in the hope of someday revising the first edition; at various places in the updated commentary of the present edition, I have drawn on those observations.

The rather lengthy endnotes that make up the updated commentary and bibliography serve as a running critique of secondary work appearing after 1981, when I submitted the manuscript for publication; I also include in the new commentary a few key primary sources not mentioned in the first edition, which came to my attention after running systematic word searches of the *Thesaurus Linguae Graecae* for some of the vocabulary listed in the appendix. I have preferred to leave mostly intact the original footnotes, with their references to the bibliography in the first edition. References to new literature can be found in the endnotes. A new index and concordance of quoted primary sources reflect these additions. Otherwise the original text, footnotes, and bibliography of *Warfare and Agriculture in Classical Greece* remain more or less as they were in 1983. I know of no major argument of the original edition that now seems incorrect or deserving of retraction. In cases where there has been scholarly discussion of or disagreements about the findings of the original thesis, I provide page references for both the 1983 monograph and the present edition.

I saw no reason to rewrite the entire book. Although I have changed some ideas about ancient warfare and agriculture since I first submitted this study as a doctoral dissertation—I was twenty-six when I finished the manuscript—its main thesis that agricultural devastation during the classical age of ancient Greece was more a tactic designed to instigate decisive infantry battle than a comprehensive mechanism for economic warfare remains sensible—even more so its corollary that *permanent* and *systematic* agricultural damage and subsequent economic collapse were difficult to achieve under the conditions of ancient warfare. And I think scholars would also now agree that the agriculture of Attica was *not* permanently destroyed by the Spartans during the Peloponnesian War— much less that such attacks explain the fourth-century "decline" of Athenian power, both material and spiritual. The Peloponnesian War was a watershed, and it caused suffering and turmoil throughout the Greek world, but the destruction of orchards, vineyards, and rural infrastructure was *not* at the heart of the catastrophe. If there was an economic collapse of the countryside in Attica and elsewhere, it occurred at least a century or more *after* the Peloponnesian War and was largely the result of taxation, changing military practice, and the erosion of the agrarian councils that had once set an agricultural, military, and political agenda that favored the middling hoplite.

It is true, of course, that as the hoplite ideal waned in the fifth and fourth centuries B.C., warfare increasingly shifted to other areas—rural skirmishing, urban fighting, sieges, ambushes, raids, and plundering expeditions. With professional and lighter-armed troops, attacks on agriculture may have increased and may have been more prolonged as ravaging became more consciously a method of economic aggression, rather than a catalyst for shock battle between agrarian heavy infantry. Still, the nature of olive trees and vines did not change; it remained an immutable fact that their permanent and widespread destruction was difficult in any age of hand-held tools, when armies were not large, logistics were unreliable, and transportation difficult. The inherent problems in destroying agrarian infrastructure were universal challenges of time, space, and technology, and not merely tied to the quasi-ritualistic nature of hoplite battle of the classical age, when the majority of the combatants were heavily armed farmers, more eager to solve their disputes decisively on the battlefield than to raid and skirmish amid the croplands of their adversaries. The flurry of publication on ancient farming and fighting in the late 1980s and the 1990s—some of it pertaining to Hellenistic and Roman events—has, I think, corroborated rather than rejected these points—so much so that the original thesis of *Warfare and Agriculture* may now appear more commonplace than novel.

Again, what catastrophes that did occur in the ancient countryside during wartime—and there were many—were the result of displaced populations, labor power losses, sieges, the unsettled conditions caused by brigandry and robber gangs, plagues, the desertion of slaves and hired hands, the loss of livestock and equipment, and the more enervating property and income taxes levied to pay for near permanent periods of hostilities. Other assumptions in the first edition—the need to distinguish plundering from ravaging in our ancient sources, the presumption of homestead and nucleated farms lived in and worked by middling hoplite farmers, the physical difficulty of covering ancient farmland, the effectiveness of cavalry sorties against ravagers, the ingenuity of evacuation measures, the failure of field walls to protect agriculture, and the haphazard record of rural fortifications serving as absolute lines of defense—seem corroborated by the later and often more thorough investigations by others.

In a subsequent, much longer book, *The Other Greeks: The Agrarian Roots of Western Civilization*, which had its genesis in the present study, I systematically explored the relationship between ancient Greek farming and fighting beyond the actual battle practice of destroying vines, trees, and cereals. If the two main arguments of *The Other Greeks* are correct—that an agrarian renaissance explains the rise of the Greek city-state, and that an ongoing agrarianism accounts for the peculiar military, economic, and political institutions of the polis between 700 and 400 B.C.—then I see no reason to reexamine those issues here.

I have many scholars to thank for the appearance of this revised edition. Article-length reviews of *Warfare and Agriculture* by Paul Harvey ("New Harvests Reappear: The Impact of War on Agriculture," *Athenaeum* 74 [1986]: 205–218) and Josiah Ober (*Helios* 12.2 [1985]: 91–101) taught me a great deal, and many of their points are now incorporated in the additions and revisions of the present edition. At the time of his review Paul Harvey also sent me an extensive list of errata that thirteen years later have proved invaluable. David Whitehead wrote a sympathetic analysis of the book in *Classical Review* (Fall 1985), which in many ways gave me the confidence to try to return to academic life after a hiatus in farming of many years. I have never met Professor Whitehead, but I owe him a debt of gratitude.

Readers for the University of California Press, David Tandy and Colin Duncan, sent along candid reports that contained a great deal of wise advice. The idea for an updated and improved edition of *Warfare and Agriculture* for a wider audience came from Mary Lamprech, Classics Editor at the University of California Press; I hope the present edition is not a disappointment to her. John Keegan has had a keen interest in agricultural devastation and in print and in private correspondence has encouraged me a great deal. Donald Kagan's advice and friendship have been invaluable, especially his generosity and sympathy with anyone investigating the practical realities of Greek history. My colleague in classics at California State University, Fresno, Bruce Thornton, kindly read this edition, and I have benefited from his suggestions and corrections. A stipend from the School of Arts and Humanities at CSU Fresno allowed Cheryln Crill and Katherine A. Becker to scan and computerize the original monograph and to assist in proofreading.

I learned a great deal about agriculture from my grandfathers, farmers both, Rees Davis and Frank Hanson, who lectured me about vines, trees, and the horrors of war as well. I hope this edition in some small way is thanks for all that they taught me.

Selma, California
September 1997

PREFACE TO THE FIRST EDITION

This study is virtually unchanged from the Ph.D. thesis I submitted to the Stanford Classics Department in June 1980. I have had some practical experience in agriculture from farming grapes and fruit trees on a family farm near Fresno, California. Professor Michael Jameson, my thesis advisor at Stanford, suggested I combine that knowledge together with my professional interest in Greek military history to study the strategy of crop devastation in classical Greece. My thanks go to him and to Professor Emilio Gabba who both made publication of this volume possible. Stanford University provided a generous fellowship that enabled me to study at the American School of Classical Studies, Athens, for the year 1978–1979 and once again helped with a timely publication grant from the Dougherty Fund of the Classics Department. Professors Mark Edwards and Ned Spofford of Stanford, Colin Edmondson, Eugene Vanderpool, and Charles Williams of the American School, John Lynch of Santa Cruz, and Leslie Threatte of Berkeley all offered their encouragement and help. My greatest thanks go to my colleague at Stanford, Dr. Lawrence Woodlock, and to my wife, Cara. Their critical insight and good sense greatly improved the manuscript.

I have tried to transliterate both personal and place-names directly from the Greek (e.g., Archidamos, Boiotia, Dekeleia); somewhat haphazardly, I have maintained more familiar English forms (e.g., Alcibiades, Corinth, Corcyra, Socrates). All Greek and Latin authors are cited in the abbreviated forms found in the *Oxford Classical Dictionary*, 2d. ed. (Oxford, 1970). The same holds true for books, journals, and periodicals on classical subjects. Secondary works frequently cited in the notes (and occasionally in the text) appear with the author's name only; a full listing of these can be found in the bibliography. I have translated most quoted Greek and Latin sources. Where the exact wording of the Greek or Latin seemed relevant, I have inserted it as well.

Selma, California
March 1981

Introduction

Armies need food. Any society that mobilizes troops must plan both to feed its own men and to seek to deny supplies to the enemy. In a preindustrial society, in which the vast majority of the population was engaged in agriculture, and armies were thus composed largely of rural folk, comprehension of the relationship of agriculture to warfare is fundamental to an understanding of the culture. All histories of Greece, it seems to me, must consider these salient facts: most Hellenes were farmers, war was endemic, and the energies of the citizens were largely consumed with either working, protecting, or attacking cropland. Nearly every major Greek author, philosopher, and statesman, despite his education and often elite status, either had a farm or served in battle: Hesiod, Archilochus, Tyrtaeus, Aeschylus, Aristides, Sophocles, Pericles, Socrates, Thucydides, Xenophon, Demosthenes, and others too numerous to mention at some time drove an ox or wore a breastplate. Most citizens of the ancient Greek polis, with whom we think to have an affinity through studying a red-figure vase, reading Euripides, or gazing at the Parthenon, spent much of their lives on tiny farms, rising at dawn, retiring at dusk, their sense of time and space confined to the changing of the seasons and the parameters of the small enclaves where they were born, lived, died, and were buried. War was physical drudgery interspersed with moments of sheer mayhem and terror, as victory required the use of edged weapons thrust by hand and with difficulty into the flesh of the enemy. The victors were probably as covered with blood as the corpses of the enemy—gore that they were accustomed to from the near constant butchery of their own pigs, sheep, goats, and cattle.

Farming was not pretty nor easy, but mostly a boring, filthy, and physically exhausting contest to eat one more day. A Greek who joined an expedition of invasion painstakingly packed his own food, which he had grown himself, took along equipment that was nearly half his body weight, and walked for hours in summertime heat, often uphill and on rocky paths—only to camp out in strange lands, where he was asked to forage for auxiliary provisions and water, to cut down trees and vines, all in anticipation of running into the spears of his adversaries and then somehow getting back to his land in one piece until the next muster. A minor puncture wound often meant a slow, solitary, and painful death, a broken leg or arm a lifetime of disability where all future encounters with the plow, ox, or spade spelled constant pain. Military navigation and information were problematic ideas in a world without compasses, good maps, binoculars, or even eyeglasses. For the farmer on the march, food tended to rot quickly, stream or pond water could make one sick, and cuts and abrasions might lead to lethal infections.

It is all too easy for us today to forget these material conditions of the past and thus the critical role of warfare and agriculture in antiquity. Few citizens of the United States have served in an army; almost none— thank God—have killed someone in battle or destroyed the property of an enemy. Our efforts at protection are limited to bars on our windows, electronic alarms, blinking lights, and automatic locks; we are not dependent on armor and weapons over the hearth and the muscular condition of our right arms. Nighttime without streetlights, police cruisers, or a powerful flashlight is full of foreboding and terror—as the panic that follows the occasional urban blackout attests. Only about 1 percent of our population now lives on farms; most of us have no idea how to grow food, build our own house, hitch up a horse, or butcher a pig. An outbreak of food poisoning at the local fast-food franchise causes national scandal. We rarely walk more than a few hundred yards a day. The majority of Americans live in temperature-controlled rooms and approach hysteria when the electricity that powers our ranges, air conditioners, televisions, and washers ceases for a few hours. The lack of running water or phones for more than a day is the stuff of lawsuits against our municipal utilities. Our knowledge of dirty work, physical violence, and the savagery of the natural landscape itself is mostly limited to what we see on television or read in newspapers, magazines, and books; those with muscular physiques owe their impressive anatomy to weight machines, high-tech sneakers, and entertaining videos. And they win such contours without the tears, wounds, scratches, and blisters that routinely accompany the physical effort to plant, prune, harvest, and plow. Instead, we work out in sanitary and often inviting gyms, where cool air, piped-in music, scented towels, and hot showers are prerequisites. The color of our complexion and the smoothness of our skin are integral to this look of fitness, not calluses and disfiguring scars, which for thousands of years were the natural wages of a hard stomach and ample biceps.

How difficult it is, then, to remember that the Greeks not only did things that we would not, but also things that we could not do. How important it is as well to keep in mind that dramatic performances, democracy itself, vase painting, Ionic columns, and bronze statues were the veneer of a culture that at its heart was in an endless war to feed and protect itself from the savageries of humans and nature. In short, we especially of the deskbound academic class who write our histories must remember that the Athenians, the Thebans, and the Argives lived lives centered around farming and fighting, lives so foreign from our own as now to be almost unimaginable.

We historians have a responsibility to go farther still: when we are told "they fought" or "they devastated the land," we must think first not of tactics or strategy, or even of economic loss or gain, but rather—as the ancient authors who wrote such histories surely took for granted—of the physical environment in which such work took place, the dirt and the danger that faced such men, the impediments of time and space to cutting, burning, and trampling, and the mentality of the farmers and the fighters, who had no doubts why such growing or destroying was so important to their survival. If we can envision that ordeal, then we can understand why an exhausted, dirty, and often terrified man thought it necessary to hack at a gnarly, towering olive tree; and we will come to imagine in the heat, with a crude ax, and among the enemy, just how difficult it was for him to cut such a tree down. And from that most basic appreciation of humankind and nature, we will forever gain a reverence for the past, a reminder to be very careful when we seek some grand theory of economic upheaval, some ingenious notion of national tragedy, or some neat model of decline in a world that is not our own. (See updated commentary, page 201 [General Considerations].)

Ravaging of cropland was central to warfare of most societies of the past. "Miserable Asiatic," wrote the Egyptian pharaoh Kamose of his conquests over the Hyksos, "I shall drink the wine of your vineyard. . . . I shall destroy your dwelling place and cut down your trees."[1] Eight hundred years later the Assyrian king Sargon likewise boasted of the destruction his troops had wrought:

> My fierce warriors rushed, and like Adad, they made the noise of
> iron axes to resound and great quantities of his fruit, which could
> not be measured, came tumbling down. . . . His great trees, the

---

1. The quote is from a stele of victory at Karnak (sixteenth century B.C.). See J. B. Pritchard, *The Ancient Near East: Supplementary Texts and Pictures* (Princeton, 1969), 554.

adornment of his palace, I cut down like millet, and I destroyed
the city of glory, and his province I brought to shame. The trunks
of all those trees which I had cut down I gathered together,
heaped them in a pile and burned them with fire. Their abundant
crops, which in garden and marsh were immeasurable, I tore up
by the root and did not leave an ear by which to remember the
destruction.[2]

The strategy of ravaging cropland in wartime did not originate with
the Greeks; it is as old as civilization, whose very armies arose as a divi-
dend of systematic and permanent farming. Today, nearly 3,500 years
after the victory of Kamose, the methods of destruction have improved
with the use of high explosives and herbicides, but agricultural devastation remains an integral part of fighting. As long as people need to eat,
and wars extend beyond the battlefield itself, generals and military plan-
ners will worry over how to protect and attack cropland. For example,
in the past half-century we have witnessed the continual devastation of
the rice fields of Korea, Vietnam and Cambodia by bomb, spray, and
fire by successive foreign and native armies. Yet, in the long history of
conflict, at no time did the ravaging of enemy farmland so dominate
warfare—culturally, spiritually, and psychologically—as during infantry
battle of the classical Greek city-state. (See updated commentary, page
202 [Protocols of Hoplite Warfare].)

For nearly 300 years war in Greece was inaugurated and often defined by a struggle to destroy, or protect, grain, vines, and olive trees.[3]

2. The text is part of a letter to Assur, "Father of the Gods," dated ca. 714 B.C.
See D. Luckenbill, *Ancient Records of Assyria and Babylonia* (New York, 1926), 2:
87–88, no. 161. For other early examples of devastation, see Judges 15:4–5 and
Harmand 1973, 16–19.

3. Cf. M. N. Tod, *Greek Historical Inscriptions* (London, 1948), 2: 303–306,
where in the ephebic oath of the fourth century B.C. the borders of the father-
land are equated with "wheat, barley, vines, olive trees, and fig trees." Cf. also a
distorted version in Plut. *Alc.* 15.7.

Even though most conflict originated over borderlands on rugged ground, armies of invasion usually entered the level ground of their enemy and either threatened, or began, to ravage their enemy's cropland. To save their farms, the agrarian defenders felt they were obliged either to capitulate and thereby submit to terms or to engage in pitched battle to drive the invader away. Why this strategy of crop devastation was able to determine the very nature of early Greek warfare has been the subject of considerable discussion.[4] The answer seems to lie in a combination of topographical, economic, social, and cultural factors unique to the particular practice of farming and land tenure found in classical Greece.

Farming was practiced, as it is today, in small, isolated plains and valleys, which extend no great distance before merging into rough terrain and mountains. The livelihood of most of the small, independent Greek city-states depended almost entirely on the harvests their yeomen farmers could produce from these holdings. Because with few exceptions (e.g., Athens, Syracuse, and Corinth), most states before the mid-fifth century B.C. had little opportunity or need for extensive commerce, and no great investments in manufacturing or industry, these food-producing plains were of vital importance. They became the natural focus of conflict among rival communities of landowning citizen-hoplites, who as voters and lawmakers determined the circumstances, the very time and the space, in which they would fight. (See updated commentary, page 205 [Centrality of Small Landowners].)

4. The three best treatments of the role of crop devastation in Greek warfare are Grundy 1948, 83–90; Gomme 1: 10–15; and Anderson 1970, 1–12. To these should be added Garlan 1974, 1–86, which contains a massive amount of evidence tracing the development of this strategy through the fourth century B.C. Garlan's too often underappreciated book forms the basis for all discussion of defense and cultural change in fourth-century Greece and has rarely been acknowledged as the storehouse of information it is.

The best way both to attack and to defend this level ground was with heavy infantry, soldiers armed with spear and shield, and well protected from head to foot with bronze armor. In the close formation of the phalanx, the success or failure of such a small army depended on forcing the opposing phalanx off the plain of battle, so that the respective troops could either devastate or continue to farm the land in question. But why, we might ask, did this closed, uniform manner of battle with agriculture at its center remain static and endure unchanged for so long in Greece?

Well-organized, if not mercenary, light-armed troops might have stopped hoplites at mountain passes on their initial descent into the plains. But such corps required greater training, specialized armament— usually mastery of the bow, javelin, or sling—and often permanent leadership and had to be deployed and supplied for long periods of time on the border. To the hoplite in the classical period, who farmed his small plot of ground and left only for the brief campaigning season, such a specialized force smelled of professionalism, involved burdening costs, and eventually might mean the end of his most important and exclusive obligation as defender of his city. And could light-armed men such as these fight face-to-face, and so shatter an army of invasion in an afternoon? In short, Greek warfare could be decisive, instantaneous, both frequent and yet relatively nonlethal within a conservative farming community only to the degree that it remained the sole domain of heavily armored, agrarian militias.

Second, the independent use of cavalry, which might have expanded the theater of war, since either mounted shock troops could break up marching columns or lighter-armed horsemen could force vulnerable and isolated hoplites off the plains, never became widespread in the classical age. The lack of stirrups and good saddles made head-on charges against spearmen difficult, while poor breeding and the lack of plentiful pasturage limited the use of horses in general in many areas of Greece. The neglect of an efficient cavalry arm was later to plague the Greeks of the city-state whenever they ventured abroad, far from the physical and ideological safety net of hoplite protocol. The horse, in short, was seen by the antiaristocratic yeoman as an uneconomical resource in the culture of intensive agriculture, and thus its usual military impotence against heavy infantry simply reflected the general diminution of the cavalryman in the cultural psyche of the polis itself.

Finally, effective siegecraft, which might have turned the center of battle away from the fields to assaults on the city itself, was still in its infancy in Greece until well into the fourth century B.C. In most cases property and people were quite safe behind mud-brick or stone walls, which were stout enough to withstand crude battering-rams and ineffective hand-propelled missiles. Furthermore, the heroic code of the citizen-soldier often made the idea of shunning decisive battle repugnant, and the policy of diverting capital and labor to fortify cities and passes with massive stone walls seemed ominous to the agrarian exclusivity of the tightfisted landowning council. Wall building and fortification in the countryside of Greece—and the arts to batter down such ramparts—are, rather, phenomena of the fourth century B.C., coinciding with the gradual diminution of the citizen as farmer-hoplite, as money, not nerve and muscle, came to determine the course of a war.

This, then, in the briefest terms, is the most common explanation for the peculiarly influential role of devastation in Greek warfare: in a world of intensive farming, where free citizens were defined by their possession of small plots of trees, vines, and cereals, those who voted as equals, held roughly the same amounts of land, and were armed and mustered identically naturally fought on, for, and about their farmland. Thus the enemies of such a system were professional troops, long campaigning, sophisticated technology, and specialized corps—anything that required capital and hence taxation to be drawn away from agriculture. Early hoplites were aware of the advantages of both cavalry and light-armed troops, but such forces became vital to Greek armies only in the late fifth and fourth centuries, when warfare became Mediterranean in scope and expeditionary in practice.

The primacy of land both as an object of attack and as grounds for infantry defense holds true for a good many Greek states in the classical period and serves well as a model against which exceptions can be illustrated. Some backward societies in mountainous areas in Crete and Aetolia, where the agrarian polis was less developed, for example, made exclusive use of light-armed troops in attacking the enemy in border passes. Effective cavalry overshadowed infantry in Thessaly and anywhere else where wide plains made their use attractive and where agriculture was practiced under different cultural and legal protocols, which emphasized aristocracy and monarchy rather than broad-based oligarchy and timocracy. We hear, too, of occasional ingenious sieges at Plataia and later at Mantineia, as the Peloponnesian War and subsequent fighting illustrated the sometime artificial and static nature of war framed solely by decisive infantry battle.

Athens, of course, as Miletus before, weighed carefully the advantages of not risking its growing urban citizenry to meet the challenge of enemy invaders on Attic soil, and so chose not to fight in pitched hoplite battle to protect its agriculture. And from the fourth century B.C. on, the widespread use of mercenaries, peltasts, artillery, slaves and freed slaves, and new emphasis on fortification changed military practice altogether: the old idea of war as solely decisive battle, and decisive battle solely as a single collision of hoplite farmers on level ground became often irrelevant. But if ravaging farmland alone no longer determined the nature of warfare in Greece, and if it was no longer integral to the rituals of hoplite fighting, it still continued to play a key role throughout Hellenistic and Roman imperial times. Such later states were not agrarian, but like most preindustrial cultures of the ancient Mediterranean they were still agricultural. And so attacks on cropland would always remain a popular tactic against any society that relied chiefly on farming for its livelihood—whether or not its food was produced by serfs, renters, and slaves, whether or not plots were middling and of like size, or enormous and owned by those in town, whether or not this tactic was a challenge to battle or an attempt to ruin the countryside.

Consequently, to the classical Greeks such destruction of grain and the cutting down of olive trees and vines were synonymous with warfare itself,[5] and thus a part of everyday life, something to be lamented, analyzed, boasted or joked about. "There is need not to be haughty," the poet Stesichorus was supposed to have told the Lokrians, "so that your cicadas don't sing from the ground" (Arist. *Rh.* 2.21.8, 3.11.6). When told that Alexander of Phereia offered beef at a cheap price to his newly found Athenian allies, Epameinondas replied: "And we will supply to them free wood to cook their meat, for we will cut down everything in their land if they make trouble" (Plut. *Mor.* 193E17). "To turn the countryside into a sheep walk" was a common promise of war (e.g., Isoc. 14.31; Diod. 15.63.2)—if rarely a real consequence of fighting.

Indeed, devastation was so common that it became institutionalized by society. Land rental agreements often contained special clauses specifying conditions to be followed by lessor and lessee in the case of enemy ravaging, instances in which farmers expected both to be attacked and to survive with some portion of their livelihood intact (e.g., *SEG* 21 [1966] 644.13–14; *SEG* 24 [1969] 151.18; *SIG*³ 966.12–14; *IG* II².411.34–37; *IG* V.2.6; *IG* XII.9.191). Military commanders routinely received fulsome praise from their city for protecting crops at harvesttime from attack (e.g., *IG* II².682.35–36; *IG* II².1299). The destruction of cropland was often written into peace treaties between sovereign states as the point where hostilities were renewed, and allied cities were obligated to fulfill their promises (e.g., Thuc. 5.23.1–2, 5.47.3–4).

5. Cf. the late Roman or early Byzantine dream-interpretation book of the prophet Daniel, which told its readers: "To dream fruit trees torn out or cut down signifies wars and the death of men and beasts" (*Byzantinische Zeitschrift* 26 [1926]: 290–314, 1.123). I wish to thank Steven Oberhelman for discussing this and other passages in the corpus of later dream-interpretation manuals.

We might think that such universal Hellenic awareness of ravaging would lead to its formal restriction in warfare among like agrarian communities who had crafted mutually understood protocols of infantry battle. Calls for reciprocal restraint and suggestions for some type of ban on devastation between Greek states, it is true, were often heard. But in typically Greek fashion they were apparently ignored, and so remained mostly a part of philosophical discussion.[6] "Do you not know", asked Socrates matter-of-factly, "that men cut the grain that others have planted, and chop down their trees, and in all ways harass the weaker if they refuse to submit, until they are forced to choose slavery rather than war with the stronger?" (Xen. *Mem.* 2.1.13). Plato in his *Republic* urged that Greeks not ravage each other's lands, nor burn down houses, but be instead content to carry away only the annual harvest (*Resp.* 470A–471B). In a particularly anguished passage Polybius much later complained:

> I never share the feeling of those who go so far in their anger
> against men of their own race that they not only take away their
> enemies' yearly crops but also destroy their agricultural

---

6. There is a similar paradox in the Hebrew Old Testament between theory and practice. At one point, fruit trees are apparently to be spared: "When thou shalt besiege a city a long time, in making war against it to take it, thou shalt not destroy the trees thereof by forcing an ax against them. . . . Only the trees which thou knowest that they be not trees for meat, thou shalt destroy and cut them down" (*Deut.* 20:19–20). But at *Kings* 2:3.19 we hear: "And ye shall smite every fenced city, and every choice city, and shall fell every good tree." Rowlands (1972, 452–453) claims that crops are sometimes protected from war in modern primitive societies: "A tacit understanding, for their mutual benefit, between hostile groups as to when and when not to indulge in warfare seems quite widespread in small-scale societies. . . . Such an understanding sets indirectly a limit on the scale of destruction possible from warfare. For example, an implicit safeguard on growing crops may explain why little care may often be taken to protect fields but, on the other hand, the concern that may be taken over the protection of granaries."

installations, thereby leaving no opportunity for reparation.
Instead, those who do that seem to me to be extremely
shortsighted: the more they assume to be instilling fear into their
enemy by ruining their land and taking away all their hopes of
earning a living—not just for the present, but even for the
future—just that much more do they brutalize others and so create a hatred of themselves that is never removed. (23.15)

These protests confirm our suspicions that in actual practice ravaging became more and more indiscriminate and unrestricted and after
the fifth century B.C. was well outside the sphere of formal challenges to
hoplite battle. How could armies who could not even restrain themselves from supposedly sacrosanct temples and grounds keep away from
more mundane farmland?[7] We know of few instances in any age where
ravagers deliberately avoid attacking agriculture out of respect for their
enemy's property. The few, rare exceptions perhaps prove the rule. For
example, during the Second Messenian War the Spartans who invaded
Messenia neither cut down trees nor demolished buildings. Instead, if
we can believe traditional accounts, they only stole cattle and carried the
harvest away. But they did so not out of empathy for the enemy, but because they considered Messenia at the time still a part of their own territory (Paus. 4.7.1–2).[8]

And when Greeks looked outside their country, they were often star-
tled at the restraint—so foreign to their own practice—shown by other

7. Cf. a random sampling of wartime violations of temples and sacred ground:
Dem. 13.32, 23.212; Diod. 14.17.11, 14.76, 31.46; Hdt. 6.75.3, 8.32, 9.120;
Polyb. 18.2, 21.11, 32.27, and esp. 5.11.3–4; Thuc. 1.139.2, 3.81.5, 4.97.2–4.

8. Even if the authenticity of this anecdote is questionable, it is all the more
revealing as a reflection of theoretical Greek attitudes toward ravaging; it is also
consistent with later authors' idealization of a more human warfare in the distant past, when protocol still limited damage beyond the battlefield. Cf.
Polyaen. *Strat.* 3.10.5 and Xen. *Ages.* 1.20, where again crops are left alone only
because of the invader's self-interest.

societies during war. India was a particularly fascinating example. Arrian remarked of the farmers there: "They work the land, and they pay the taxes to the kings and to the cities such as are autonomous; and if there is civil war among the Indians, it is not lawful to touch these workers, nor even to devastate the land itself" (*Ind.* 8.11.9). Diodorus adds:

> Among other peoples enemy forces through devastation cause land to become unfarmed. In India, however, farmers are considered sacred and inviolable: those who farm near war zones are unaware of any danger. While opposing sides kill each other in battle, they allow those at work on the farms to remain unhurt, acknowledging them as the common benefactors of everyone. Neither do the Indians burn the lands of their enemies nor chop down their fruit trees. (2.36.6–7)

Perhaps the restraint shown by other cultures fascinated these later Greek writers because it reminded them of the earlier protocols of city-state warfare, when ravaging had served to begin pitched battle and was not an end in itself nor very serious in its consequences. We should keep in mind also that it was not merely the land that was purportedly left untouched in India, but the caste of farmers themselves—in contrast, the lethality of unrestricted Greek warfare in the countryside sometimes involved the killing and dislocation of the agrarian populace in addition to merely burning and cutting down crops. (See updated commentary, page 206 [Ravaging and the Historiography of the Greek State].)

It might seem a simple matter to analyze this strategy of crop destruction in classical Greece, given the many references in the ancient literary and epigraphic sources. Unfortunately, the very opposite is often true. Because the Greeks took devastation for granted as a commonplace activity, they naturally felt no need for much elaboration or even explanation. That is, they rarely tell us what kind of troops are engaged, which precise crops are targeted, or exactly how they are destroyed. We miss especially an analysis of the degree of damage done and subsequent reference to the long-term effects of earlier attacks. What information we can obtain often must be gleaned through inference and assumption, with attention paid to practical considerations. In much the same way, modern historians, when referring to strategic bombing, sometimes merely state that the "enemy was bombed" and give no further detail or explanation. They rightly assume that as witnesses of the last fifty years of warfare, we understand automatically that multiple-engine aircraft, flying in formation over enemy territory, drop explosive charges that are designed to destroy industrial centers or kill people. Yet readers 2,500 years hence may find the phrase "bombed" as nondescript and hazy a term as we do "ravage," and so may wonder how this frequent twentieth-century tactic was carried out, and just how effective were the results it produced. Indeed, even today scholars cannot agree on the exact purpose, damage, and effectiveness of much of the strategic bombing undertaken against Germany during World War II.

No comprehensive study of ravaging in classical antiquity has yet appeared. Consequently many wrong assumptions have been made. For example, plundering, where troops seek booty, is sometimes considered the same activity as crop destruction. We are often told, too, that olive trees were uprooted, not cut down, and thus forty to sixty years passed before their replacement plantings reached full production. Nor is this confusion always limited to such esoteric points. Often a basic question of Greek history is involved. For example, we hear that all the land of Attica was destroyed in the Peloponnesian War and never regained its productivity, with farmers fleeing their wrecked holdings and flocking into the city. This assumption of a radical change in Athenian land tenure and agricultural practice has too rarely been seriously questioned. A simple phrase in an ancient source that "the land was ravaged" leaves too much room to the imagination. Indeed, it is nearly the case that the more an ancient author records particular cropland as being ravaged, the more we might ask why such continual devastation is necessary in the first place. In general, this book suggests that the damage that did occur to farmland during war was more often a result of dislocation—the evacuation of farmers, the driving off of slaves and livestock, the deaths in battle of farmer-hoplites themselves—than of the physical destruction of trees, vines, and cereals.

My purpose is to examine how the Greeks in the classical period destroyed agriculture in wartime. Through an examination of the manner of crop destruction (part 1), and the methods of defense (i.e., fortification, evacuation, and retaliation [part 2]), I hope to determine the effectiveness of the tactic. These findings will be compared to the best-known and most important example of repeated, well-organized ravaging campaigns: the invasions and occupations of Attica by the Spartans in the Peloponnesian War (part 3).

Finally, I should note that plundering, pillaging, piracy, and the profits of war are not dealt with here. They have long been the subject of ample study and were, I suggest, often quite separate activities, distinct from both the strategy and the practice of agricultural devastation. (See updated commentary, page 209 [Plunder and Devastation].) The fifth and fourth centuries B.C. (ca. 500–300 B.C.) are the focus of this study. Some evidence, however, is drawn from both earlier and later times, as absolute chronological limits have not been possible for all chapters, given the paucity of information.

I hope to leave the reader with five valid generalizations about ancient farming and its role during wartime: (1) permanent agricultural devastation of crops in Greek history was difficult, and so not usually in itself the cause of economic crises; (2) the ritualistic nature of crop ravaging and its relationship to decisive hoplite battle should be seen as part of the protocols of early classical Greek infantry practice—a remarkable and revolutionary system where warfare originally was made to reflect the interest of the citizens rather than vice versa; (3) despite differing strategies and practices of ravaging throughout Greek history, it remains a general truism that trees and vines are hard to destroy systematically, and cereals rarely are burned or trampled into oblivion—and such generalizations apply to other military theaters and histories of the Mediterranean as well; (4) rural impoverishment and depopulation during periods of war were more often insidious processes—the results of infrastructure and labor power losses, taxation, and general periods of banditry and unrest— than the immediate consequence of invading armies that destroyed trees, vines, and cereals; (5) because most of the population of Greece was rural and engaged in agriculture, and because the Greeks saw warfare as the decisive experience of the citizenry, any analysis of farming and fighting of the city-state is nothing less than a valuable reflection of the culture at large.

PART ONE

The Attack on Agriculture

ONE

Military Organization

An army of invasion in the classical age usually sought decisive battle, but it needed to utilize the countryside of its adversary to accomplish that goal—both to feed itself and to provoke the enemy to fight by attacking farmland. Consequently, Greek armies brought along mobile light-armed troops, built field camps from local materials, had specialized tools, and were careful to time their arrival to particular cycles of the farming year. Almost every consideration of a Greek army—logistical, tactical, strategic, psychological, and technological—was in some way connected to agriculture.

THE USE OF LIGHT-ARMED TROOPS AS RAVAGERS

After entering enemy farmland an invading army attempted to keep its phalanx in formation and its hoplites in rank, whether or not enemy forces appeared. So, for example, King Archidamos on his initial entry into Attica reminded his soldiers:

> Although we appear to be invading in overwhelming numbers,
> and it seems assured that our enemy will not face us in battle, still
> we must not for these reasons let down our guard while on the

march. The officers and soldiers of each city must on every occasion expect to find themselves in danger. . . . Follow wherever your officer leads, and above all, be careful to stay in formation, keep up your defense, and promptly follow the orders you receive. (Thuc. 2.11.3)

During the five Peloponnesian invasions of the Archidamian War, hoplites were rarely free to leave their ranks, lay down their arms and armor, and scatter to ravage cropland.[1] Similarly, during Teleutias's march on Olynthos (382 B.C.), he kept his "very large" army in close order as he advanced, burning and ravaging the countryside (Xen. *Hell.* 5.2.39). When the Thebans once sent out their entire army on a punitive expedition against Thespiai, enemy peltasts initially forced their retreat and "at no point allowed them to scatter from their phalanx" (*Hell.* 5.4.42). Another large Theban army overran the Corinthia in 369 B.C. and destroyed "whatever was of value in the plain" but still had to be kept in some order the entire time as a precaution against the numerous enemy cavalry patrols in the area (*Hell.* 7.1.20).

Since hoplite troops were expected to remain in rank in case of sudden attack, naturally they could not always cover the countryside effectively, and thus were not well suited for the task of destroying enemy crops.[2] Instead, we should imagine that light-armed troops, unencum-

---

1. See Hardy 1926, 348; Delbrück 1890, 111. Cf. also Onasander 27: "Quite simply, the general must stress that nothing is more important to his troops than keeping in formation, nothing more dangerous than breaking formation." We should understand that no enemy territory was ever completely evacuated or free from reconnaissance patrols and sudden sorties. The orders of General Sherman to his men at the outset of his march to the sea were similar: "Of all things, the most important is, that the men, during marches and in camp, keep their places and do not scatter about as stragglers or foragers, to be picked up by a hostile people in detail" (*Memoirs of General W. T. Sherman* [Chicago, 1875], 2: 171.

2. Of course hoplites marching in formation could sometimes be very effective in trampling all the pasturage, cereal crops, and even small vines in narrow

bered by body armor, accompanied hoplites and fanned throughout farmland in small patrols while the main infantry force either stayed in protective formation or marched more slowly in mass. Ancient writers of military tactics continually stress this point. Onasander, in his treatise on the duties of the general, warned against allowing unorganized foraging and ravaging parties to venture forth. The ideal practice was "to dispatch along with the light-armed and unarmed men protective forces of cavalry and infantry who shall have no concern at all with booty but rather are to stay in formation and guard the raiders" (10.8). Aeneas Tacticus took for granted that any well-organized, sensibly led army followed this universal practice:

> It is necessary that you realize that when the enemy goes to war
> with good sense and skill, he first of all brings up his strongest
> contingents in formation, keeping on the lookout for a counterre-
> sponse and ready to go on the defensive. In the meantime, some
> of his forces spread out and ravage the countryside. (16.4)

We can be sure that in actual practice invaders relied on light-armed parties, not hoplites, to destroy agriculture. (See updated commentary, page 210 [Light-Armed Troops].)

During the Athenian seaborne retaliation raids against the Peloponnese, scattered bodies of light-armed troops did the actual devastation. Hoplites were deployed for protection and marched in rank to keep the vulnerable ravagers safe from enemy sorties (Thuc. 4.56.1). Another example can be found during the annual Athenian invasions of the Megarid, when there was little enemy opposition, and agricultural devastation was the key objective. Then we hear that a "considerable number" of *psiloi* (lightly armed troops) went along (2.31.2). The only explanation for their inclusion on these punitive campaigns was the need to attack enemy cropland—pitched battle was not imminent, and so they

---

swaths along their path of entrance and exit. We hear, too, of rare occasions when the main army joins in burning enemy property (e.g., Xen. *Anab.* 6.3.19).

were not really required on the flanks of the phalanx nor as skirmishers before the initial clash. Their value was to sweep the Megarid, searching out farms and hamlets, while the presence of the Athenian phalanx ensured heavy infantry response would be either decisive or nonexistent.

It should be assumed also that the Peloponnesians used chiefly light-armed soldiers during their ravaging activity in Attica. At one point, patrols who seek to reach the rich fields near the city are mentioned (Thuc. 2.22.2); these advance parties must have been made up of cavalry and light-armed contingents, who could run suddenly onto farmland and then depart at the first sign of resistance. This assumption seems confirmed later when Thucydides relates how Athenian cavalry prevented "the mass of enemy light-armed troops from leaving the protection of their hoplites and ravaging the croplands near the city" (3.1.2).

If we can believe a passage in Diodorus (13.72.4), King Agis in 408 B.C. attempted to march on Athens from Dekeleia with a large force, half of which was composed of light-armed troops. They, too, must have come along solely to ravage the rich land near the city's walls, while the hoplite body intended to keep the Athenian defensive forces busy. Nor should we forget that many states relied on their cavalry to check ravagers—a strategy that could be effective only against vulnerable light-armed troops, not really directed at hoplites in formation. Elsewhere, there are other instances that confirm the key role in agricultural devastation played by light-armed parties (e.g., Xen. *Hell.* 1.2.2–3, 5.4.42; and cf. other suggestions of this strategy at Arr. *Anab.* 3.30.10; Thuc. 8.41.2).

One wonders who served in this loose corps of light-armed troops. We do know that the great majority of hoplites were accompanied on expeditions by at least one servant, usually a slave.[3] It seems logical, and

---

3. Gomme (2: 275) denied (wrongly, I think) the presence of hoplite attendants on campaigns. See instead Anderson 1970, 30, 46; Pritchett 1971, 49–51. The presence of slave attendants on hoplite campaigns is the natural corollary

is sometimes suggested, that this large service body of slaves could also engage in ravaging the countryside once the hoplites had driven the enemy from the field. But for obvious reasons this practice cannot have been widespread.[4] Would not slave attendants be the worst troops to turn loose in the countryside to destroy crops? Even as mere camp followers they were not always trustworthy, and often liable to desert their masters (e.g., Thuc. 7.75.5). Once they were given the relative freedom to roam through fields and orchards with either weapons or tools they might well not come back. Second, by definition they were servants, charged with carrying a hoplite's weapons, provisions, and bedding and doing other odd jobs.[5] We should assume, then, that they kept near the phalanx, attending to their masters, and tending to their tasks. (See updated commentary, page 211 [Hoplite attendants].) Instead, the light-armed troops were in large part "the very poor, landless men, despised and neglected."[6] This group provided a great deal of the labor power for devastation, and it must have operated in a manner often independent from the main body of heavily armed troops. All soldiers who were not hoplites must have been included, with the exception of archers, slingers, and other special corps of peltasts or light-armed contingents, who were highly trained and at times expected to join in against hoplites in battle (as, for example, at Aitolia, Amphipolis, Spartolos, and Sphakteria). Thucydides remarks on the eve of the battle of Delion:

---

of servile workers in freeholding agriculture; we should understand that many farmers would simply bring along on campaign their family servants, who worked on the farm beside their masters, to carry breastplates, shields, and provisions. In at least one case (viz., Is. 5.11), a relative, rather than a slave, served as an attendant. Cf. *REG* 39 (1926): 354–366 for support personnel in Hellenistic times.

4. Delbrück (1890, 111) rightly objected to Müller-Strubing's suggestion that slave-attendants participated in the devastation of Attica by the Spartans.

5. For these possible duties, see Pritchett 1971, 51.

6. Gomme 1: 15. See also Plut. *Phoc.* 12.3; Arr. *Tact.* 2.1.

At that time no standardly equipped light troops were present, nor were any available to Athens. Those who had marched along on this expedition were many times more numerous than their enemy counterparts—but the majority of them had followed along without adequate armament, part of the many citizens and foreigners on hand in the city who made up this invasion force. Because they were the first to leave for home, only a small number still remained. (4.94.1)

The implication is clear that a large, loosely organized group from Athens had followed the hoplites into Boiotia, helped with the fortification of Delion and the ravaging of the countryside (we hear of vines being cut down), and then left for home when they were no longer needed. The idea that ravagers might plunder as they destroyed obviously was an added incentive to many irregular troops who followed in the wake of the invading hoplite corps.

So it seems likely that a prime purpose of bringing any light-armed troops along at all on campaigns in the fifth and early fourth centuries B.C. was to have a substantial force of ravagers on hand. For example, when Epameinondas entered Lakonia unopposed in 370 B.C., "many light-armed and unarmed troops also followed along in hope of plunder so that a massive wave of 70,000 soldiers entered the country. . . . They invaded an unravaged and untouched land and burnt and plundered as far as the river and the city" (Plut. *Ages.* 31.1–2). Indeed, in the fifth and early fourth centuries B.C. light-armed troops were not especially valuable for anything else. Their role in pitched battle was not impressive, since they were extremely vulnerable to both cavalry and hoplite charges.[7] Even after the revolution in tactics and armament in the

7. Light-armed troops were, of course, used on sentry and garrison duty (e.g., in Athens and as *peripoloi* in Attica) where their mobility was needed and valuable protection while on patrol was offered to them by rural fortifications. Elsewhere, they had some use on the wings of a phalanx and as skirmishers before and after battle. But in general before the late fifth century B.C. they were

fourth century B.C., a chief attraction of organized light-armed companies and peltasts remained their success at ravaging (e.g., Isoc. 4.144), for which their speed and mobility were advantageous.

To sum up: armies of invasion were accompanied by lighter-armed auxiliaries, whose job was to range over the countryside destroying and plundering property as they ravaged cropland. Such troops were mobile and quick, but they were also vulnerable to sudden enemy counterattacks, inasmuch as they were loosely organized, poorly disciplined, and relatively unprotected.

FIELD CAMPS

It was the frequent practice of the Greek army of invasion bent on the ravaging of the countryside to build a temporary, fortified camp. Naturally, protection at night in hostile territory was needed, and in daytime a headquarters was desirable to coordinate light-armed ravaging patrols and hoplite protective cover. In his description of Archidamos's invasions into Attica, Thucydides implies that the Peloponnesians routinely first established a camp, and then proceeded to use this as a base for ravaging (Thuc. 2.19.2; cf. 3.1.2, 4.2.1). Likewise, during an Athenian ravaging expedition into Boiotia, troops first established a camp, devastated the land, and then returned there for protection at night (3.91.5). In fact, we should assume that in most cases armies ravaged only after establishing a secure base of operations (e.g., Thuc. 4.45.1, 4.54.4, 5.64.5; Xen. *Hell.* 3.2.2–3).

Besides offering security, the construction of temporary ramparts could directly aid in destroying cultivated crops. Unlike their Roman counterparts, who constructed their stockades from finished stakes that were transplanted from camp to camp, Greek armies cut down

---

"as lightweight as their weapons" (Adcock 1957, 16; see also Garlan 1975, 127–128; Grundy 1948, 274–275; and Kromayer and Veith 1928, 87–88).

trees on the spot and piled the brush and timber into the rough form of a wall.[8] Consequently, nearby orchards of cultivated fruit trees were prime targets each time a new camp was constructed. The Thebans during their stay in Lakonia (369 B.C.) built their stockade using as "many of the fruit trees that they had cut down as possible, and so in this way guarded themselves" (Xen. *Hell.* 6.5.30). At Syracuse the Athenians recognized this dual advantage of protection and simultaneous devastation when they felled the surrounding trees to form a palisade around their ships.[9] Before the battle of Mykale the Persians cut down fruit trees belonging to the Milesians in order to form a walled camp against the Greek seaborne attack.[10] We hear that Agesilaos during his invasion of Boiotia was able to force his reluctant allies to ravage the orchards around Thebes by moving his camp three to four times a day. In this way, his men "became obligated to cut down fruit trees for wood in order to build their huts" (Polyaen. *Strat.* 2.1.21; cf. Xen. *Hell.* 5.4.38).

Nor were fruit trees the only property liable to destruction and subsequent use in fortification. The Athenians under Hippokrates at De-

8. The difference between the two practices is explained in Polybius (18.18) and Livy (35.5.5–12). For general information about the Greek temporary field camp, see Anderson 1970, 43–66; and especially Pritchett 1974, 133–146.

9. Thuc. 6.66.2. For other examples that suggest that the practice of destroying fruit trees and then using the wood for fortification was commonplace, see Diod. 13.108.5, 13.110.3; Thuc. 4.69.2, 6.99.1. The Spartan stockade around Plataia was constructed from the wood of the surrounding fruit trees; for support and reinforcement of the accompanying mound, timber from the nearby mountains was used.

10. Hdt. 9.97. How and Wells (*A Commentary on Herodotus* [Oxford, 1928], 2: 330) fail to recognize the true intent of the Persians: "The destruction of fruit-trees, although there was a large forest close by the hill, showed reckless disregard of the Milesians' property." The Persians were not merely reckless; in addition to providing protection for themselves, they wished at this stage to injure the Milesians, who were of questionable loyalty (see, for example, Hdt. 9.99).

lion, besides using native timber for stakes, also cut down the surrounding vines and threw them into their rampart along with stones and bricks pulled down from the houses nearby (Thuc. 4.90.2).

Xenophon relates how the Spartans moved their field camps frequently (*Lac. Pol.* 12.5; cf. also Onasander 6.13; Xen. *Hell.* 5.2.38). This had two results: damage to friendly territory could be distributed equitably,[11] and in enemy country devastation could be spread as far as possible. Sometimes even defensive troops and residents alike were obligated to ravage their own territory to obtain wood for fortifications against the enemy. Lycurgus recalled of the Athenian defensive measures after Chaironeia: "The land gave up its trees, the dead their gravestones, and the temples arms. Some began to build walls, others to make ditches and palisades" (*Leoc.* 44). When Mardonios retreated into Boiotia he "ravaged the surrounding countryside, even though the Thebans had gone over to the side of the Medes. This was not because of any enmity of the Thebans, but on account of his own pressing needs, for he wanted to build a fortified camp for his army" (Hdt. 9.15.2). Likewise, Thucydides relates that in the face of an advancing Athenian wall, the Syracusans were forced to use their own olive trees in a counterfortification (6.99.3).

So, before enemy contingents had begun formal agricultural devastation, we can assume that their mere presence in a fortified camp caused some degree of damage, mostly to fruit trees and on occasion vines and vine stakes. While such ravaging was probably limited to a very small

11. Cf., for instance, *IG* II².1241.4–17, a rental agreement of the Dyaliens, where the lessee is not responsible for crop losses resulting from either enemy incursions or the camp building of friendly troops. A somewhat similar situation arose in the South during the latter part of the American Civil War. Residents asked to be saved "from our friends" as Confederate troops inhabited the area. Southern papers complained: "Our own army, while falling back from Dalton, was even more dreaded by the inhabitants than was the army of Sherman" (B. H. L. Hart, *Sherman* [New York, 1960], 335).

area around the camp and not so flagrantly designed to prompt an immediate enemy counterresponse, it, nevertheless, utilized, in a most effective way, available labor to do two necessary tasks at once. A strong invading force also could sometimes require the local population or opposing troops hastily to protect themselves by using timber from their own orchards and vineyards—and in a way ravage their own territory. M. D. Gutman describes these exact circumstances in the Low Countries during the late seventeenth century:

> War led to the destruction of crops and farmers' resources in two significant ways. First, some armies destroyed property inadvertently or through the necessary undertakings of war. For example, troops who marched through a region, stopped overnight, or built a camp destroyed growing crops. . . . Also, the construction of lines of fortification had the same result because the armies needed a clear view of their surroundings and the approach of potential enemies.[12]

A rather different type of camp in hostile country was the *epiteichisma* or *epiteichismos*, a permanent, fortified garrison aimed at plaguing the enemy year-round. A great deal has been written about the strategy and function of *epiteichismos*,[13] and there is little that needs be contributed to the discussion. One small point, however, requires brief clarification, because it relates directly to the question of agricultural devastation. It is usually assumed that the chief purpose of a year-round fortification in enemy territory was simply to devastate the cropland more thoroughly. For example, according to this line of reasoning, the Spartans sought and achieved a much greater degree of agricultural destruction once

12. Cf. Gutman 1980, 77.

13. See, for example, Adcock 1947, 2–7; Boardman 1956, 41–55; Brunt 1965, 267–270; Garlan 1974, 33–38; Grundy 1948, 335, 446–447; Salmon 1946, 13–14.

they had occupied Dekeleia than earlier, when they came only seasonally under Archidamos. Although there may be some truth to this, the practice of *epiteichismos* seems to have had rather a different aim: "L'installation d'un '*epiteichismos*' pouvait donc avoir deux objectifs: un objectif économico-militaire, le controle d'un territoire, et un objectif plus largement politique, l'incitation à la révolte."[14] Cropland, of course, could be and was ravaged, but this activity was incidental in comparison. Effective devastation was often better accomplished by large yearly invasions in force when a sufficient body of ravagers could overrun the countryside as part of a more direct challenge for the enemy to march out and fight.

Epiteichismos, on the other hand, was the only lasting way of inciting slave desertion, causing political turmoil by providing sanctuary for exiles and troublemakers, interrupting food supplies to the city, keeping enemy forces on constant patrol, and staging bothersome raids to get plunder and cause terror. Consequently, in the classic instances of *epiteichismos*—a tactic more common during the Peloponnesian War and its aftermath—we usually hear of the activity of thieves and plunderers, exiles, and runaway slaves and the loss of access to farms. Very rarely, if at all, is there mention of systematic destruction of cropland by the enemy garrison.[15] *Epiteichismos* had a different purpose than annual invasion of the countryside and was more part of a strategy of exhaustion than a catalyst for decisive pitched battle between hoplite phalanxes; it may not be

14. Garlan 1974, 40.

15. Consider, for example, Atalante (Thuc. 2.32); Corcyra (Thuc. 13.85.2–4), Dekeleia (Thuc. 6.91.7, 7.27–28), Delion (Thuc. 4.76.5), Delphinion on Chios (Thuc. 8.38.2), Methana (Thuc. 4.45.2), Minoa (Thuc. 3.51.1–2), Notion (Thuc. 3.34), Pagai (Thuc. 4.66.1), and Pylos (Thuc. 4.3). *Epiteichismos*, of course, could have a psychological effect, as farmers worried about the proximity of enemy troops and their own inability to reach their farms and fields. But the simple presence of the enemy in a standard fortified position did not mean automatically the physical loss of crops such as trees and vines.

an exaggeration at all to say that it did not involve the traditional strategy of agricultural devastation. (See updated commentary, page 212 [*Epiteichismos*].)

RAVAGING TOOLS

Hoplites could sometimes merely use their feet to trample cereal crops as they marched along through enemy farmland, and dry grain and farmhouses could in some instances be destroyed with fire. But in the great majority of cases some specialized tools were needed for the light-armed soldiers who roamed the countryside on ravaging patrols. Spears and javelins were of little use in cutting down vines, trees, and grain.[16] Although direct evidence is very scarce, armies must have brought along a sufficient supply of axes, hatchets, hoes, shovels, scythes, sickles, and other tools. For example, Kleomenes' troops who invaded the Argive Plain (222 B.C.) carried specially made wood shafts to beat the grain down, "not like most ravagers who cut it with sickles and knives" (Plut. *Cleom.* 26.1).[17] The implication is that other ravagers, unlike Kleomenes' innovative soldiers, were usually equipped with sickles and knives on the march in order to plunder and devastate green grain. Xenophon tells us that during the march of the Ten Thousand, Klearchos was almost killed by a flying hand ax thrown by a disgruntled

---

16. Cf., for example, Anderson 1970, 3. Alexander at one point had his men lower their *sarisai* to beat down a path through a grainfield, but his aim was to advance his troops quickly through the area, not the systematic destruction of crops (Arr. *Anab.* 1.4.1–2).

17. The *machaira* was a long, curved knife used as a secondary weapon by most Greek troops, and so often a part of a soldier's offensive armament. Cf. Anderson 1970, 281 n. 126. The ravaging contraption noted by Plutarch is characteristic of Hellenistic military practice, where attention to economic aspects of warfare was more pronounced, as the support of mercenaries, siegecraft, finance, and logistics came to be as much a part of warfare as pitched battle itself.

soldier who was chopping wood (*Anab.* 1.5.12.). This need for implements of devastation caused an army no inconvenience, since most well-
organized expeditions were equipped with all sorts of tools to make
camp, gather wood, clear roads, build bridges, construct siege works,
and harvest crops on foraging patrols. These engineering and farm implements would easily double as tools for crop destruction. This may explain why we rarely find reference to specific "ravaging tools."

Wagons were usually used for easy transportation. Xenophon relates
that before the Spartan army marched out, all the tools that could possibly be needed were placed on carts or pack animals (*Lac. Pol.* 11.2). We
hear of such wagons at the battle of Mantineia when the Argives and
Mantineians swept into the Spartan rear and found them guarded by the
older men of the army (Thuc. 5.72.3). No doubt they carried the tools
that the Spartans used the day before to ravage the Mantineian countryside (5.64.5). Similarly, when Archidamos attacked Plataia and found
the citizens unreceptive to his demands, he immediately had nearby orchards felled to build a palisade. Timber was cut and hauled from Kithairon to frame out a mound onto which earth and stones were heaped
(2.75). The army obviously had arrived with a plentiful supply of axes
and shovels.

In the *Cyropaedia*, we hear that arrangements were made at one point
to have every wagon of Cyrus's army equipped with a shovel and mat-
tock; each pack animal was to have an ax and sickle. Such tools were
considered by the army as "always useful to the owner, and often helpful to all" (Xen. *Cyr.* 6.2.34–36).[18] Even the Athenian armies, which
were probably less well organized than their Spartan counterparts, must
have brought along tools to be used in devastation. At Delion the
light-armed troops hastily cut vines and timber and pried up stones and

18. Light-armed troops, we are told, were chosen to use these tools for various
engineering tasks. In much the same way, they would have been responsible for
ravaging enemy cropland as the army progressed.

tiles for the fortifications.[19] And the legendary Macedonian army that frowned on the use of slow-moving supply wagons nevertheless brought along picks, shovels, and axes on its pack animals.[20]

There is little evidence for the wartime use of pack animals themselves as tools of destruction. This may seem surprising, but we should remember that fruit trees could not be easily or quickly uprooted, even with horse or mule power. Vines could be uprooted, but the sources suggest that they were usually trampled or cut. Hitching a mule, donkey, or horse to each of the numerous vines in even a small vineyard would be a slow, and thus hazardous, process during wartime. I have snapped heavy steel chains in the process of pulling out fruit trees with tractors of sixty horsepower and more. Usually, even with mechanized power, extensive amounts of dirt must be cleared from the roots or the ground flooded to yank the tree out. We are left with the conclusion that horses and mules were used only to trample grain or fodder. For that task, they would certainly be useful.

SEASONAL CONSIDERATIONS

Since the destruction of agriculture played such a central role in the strategy of invading armies, it would seem logical that the harvest dates of particular crops might help determine the time of arrival in enemy territory. Wheat and barley, for example, the most important of all crops in the Greek world, ripen anytime from the middle of May to the end of June, depending on the terrain, elevation, soil conditions, and local climatological factors. It was during this period of six to eight weeks in late spring that there were definite advantages for an enemy to

19. Thuc. 4.90.2–4. Cf. also the naval inventory inscription *IG* II².1631. 407–409, where axes (among other household implements) were apparently regular equipment on a trireme—perhaps used for encampment, foraging, and crop devastation while on shore.

20. Engels 1978, 16–17.

invade. In the first place, grain would still be exposed in the field, not yet harvested and gathered behind the city's walls.[21] Troops could ravage the vulnerable crop as it ripened, or at least keep farmers away from their harvests, and so ruin their entire year's investment. Second, since the grain was "in ear" at this time and the stalks becoming dry, in theory entire fields could on occasion be torched, letting the flames run rampant over the countryside. (See updated commentary, page 212 [Seasonal Considerations].) True, earlier in the winter and spring the crop was out in the field and thus vulnerable, but it was still green then, and not liable to ignite—requiring the more time-consuming process of trampling or cutting to achieve its destruction.[22] Finally, an army entering enemy country near or at cereal-harvesting time would find a plentiful supply of food and fodder.

Fortunately, a great deal has been written about the provisioning of ancient armies. From examination of ancient sources and practical considerations of logistics, we know that troops usually relied neither entirely on the supplies they had brought along nor on foraging from the crops of the enemy. Instead, soldiers were expected to be provided with anywhere from three to thirty days or more rations, depending on the distance and time of the expedition. Then, after entering enemy territory, additional food could be supplied from the local produce as provisions ran out.[23] Consequently, in May and June alone ravagers out in the

21. This is true of any well-fortified city (e.g., Miletus, Athens, Syracuse). Even small towns like Plataia could evacuate harvested produce inside the walls and prevent entry by the the enemy—given the ineffective art of siegecraft in the fifth century B.C. But later also, during the siege of Gaza (332 B.C.), Alexander was forced to import his entire supply of grain because he had arrived too late to catch the crop in the field, and the enemy had evacuated it behind the walls. See Engels 1978, 59. Cf. also Westlake 1945, 80 n. 4.

22. For the methods of grain destruction, see chapter 2.

23. See the extensive studies of Anderson (1970, 43–59), Pritchett (1971, 30–51), and Engels (1978, 119–122). Engels (pp. 27–28) observes that when Alexander left Greece in late March or April his army brought along thirty days'

countryside could carry off any ripening, unharvested grain that they did not destroy.[24] In a purely military sense, these months were favored for campaigning, since water was available for men and animals, as rivers often were not yet dry, and most flooding had long ago subsided, and mud dried out. Phalanxes needed the firmer ground of late spring and summer, when the plains of Greece were free of runoff, and inclement weather was rarer.

The twelve successive invasions of Miletus by Alyattes offer a good illustration of the advantages in ravaging during this period of the year. Alyattes always arrived right when the grain ripened (Hdt. 1.17.1). In this way his troops were able to destroy the crop while it was still out in the countryside before the besieged Milesian farmers could gather it behind their walls (1.17.2). Since the grain was now drying, the far easier technique of burning the fields was sometimes successfully carried out

---

rations—roughly enough supplies to last until early May, when the grain crop along his route would be "milk ripe," and just able to be harvested and consumed.

24. I have made the assumption throughout that there is a fundamental difference between the activity of plundering and that of ravaging cropland. Mercenaries, exiles, small raiding parties, professional armies, pirates, and troops of occupation all seem more intent on personal gain and booty than citizen-hoplites, who march in force into enemy territory, destroying agriculture and expecting battle. But that is not to say that the two activities did not frequently overlap. We should assume that there was always incidental plundering during any invasion; all ravagers saved and carried off enemy produce as needed, and stole small valuables and looted dwellings while engaged in crop destruction. On the other hand, plunderers in search of booty might stop and destroy property they could not use: "The pillager disappointed of detachable loot easily finds vent for his feelings in the destruction of fixtures" (B. H. L. Hart, *Sherman* [New York, 1960], 334).

For simultaneous plundering and ravaging by invading armies, see the following: Diod. 14.62.5, 15.65.5; Onasander 6.12; Plut. *Cleom.* 25.4; *Ages.* 31.2; Polyb. 2.32.4, 4.45.7, 16.24.7–8, 21.10.12–13; Thuc. 7.49.2; Xen. *Hell.* 3.2.26, 5.4.42, 6.5.37.

(1.19.1). Any grain needed for Alyattes' own army was simply plundered and carried off (1.17.3).[25] Alyattes thus accomplished the dual goal of maintaining his army and destroying the year's work of his enemy.

An even better-known example are the Archidamian invasions of Attica during the Peloponnesian War.[26] In the years 431, 430, 428, 427, and 425 B.C. the Peloponnesians arrived in Attica around mid- or late May and, except for the last occasion, stayed on average thirty days. Thus in theory they were able to ravage grain (much of which had been planted each year regardless of the threat of invasion) before Attic farmers had a chance to harvest and transport it behind the long walls. Although the method of grain destruction is never indicated, we can assume that the Spartans would burn, not trample or cut, all the stalks that were drying and becoming flammable. In addition, soldiers were able to supply themselves with food and gather fodder for their animals from the local crop. Indeed, during the invasion of 425 B.C. the Peloponnesians left Attica after only fifteen days. They had timed their invasion too soon that year, when it was still cold and the crop still green, and so were not able to supplement their diminishing provisions with Attic grain (Thuc. 4.6.1). Thucydides gives little other information, but we can assume also that Peloponnesian ravagers could not yet ignite cereals and were forced to take on the more time-consuming task of trampling

25. See also other examples of springtime invasion and crop destruction: Thuc. 2.79.1 (Athenian troops invaded Boiotian Spartolos in mid-May and destroyed grain out in the field); Polyaen. *Strat.* 4.6.20 (Antigonos invaded Attica at harvesttime, when the Athenians had nearly exhausted their past year's supply of grain and were then on "short rations"; they came quickly to terms rather than lose their ripening crop). See chapter 4 for various honorific decrees praising military officers who protect the city's grain harvests from springtime enemy invasions—just when grain was becoming combustible, harvesters would be out in the field, the city would be hungry after consuming the prior year's stores, and the invaders would be looking for additional local food and fodder.

26. For details of these invasions, see chapter 6.

and cutting; after leaving some of the highland plains of the Peloponnese it must have been difficult for their generals to calibrate the exact ripening status of the year's cereal crops in distant Attica.

Thus mid-May to the end of June was the ideal, but not the only, time to plan on arriving in enemy territory. Many factors—political considerations, supplies, weather, reluctant allies, seasonal variations in grain harvests, and grape and olive harvest times—were involved in deciding whether a proposed expedition would have an earlier or later arrival. For example, as long as the Peloponnesians occupied Attica, the Athenians were determined not to send out a large hoplite army from their walls. Consequently, their own forces invaded the Megarid in force and ravaged the land later in the summer, at the beginning of August, after their own enemy had left Attica.[27] Also, since most armies in Greece were composed of small farmers, agrarian hoplites on campaign would miss out on their own harvests at home if they left on a foreign expedition. They could stay in enemy territory in May and June only as long as they were willing to give up that amount of time for their own grain crop; in coalition armies, some agrarians among the troops would have harvest commitments nearly every week from late May to July.[28]

27. Thuc. 2.31.1, 4.66; Plut. *Per.* 34.2. Cf. the similar situation in 418 B.C. when for political reasons the Spartans did not mount an invasion into the Peloponnese until late summer (August and September). Their ravaging of the territory of the Mantineians (Thuc. 5.64.5), then, must have been aimed at vines and olives, since the grain had already been harvested and carried to safety.

28. In August and September, grapes, and then later olives in the early autumn, would be ripening, and the same situation would then also arise. So, for example, the allies of the Spartans, worried about these crop harvests, were reluctant to march off to Attica on a second invasion the same year (Thuc. 3.15.2). No doubt this displeasure at leaving one's own harvests in part resulted in the short campaigning season so characteristic of classical Greek warfare. As long as agrarian hoplites remained the exclusive military arm of the polis, a paradox predominated: invading armies that sought to attack enemy cropland at its most vulnerable stage were, by their absence from home, neglecting their own crops at the critical harvest period. See, for example, Thuc. 1.141.3, 5; 1.142.7;

Late June and July were also sometimes advantageous for ravaging raids, especially by seaborne forces. It was during this period that the grain had just been cut and was being gathered; the entire crop, then, would be concentrated on threshing floors out in the field or taken to storage. If carefully planned attacks could be aimed at selected, small, unfortified villages and scattered farms, there was a good chance of burning or plundering much of the crop right after it had been collected. If the timing were just right, this tactic might even have been easier than sending troops throughout the countryside to torch unharvested dry grainfields.[29] For example, the Athenian seaborne forces that attacked the Peloponnesian seaboard during the first years of the Archidamian War usually set sail from Attica at or near the end of June, right after the cutting of the grain. In these raids, small, isolated towns, without good walls, along the coast of the Peloponnese, the Argolid, and northeastern Greece (e.g., Astakos, Kephallenia, Prasiai, Sollion, Thronion) were usually targeted. Troops went ashore and often caught the surprised inhabitants unaware. Then they attempted—often with success—to storm the poorly fortified village and drive away the enemy. Their "ravaging" consisted of the easy task of destroying newly harvested produce that was already collected inside or near the walls.[30]

Grundy 1948, 257; Gomme 1: 11–12. Women, children, slaves (those not on campaign as personal servants), and older people could probably have taken up the slack of absent hoplites in the brief "low" season of the farm year but would not have been able to bring in the entire harvest alone.

29. Sheridan's devastation of the Shenandoah Valley during the American Civil War was particularly effective, since the ripe crops had recently been harvested and were all concentrated in storage barns: "Sheridan reported that he had burned 2,000 barns, 120 flour mills, destroyed or carried away 874 barrels of flour, 22,000 bushels of oats, 460,072 bushels of wheat, 51,380 tons of hay, 157,076 bushels of corn" (J. Davis, *The Shenandoah* [New York, 1945], 260; see, too, B. Catton, *A Stillness at Appomattox* [New York, 1953], 286–287).

30. Thuc. 2.25.1–5, 2.26.1–2, 2.30.1–2, 2.56.1–6; and see also Westlake 1945, 75–84.

On occasion, an army could also invade later in the summer in order to arrive at the vintage season. Brasidas marched on Akanthos (a small city dependent on its wine export for needed cash) in mid-August. Rather than watch the Spartans destroy their grapes right before harvest, the entire citizenry apparently acknowledged the importance of local viticulture and as a collective body agreed to meet Brasidas's demands, thus saving their crop (Thuc. 4.84.1–2, 4.88.1–2). In general, summer ravaging was more conducive to burning; low humidity and high daytime temperatures assured a greater presence of dry grasses, undergrowth, and brush that fuel fires; similarly, woodwork, timber, and any assorted wood structures would ignite and burn more easily after weeks of arid weather.

Still, we hear on occasion of agricultural devastation in midwinter. The Athenians were forced to ravage the Aeolos Islands during the winter months, the only time of year water was available (Thuc. 3.88.1). Sitalkes sent his massive Thracian army on a winter march into Macedonia to ruin the countryside, although, not surprisingly, his troops suffered from the cold and lack of food (2.95–101). The Thracians were not able to induce the Macedonians to pitched battle, nor to starve them out, and suffered from constant attacks of the enemy's heavy cavalry. After thirty days Sitalkes went home.

In the winter of 416/415 B.C. the Spartan army invaded Argive territory, ravaged "a small amount of land," and carried back some produce in wagons. Apparently they overpowered the meager defenses of small towns and villages, and so were able to raid their storage bins (Thuc. 6.7.1).[31] The Arcadians also made a midwinter expedition against

31. From the description of the campaign, there is little suggestion of large-scale losses (cf. Gomme 4: 222). When Thucydides expressly states that the army "ravaged a small amount of land and took away a little grain," we should not imagine much damage. Some grain must have been stored in isolated farmhouses and granaries. In such a brief invasion not all these farms could be reached, much less plundered.

Heraia and found plenty of suitable targets as they burned houses and cut down fruit trees (Xen. *Hell.* 6.5.22). The drama surrounding Epameinondas's great invasion of Lakonia in 370/369 was not merely the enormous size of his army, nor even his audacious entry into an inviolate countryside, but his decision to march in midwinter. Apparently, he felt that the December departure was critical to answer the frantic appeals of his Arkadian allies, who were threatened by Spartan attacks— even though his troops for the rest of the winter were bothered by short supplies and had to confine their attacks mostly to plundering farms and cutting trees (Xen. *Hell.* 6.5.20, 50; Diod. 15.65.2; Plut. *Ages.* 33.8). In theory, the cutting of vines and trees might be easier during the dormant season, when trunks, limbs, and canes were free of foliage, and ravagers not exposed to excessive summertime heat.

While mid-May to late June was the preferable time for the most effective devastation of crops, it seems clear from even these few examples that troops could invade an enemy country at any time of the year to ravage farmland. After all, vines and fruit trees could be cut down during all seasons, and farmhouses could be torched throughout the year.[32] Green grain was exposed and vulnerable in the field much of the winter and all spring; in small, unwalled villages previously harvested stored crops could be looted or ruined, causing particular problems in food-scarce winter months. And since the triad of Greek crops—cereals, olives, and grapes—all ripened at different times, the enemy had the option of arriving in late spring, late summer, or autumn, and thereby causing considerable damage and psychological distress by ruining the

32. Consider, for example, the complaints of the Spartans during the winter invasion of their homeland in 370 B.C.: "The Thebans have invaded our land and have cut down trees and burned down houses and seized property and stock" (Xen. *Hell.* 6.5.37). They apparently felt that such devastation was considerable, even without the loss of their grain crop (which must just have been sown at this time and thus was not so vulnerable) or their tree-fruit and vine harvests.

mature fruit right before harvest.[33] This wasted an entire year's work. Winter was the least favorable season to march, since grain was in short supply and marching and camping were difficult in the cold and rain.

CONCLUSION

Most Greek armies made special arrangements for the devastation of enemy cropland. As they marched through hostile country, the phalanx stayed in protective formation while bands of light-armed soldiers, often poorly organized and trained, followed and spread out over the fields to destroy crops. But because the main army usually could not itself break up and scatter into smaller ravaging parties, and the light-armed that did were extremely vulnerable to enemy sorties and cavalry patrols, the destruction of farmland must have proceeded cautiously. For this reason alone devastation was a slow process. Camps, usually fortified, were nearly always constructed as troops destroyed surrounding small acreages of orchards and vineyards for needed brush and timber. Wagons or pack animals brought along the tools needed for devastation, nearly all of which were also used for road building, construction, and foraging. May and June were the best, and most common, months to invade and devastate—and especially burn—an enemy's important grain crops; but, in fact, ravaging occurred at all times of the year. The complexity of the operation—with such considerations as the season, the extent of enemy resistance, weather and terrain, and the maturity of crops—suggests that systematic devastation was not uniform;

33. See, for instance, Polyb. 4.45.7. And see also Plut. *Agis* 15.2, where Aratus was able to pass up an opportunity for pitched battle "because he thought it wiser—since the farmers had now harvested nearly all their crops—to let the enemy go on by than to risk everything in battle." Obviously the time of invasion had much to do with the response of the invaded; capitulation or pitched battle was more likely during harvesttime invasions—which made the Athenians' apparent inaction during the Peloponnesian War so atypical.

indeed, ravaging was often incidental to other activities, such as plundering, challenging the invaded to pitched battle, and providing dramatic displays of force in enemy territory, the resulting damage from which may have been as much psychological as economic. In general, it is critical to keep in mind that even successful armies of invasion found themselves amid thousands of acres of cropland, often unfamiliar, sometimes inaccessible, and occasionally not entirely evacuated. Because their own supplies were often precarious, and since the systematic destruction of trees and vines often entailed strenuous chopping and cutting, even light-armed troops equipped with axes might find the task of complete devastation nearly impossible. Hoplites would largely stay in formation to prevent sudden counterattacks; and the agrarians in the ranks would be reminded of their own harvests left largely unattended at home as their own army attacked their enemy's ripening crops.

TWO

The Methods of
Agricultural Destruction

Under the diverse conditions of Mediterranean farming in ancient
Greece, "agriculture" is, of course, an abstraction and can refer to radically different types of crops—olives, figs, and other deciduous fruit
trees, barleys and wheats, vegetables, and various species of grapes.
Moreover, since these fruits were both permanent and annual, cultivated under different practices, and part of a larger rural infrastructure
of fences, sheds, houses, terraces, and walls, a review of the ancient
Greek farm and its more important crops is critical for any understanding of agricultural devastation.

GREEK FARMS

A brief outline of the size and physical nature of the Greek farm itself
helps to clarify how invading enemy troops attempted to destroy fruit
trees, vines, grain, and farmhouses.[1] In the first place, landholdings in
Attica were relatively modest in size, and worked for the most part by

---

1. See Jameson's brief remarks (1978, 125–126 n. 1) about the traditional
absence of scholarly interest in ancient farming.

small, independent farmers—the *geôrgoi, mesoi,* or *autourgoi* who appear so frequently in Attic philosophy, comedy, and oratory. From an abundance of literary, epigraphical, and archaeological evidence, we learn that individual plots throughout most of Greece often averaged only 40 to 60 *plethra* (8.9 to 13.3 acres) in extent, rarely, if ever, exceeding 400 to 500 *plethra* (89 to 111 acres).[2] Vast, unbroken parcels owned by absentee landholders were rare in most areas of classical Greece, if not unknown.[3] Ravagers would not be roaming over uninhabited monocropped estates, but through a patchwork of small orchards, vineyards, and grainfields. (See updated commentary, page 213 [Size of Farms].)

Not only were Greek farms rather small in size, but many also were often surrounded by a fence or field wall of rubble (easily collected from almost any Greek field), earthen banks, or planted hedges. In this way, boundaries could be delineated, holdings kept separate, and flooding prevented; as farmland ranged vertically up hillsides, terraces were often common and aided in marking private property.[4] It may seem to us surprising that on farms of such small size it would be economically feasible to fence in a few vines or trees, or even a small grainfield. Yet we see

2. For the epigraphical material, see Andreyev 1974, 14–15; Finley 1952, 58–60; Lewis 1973, 187–212. Cooper 1977, 168–172, contains a valuable synopsis of the primary and secondary sources. For the rarer, relatively larger holdings, see Langdon and Watrous 1977, 175; their field survey and reexamination of the Cliff House in southern Attica revealed a farm of about 180 *plethra* (50 acres). De Ste. Croix (1966, 109–114) has demonstrated that the estate of Phainippos—usually thought to have been the largest farm in Attica—was nowhere near the assumed 3,000–3,800 *plethra* in size, but probably no larger than 400–500 *plethra* (i.e., around 100 acres).

3. Scholars have traditionally been in unanimous agreement on at least this point; see, for instance, Bolkestein 1958, 26–27; Ehrenberg 1951, 80; Finley 1952, 58, 63; Glotz 1927, 247–250; Guiraud 1893, 391–394; Jardé 1925, 120–122; Michell 1957, 43; Pritchett 1956, 275–276.

4. In Greece, where farming is carried on in rough terrain, terrace walls also serve both as retaining walls for soil and as boundaries. The literary evidence for

the same phenomenon often in Greece today. For example, twenty or thirty olive trees can be surrounded by a chain-link fence supported by a concrete foundation. One suspects that the reasons for fencing land are—and were in the past—not entirely economic: small farmers frequently are suspicious of each other, and of strangers in general. The cost of fencing minute holdings may be acceptable if a farmer is convinced that his crops or grazing lands, however small, will be left alone. Pride in one's holdings, the fear of trespassing (by people or animals), and the natural inclination to keep one's possessions separate ("good fences make good neighbors") should also be considered. In any case, the image of a checkerboard of small parcels is strengthened by the notion of fences and stout borders—further obstacles to enemy ravaging of crops. (See updated commentary, page 214 [Fences and Terrace Walls].)

Whether individual, rural farmhouses were part of these small farms is a more difficult question. On the basis of scattered bits of literary and epigraphic evidence, and the long absence of any archaeological remains of farmhouses, settlement in ancient Greece was once thought to

---

field walls is abundant. See Dem. 55.12; Hom. *Od.* 18.358–359; Plut. *Cim.* 10.1.; *Per.* 9.2; Theoc. 1.47. At Lys. 7.28 a plot of ground is specifically described as unfenced. Democritus was said to have disapproved of the unnecessary expense involved in constructing walls (Columella 11.3.2). The field wall running around the perimeter of the Cliff House and farm extends more than three kilometers (see Langdon and Watrous 1977, 173–175, fig. 6, p. 174. Bradford (1956, 172–176) describes farms in the Pinari Valley near Mt. Hymettos that were separated by stone orthostates, as well as by extensive terracing. For the stone field wall belonging to the Salaminioi at Sounion, cf. *Hesperia* 7 (1938): 9; Young 1941, 177–178, 190. Pecírka (1973, 140–145; 1970a, 140ff.) notes the extensive walls surrounding the farm plots in the Crimean Chersonesos. See White 1975, 24–28, for the Roman evidence. The *aulê*, or courtyard, could often extend well beyond the house and so enclose an extensive "barnyard"; see, for example, Jones, Sackett, and Graham 1973, 370–372; Kent 1948, 294–295.

have been centered solely around the city proper or among the smaller, rural villages that were satellites of the polis:[5] "The isolated farm in the middle of a hundred acres or more was unknown."[6]

The excavation of a few isolated, rural Greek farmhouses has now shown that assumption to be false. In Attica alone several homestead farms have been excavated,[7] and many more have been noticed, though not yet explored.[8] The most striking published examples are two pastas-style houses: the so-called Dema House of the late fifth century B.C., situated in front of the later fourth-century field wall spanning the Aigaleos-Parnes gap,[9] and a similar, though smaller and more isolated, fourth-century house near the Cave of Pan at Vari.[10] Less elaborate but more numerous are the well-built farm buildings in the grain-growing

5. Pecírka devotes an entire article to the "problematique" of the isolated, rural farmhouse in the Greek world (1973, 113–147). But compare the traditional view of Bradford (1956, 180), Bolkestein (1958, 19–21), Finley (1952, 62–63), and Semple (1931, 539), all of whom denied the existence of isolated homesteads outside the polis or village, citing in support of their view the lack of available water in the Greek countryside, problems of protection and defense, and the social desirability of living in communal areas. Dem. 55.11, Lys. 1.11, Thuc. 3.88.2, and Xen. *Hell.* 5.2.7, 5.4.3, and 7.5.14–15 may offer examples of farmers who must commute from their homes in town to their fields in the countryside, but do not (as some believe) rule out the possibility of the simultaneous presence of isolated farmhouses in the country.

6. Michell 1957, 4.

7. See Jones 1975, 63–140, for a summary of excavated farmhouses in Attica.

8. Random notices of unnamed, unpublished farmhouses can be found in Eliot 1962, 43–44; Jones 1975, 135 n. 59; Langdon and Watrous 1977, 162 n. 2; Pecírka 1973, 136–137.

9. Jones, Sackett, and Graham 1962, 75–114. The Dema House unfortunately has become completely obliterated under the trash of the Athens municipal dump.

10. Jones, Sackett, and Graham 1973, 355–452. For comparative studies of the two houses, see Jones 1974, 303–312; 1975, 110–116.

regions of the Laureion hills in southern Attica. They are easily recognizable by their characteristic towers.[11] At Cape Zoster near present-day Vouliagmeni, an isolated homestead, the so-called Priest's House, was found and excavated over forty years ago.[12] Outside of Attica there are even more examples. On the southwest tip of the Crimean Chersonesos there is a complex of separate farms and farm plots covering almost 10,000 hectares.[13] And in the Aegean, isolated farmhouses are known to have existed on Chios,[14] Delos, Rheneia, and Mykonos.[15]

This archaeological evidence for the existence of isolated rural farmhouses throughout the Greek world is corroborated by literary references that have usually been ignored or misunderstood. For example, in Thucydides' famous description of the Thebans' night attack on Plataia, Plataian citizens are mentioned as caught with their property on their farms outside the walls of the city (Thuc. 2.5.4; cf. 2.5.5, 2.5.7). Since the events took place at night, and in very early spring (e.g., 2.2.1), when neither planting nor harvesting was taking place, these Plataians must have been permanent residents of rural farmhouses, not city dwellers temporarily residing in harvesttime shacks in the fields or members of satellite villages surrounding a large mother polis. Similarly, when Brasidas surprised the city of Amphipolis, he caught many inhabitants who were living at the time scattered about the countryside (Thuc. 1.103.5, 4.104.1).

11. Young 1956b, 122–146; Langdon and Watrous 1977, 162–177. Young's "red" and "hilltop" towers are uncomfortably devoid of surrounding agricultural land (bee-keeping, however, could have been practiced) and were probably storehouses or guardhouses for slaves and equipment associated with the mining operations.

12. P. D. Stavropoulis, "Ieratikê oikia en Zosteri tês Attikês," *Archaiologikê Ephêmeris* (1938): 1–31.

13. Pecírka 1970a, 459–477; 1973, 113–147; 1970b, 123–174 (with M. Dufkova).

14. Boardman 1956, 41–45.

15. Kent 1948, 243–338.

In numerous descriptions of agricultural devastation, attacks on rural farmhouses are constantly mentioned; it is likely that in the majority of cases the isolated homestead or very small cluster of houses is meant, rather than the larger, centralized rural village or deme. For example, when the Lydian king Alyattes invaded the territory of the Milesians each year, he left their rural farmhouses intact (Hdt. 1.17) but destroyed their crops. His hope was that the Milesians would have their homes outside the walls and thus a base from which they could plant and cultivate their land. That way he could ravage the farms the next year. We also hear of Aitolian plunderers who stage border raids, steal stock, and break into farmhouses clearly described as "houses on farms" (Polyb. 4.3.10). When Mnasippos overran the countryside (but not the city itself) of the Corcyraeans, he devastated the land and "the extravagant houses and wine cellars that had been built on the farms" (Xen. *Hell.* 6.2.6).[16] When the attack is against houses that are clustered into rural villages, on the other hand, it is usually so specified (e.g., Xen. *Anab.* 4.1–5; *Hell.* 1.2.4; Polyaen. *Strat.* 1.32.3). To assume that these dwellings are all clustered or simply temporary shacks is mistaken.

There are, of course, also many references to rural settlement and houses in the countryside in which it is not stated whether citizens are assumed to be living in isolated farmhouses or in small villages and demes (e.g., Aeschin. 1.105; Dem. 21.157–158; *Hell. Oxy.* 12.5; Isoc. *Areop.* 52; Thuc. 2.14.2, 2.16.2, 2.62.2). Nor is it clear whether there were always two distinct types of settlement. A few houses along a small roadway, while not examples of isolated farmhouses, are hardly, on the other hand, a real village. A good example are the interesting, but scantily published and often overlooked, remains of the late fifth century B.C. at Draphi in the foothills of Mt. Pentelikos. There a street, a cemetery, and two small, separate clusters of houses have been uncovered. One

---

16. See also, for example, Xen. *Hell.* 5.4.21; 6.5.28, 30, 37.

contains a very impressive split-level home with hearth and mosaic bathroom.[17]

We should assume that in the ancient Greek countryside, as today, there were all types of rural settlement. Small villages may have been common, to be sure, but there were countless farmers who, for whatever reason, chose to live on their land in single, isolated farmhouses. Likewise, others, perhaps family or kin groups, would cluster together at favored places (like Draphi) out in the countryside, living neither alone nor in the more urban environment of the nearest village. (See updated commentary, page 214 [Rural Residence and Isolated Farmhouses].)

In conclusion, rarely did wide-open expanses of unoccupied cropland await the enemy army of ravagers. The small valleys and plains of Greece were instead broken up into small parcels whose borders were clearly delineated and often fenced; terraces on hillsides could serve as additional boundaries. Occasionally plots were occupied by isolated farmhouses, whose occupants might defend not merely their cropland but their homes as well. Nor were all farms on level, accessible ground. Many were situated on hilly, if not rugged terrain—such as the *eschatiai* so frequently mentioned in Greek inscriptions and literature.[18] These factors should all be kept in mind as we turn to the discussion of the methods of agricultural destruction. For physical reasons alone, ravagers could not gallop wildly through the Greek countryside, spreading fire and ruin at will. Fences, terraces, hills, small orchards, and vineyards all made progress slow and will help to explain some of the difficulties in agricultural devastation mentioned later. (See updated commentary, page 217 [Nature of Terrain and Farm Plots].)

17. Cf. a series of articles in *Bulletin de Correspondance Hellénique* and the *American Journal of Archaeology*: *BCH* 80 (1956): 246–247; *BCH* 81 (1957): 515–519; *AJA* 60 (1956): 269; *BCH* 82 (1958): 680–691.

18. See Guiraud 1893, 66–68; Lewis 1973, 210–212; de Ste. Croix 1966, 109–112. The Cliff House and farm in southern Attica and the estate of Phainippos come quickly to mind as examples of large farms on difficult terrain.

In describing the way in which ravagers devastated agriculture, I limit my remarks to farmhouses and grain (i.e., barley and wheat), olive trees, and vines—the triad of crops that made up the bulk of Greek farming. Of course, other fruit trees, such as apple, fig, pear, and pomegranate trees, as well as flax and vegetables, were cultivated, and thus were subject to attack during wartime. (See updated commentary, page 218 [Fruit Trees Other Than Olives].) But in comparison, these were not so important in Greek agriculture, and the methods of their destruction will have not differed too greatly from those used on the usual triad discussed below.

GRAIN

In many parts of Greece, particularly landlocked or mountainous regions such as Arkadia or Akarnania, the loss of one year's grain crop meant hardship, while two years' deprivation could bring on hunger.[19] The destruction of grain, then, was potentially the most lethal of all forms of agricultural devastation, involving as it did the staples of everyday life.[20] Unfortunately for our purposes, very rarely is any information given about how grain was actually destroyed, or the effectiveness of the attack. There is usually only a line acknowledging that "the land was

19. See, for example, Xen. *Hell.* 4.7.1, 5.3.26, 5.4.56; Anderson 1970, 2; Grundy 1948, 90–91, 246–247. Few Greek poleis could afford to stockpile vast supplies of grain in case of sudden emergencies (unlike Babylon, which paid no attention to the siege attempted by Cyrus, "since they [the Babylonians] had stored up a supply of provisions for many years" [Hdt. 1.190.2]). Belt tightening and imported supplies, however, could keep a Greek city alive for surprisingly long periods: see, for instance, Xen. *Hell.* 5.3.21, 7.2.17.

20. In using the term "grain" I am referring to wheat and barley, the chief cereals of classical Greece and of antiquity in general; see L. A. Moritz, *Grain Mills and Flour in Classical Antiquity* (Oxford, 1958), xx–xxi. Both were usually planted by mid- or late November and harvested from mid- or late May until the end of June, depending on the region and species. See Jardé 1925, 45 n. 2; Shear 1978, 69; White 1970, 141; Zimmern 1931, 42; and Hes. *Op.* 385, 614.

ravaged." Even in the few cases where grain is specifically mentioned as the target of attack, there is still frequently no hint of what method of devastation was used (e.g., Xen. *Hell.* 4.7.1; cf. 5.3.18; Thuc. 2.79.2; Isoc. 16.13; see also Diod. 16.56.2).

At first glance, wheat and barley would seem the most vulnerable of all crops to devastation, liable to burst into flames that could sweep an entire field[21]—an operation that requires little, if any, work by ravagers. Thus one recalls the biblical feat of Samson, who lit the tails of 300 foxes and released them into the fields of the Philistines, where they ignited the standing grain (as well as vines and olives) (Judg. 15:4–5). In classical times, the best-known example again comes from the Lydian invasions of Miletus. Herodotus (1.19) relates that in the twelfth year of the war when the Lydians were routinely burning the Milesian grain, a violent wind came up and carried the flames against the temple of Athena Assesia, razing the structure. Curiously enough, however, there are very few other examples in our literary sources where standing grain in the field is described as being burnt during wartime.[22]

There are probably two different reasons for this surprising silence. We should first consider the time of enemy invasions. Should the enemy advance at the beginning of the campaign season—that is, in March, April, or early May—the grain would still be green and hardly

21. Dry grain, of course, is flammable, in fact almost explosive when stored in large quantities. In Greece today the stubble left after the grain harvest is burnt away in the early fall: see Xen. *Oec.* 18.2; McDonald and Rapp 1972, 50; White 1970, 184. In the Boer War the British had great success burning entire fields of dry grain in the arid South African countryside; see T. Pakenham, *The Boer War* (New York, 1979), 500–501. During Sheridan's devastation of the Shenandoah Valley (summer 1864), the shocks of corn still left out in the field were torched; see J. C. Andrews, *The South Reports the Civil War* (Princeton, 1970), 421; see, too, *Memoirs of General W. T. Sherman* (Chicago, 1875), 2: 191, where dry fodder left unharvested on Southern farms was burned.

22. See Arr. *Anab.* 1.12.9; Polyb. 5.19.8; and Xen. *Anab.* 1.6.1 for the burning of fodder. See also Xen. *Hell.* 1.2.4–5.

combustible. It would have to be either trampled or cut. When Thucydides tells us that the Athenians burnt the grain of the Sicilians in early spring, we should understand the firing of the prior year's stored grain only (Thuc. 6.94.1–2; cf. Gomme 4: 368), not the current crop that was still green and presumably destroyed by other means. Burning standing grain that is even partly green is impossible, as I can attest from personal experience. (See updated commentary, page 219 [Destroying Grain].)

On the other hand, attacks in mid- or late summer or early winter would be too late to catch the standing grain at all, green or dry, because the crop would already be harvested and stored. For example, when the Peloponnesians mounted a winter invasion of the Argolid, they brought along wagons to carry back the enemy's stored grain and ravaged trees and vineyards out in the field (Thuc. 6.7.1; Gomme 4: 222). Therefore, there was only that ideal—but short—period of a month or so in which to burn grain. Enemy invaders would have to arrive right around mid- or late May, when the grain (barley usually ripens anywhere from a few days to weeks before wheat, depending on the individual species) was just becoming combustible but had not yet been harvested and stored behind strong walls. (See updated commentary, page 220 [Regional Considerations].)

The second reason for the general silence in our sources concerns terminology. When troops are described in the frequent operations of taking part of the enemy's crop for themselves and destroying the rest,[23] we can automatically assume that they occupied the fields at or near harvesttime and so burned the ripe grain they could not use.[24] Burning,

---

23. As was sometimes the case perhaps with the Peloponnesian armies during the invasions of Attica in the Archidamian War.

24. It should be taken for granted that anything combustible was always burned by ravagers—this was the easiest method of agricultural devastation. Before the advance of Alexander, for example, the natives burned their dry grain but were forced to trample their still green pasturage to achieve its destruction (Arr. *Anab.* 1.12.9).

then, was probably somewhat more common than the rare detailed descriptions in our sources suggest. Soldiers who were able to occupy fields in May or June (the preferable period of arrival in hostile territory), and who are described in general terms as "ravaging" the land, were probably attempting to burn the bulk of the grain crop that was dry, ripe, and unharvested.[25] If they arrived at just that critical time, then broad devastation was indeed possible.

Many invasions, of course, could not catch the ripe grain while it was still unharvested. Some Greek armies were already engaged in March, April, and early May, when the crop was green. Ravagers during this time were forced either to trample or to cut down grain crops. Both operations are sometimes mentioned, and there are no real indications which was preferred. Cutting the green grain was probably both the more efficient and the more time-consuming method; trampling was less thorough—stalks were often bent, not broken or crushed—but much easier, since large bodies of troops aided by cavalry or pack animals could cause havoc by merely marching through the fields. During the combined Argive-Arkadian invasion of Phleious in 368 B.C., the Phleisian cavalry was careful to keep the enemy forces close under the mountains, "as if they [the enemy] were cautious not to trample the grainfields of their friends" (Xen. *Hell.* 7.2.10). In the retreat before Alexander's advance, native soldiers trampled their green fodder by riding their horses over the fields.[26] At one point, Alexander himself led his

25. We should remember, however, that there were always variations in the harvest period of grain, even within one region. For example, grain planted on marginal land at higher altitudes would ripen later in June. Thus it might still be green in late May and have to be cut or trampled—not burned like the bulk of the crop in the plains below.

26. Arr. *Anab.* 1.12.9. Cf. the text recounting the eighth campaign of Sargon (ca. 714 B.C.): "His pleasant fields, which were spread out like a platter painted lapis lazuli—the surrounding plain planted to grass and habburu, with the chariots and horses of my destructive advance, like Adad I overwhelmed and made the meadows, the support of his horses, like plowland" (D. Luckenbill, *Ancient*

troops through a grainfield and cleared a path by having his men hold their spears down to flatten the crops (Arr. *Anab.* 1.4.1–2). An especially innovative tactic is reported by Plutarch in a passage that sheds much light on the entire process of grain destruction:

> Kleomenes swiftly marshaled his troops and eluded the enemy by taking a different route. At daybreak, he appeared at the city of Argos and began devastating the surrounding plain and grainfields. He did not cut the grain down with sickles and knives (as most others did) but rather had it shattered by the use of special timber planks cut into the shape of shafts. With these, his men, as if on some playground, traversed the field, crushing and ruining the entire crop with little effort at all.[27] (*Cleom.* 26.1)

From this account it seems that troops in special teams with such tools could beat down a grainfield quickly.[28] But we should keep in mind that Plutarch does say that most other armies cut the grain down with sickles and knives. The implication is that in the past (i.e., the fifth and fourth centuries B.C.), before this (rarely followed and mostly atypical?) innovation, the normal way of destroying grain in the field was to cut it down.[29] This process was both strenuous and time-consuming. We should also keep in mind that even the more remote, smaller villages could possess vast tracts of cultivated grainfields, some widely separated

---

Records of Assyria and Babylonia [New York, 1926], 2: 88, no. 161). During Sherman's march to the sea in the American Civil War (1864), livestock was driven into Confederate farmland to trample the growing crops; see R. Wheeler, *Sherman's March* (New York, 1978), 118.

27. This invasion took place in winter (e.g., Plut. *Cleom.* 25.4, 26.1), when the immature, green grain could not be torched.

28. But the idea of covering an entire field with any hand-held implements seems difficult. Farmers in Greece on occasion thin winter grain by allowing flocks to graze in the fields.

29. See, for example, Xen. *Mem.* 2.1.13, where Socrates is made to ask: "Do you know that men cut the grain that others have sown, and chop the trees they have planted?"

and terraced on rugged ground, hard to get to, at various elevations, and ripening at different times.[30] Hans Delbrück, for example, pointed out that the destruction of grainfields requires much time and extensive effort, adding that in the Middle Ages troops resorted to bringing along reapers to mow down the enemy's crops.[31]

In conclusion, the manner and efficiency of destroying annual crops such as grain, unlike olive trees or vines, depended almost entirely on the season in which armies invaded.[32] If the enemy came in winter or spring, grain had to be trampled or even cut, and this could take time. Burning was relatively easy and could wipe out much of a small, landlocked state's annual food supply; but combustion was possible only from around mid-May onward if the crop could be reached before it was harvested. In late summer and early winter, when there were not yet again standing crops to destroy, ravagers could steal or torch grain in storage—if the crop had not been evacuated behind strong, defensible walls (e.g., Thuc. 6.7.1, 6.94.9; Xen. *Anab.* 7.4.5; *Vect.* 4.45).[33] And if a

30. For example, towns of only a thousand or more people, were they self-sufficient in wheat, might farm about 2,000 acres (Jameson 1978, 131, relates that a family of four or five would need about four hectares [ca. ten acres] of land sown in wheat per year). According to this formula, entire rural districts such as Arkadia, Elis, or Akarnania, which were probably self-sufficient in wheat production, with populations of 80,000 to 100,000 (see *OCD²* s.v. population), might have nearly 180,000 acres under grain cultivation alone.

The idea of trampling or cutting down such acreage in one invasion seems difficult (if an invading army could field, feed, and protect 10,000 full-time ravagers for two uninterrupted weeks of continuous devastation, each man would, nevertheless, need to destroy over an acre himself each day). Anyone who has traveled at grain harvest through the miles of various plains and valleys in Boiotia—one of the flattest and most accessible regions of Greece—can imagine how difficult it would be even to reach, much less destroy, all those fields.

31. Delbrück 1890, 110.

32. This point is nearly always overlooked by modern scholars. They usually mention only one constant method of grain destruction, namely, burning (Michell 1957, 85; French 1964, 82).

33. See Westlake 1945, 80 n. 4.

force could just occupy an area for a few weeks in the late fall and early winter, the sowing of grain could be delayed or prevented altogether, and the year's crop automatically imperiled or even lost—without even ravaging the countryside.[34]

OLIVE TREES

The ubiquity of the olive tree and vital importance of olive oil in the ancient Greek world are well known.[35] Not surprisingly, then, destruction of olive trees was a common tactic in warfare of the Mediterranean. No one can read Herodotus, Thucydides, Xenophon, or any other writer of Greek history without noticing the constant references to invading

34. Agesilaos considered disrupting the Akarnanians' sowing but chose not to so that they might fear for their crop in the upcoming year and so desire peace (Xen. *Hell.* 4.6.13–14; Polyaen. *Strat.* 2.1.1, 4.6.20). The mere presence, then, of the enemy for only a few weeks at grain sowing time or during the harvest period for grain, vines, or olives could cause considerable problems for farmers (e.g., Xen. *Hell.* 3.2.8; 6.2.7, 8; and cf. 1.1.35). Special release clauses were inserted in many farmland rental agreements to allow for the possibility of a farmer not being able to reach his fields to cultivate or harvest his crops because of the enemy's presence. See, for instance, *SIG*³ 966.12–13; F. Sartori, "Eraclea di Lucania," *Herakleiastudien: Archäologische Forschungen in Lukanien* 2 (1967), 1.152–154 (pp. 40–57); *IG* XII.9.191; *IG* V.2, 6; and see also *IG*².411.34–37.

35. For the cultivation of olive trees in ancient and modern times in Greece, and for general information about the tree, see the following: F. Bioletti and W. Oglesby, "Growing and Grafting Olive Seedlings," *University of California Agricultural Experimental Station, Bulletin 269* (1916); Detienne 1973, 293–306; H. Forbes and L. Foxhall, "The Queen of All Trees," *Expedition* 21.1 (1978): 37–47; N. Gavrielides, "A Study in the Cultural Ecology of an Olive-Growing Community: The Southern Argolid, Greece" (Ph.D. diss., University of Indiana, 1976); H. T. Hartmann and K. W. Opitz, "Pruning Olive Trees in California," *University of California Agricultural Experimental Station, Circular 537* (1966); McDonald and Rapp 1972, 53–55, 195–196; Michell 1957, 76–77; *RE* 17.2 (1937) 1998–2022, s.v. Olbaum (A. Pease); R. Standish, *The First of All Trees: The Study of the Olive* (London, 1961); White 1970, 225–227.

troops who seek to destroy the olive orchards of their enemy. Scholars often cite a passage or two describing the ravaging of olive trees, assume total destruction, and then speculate on the resulting long-term economic disruption—often surmising periods of agrarian depression of up to a half-century. Yet very little is known about the actual methods (e.g., uprooting, burning, girdling, cutting) and effectiveness of this routine ravaging. (See updated commentary, page 221 [General Information].)

Troops rarely, if ever, attempted to uproot the olive—the only sure way of absolutely destroying the tree. The sole explicit reference to the use of this method during wartime seems to be Polyaenus, *Strategemata* 2.1.10. In this instance Agesilaos tears up the trees of the Akarnanians by the roots.[36] Interestingly enough in this case, the Akarnanians quickly leave their mountain garrison because Agesilaos appears to be bogged down in this exhaustive task—the Akarnanians, Polyaenus reports, "despis[ed] his slowness and preoccupation with the trees." The olive's tough wood and extensive root system explain why olive trees were not normally uprooted during war.[37] While the roots do not penetrate to any unusual depth, they do spread out laterally quite a distance. This root expanse provides a wide base for the tree and makes it nearly impossible to topple the tree over (as is possible, for example, in the case of the almond). R. Standish, for instance, recounts a particularly vivid illustration of difficulty in removing the roots of an olive tree:

36. I make the assumption always that *dendra* in Greek usually refers to fruit trees alone and, in most cases, meant olive trees (see, for example, Gomme 2: 207; F. W. Walbank, *A Historical Commentary on Polybius* (Oxford, 1979), 3: 247; Zimmern 1931, 37–38). We cannot of course exclude the occasional use of *dendra* to refer to citrus and fig–trees. Xenophon's parallel account of this same campaign in Akarnania makes no mention of the uprooting of trees. Instead, Agesilaos is described as burning and cutting the land (Xen. *Hell.* 4.6.5, 4.6.12). If one does believe Polyaenus's story, he may be referring to tiny sapling olive trees recently transplanted from seedbeds—thus easily dug out to ensuring lasting destruction.

37. See, for example, Plut. *Sol.* 23.5–6; Theophr. *Hist. Pl.* 2.5.6, 4.13.5.

Fuel was dear and scarce in France after the war, so I had these olive roots dug out of the ground. It was fascinating to watch. First the men dug a circle about twenty feet in diameter around each root, exposing all the lateral roots. These they cut with an ax. Then they set to work with sledge-hammers and wedges breaking the roots into pieces small enough to be moved by hand. . . . The roots were enormous, almost like boulders. They had a great resiliency, so that sledge-hammers bounced back without making any impression. This was especially true of old wild olives on to which had been grafted one of the cultivated varieties.

The men who did this work preferred fuel to money, so they worked on a fifty/fifty basis. This is how the roots came to be weighed. One weighed out at 2,305 kilograms, or close on two and a half English tons.[38]

When we do hear of olives being uprooted it is during peacetime, when the situation is completely reversed. Then the thoroughness, not the speed, of removal of the olive tree is most important. Farmers, consequently, are obliged to undertake the time-consuming task of uprooting the tree in order to remove the bothersome dormant stump and retrieve the valuable wood. A good illustration is found in Lysias's seventh oration. After the war, the speaker is accused of clearing his land, and in the process taking out a sacred olive stump by the roots (7.26), since the tree had recently been cut down (7.6–8), but *not* uprooted by the enemy during the war. Likewise, in Demosthenes' forty-third oration, the heirs of Hagnias's estate, who apparently wanted their newly acquired orchard removed, were accused of having the trees rooted out (43.69) and sold for wood at a great profit. In the same speech, an Athenian law listing penalties for the uprooting of olive trees is quoted (43.71), again suggesting that this was the usual way to remove olive trees during

38. Standish 1961, 60–61. This method of propagation was common in ancient Greece, as it still is today.

peacetime. Olive trees, then, clearly were dug up by the roots only in peace, when there could be advantages (even if sometimes illegal) to this process, and not during war, when there was no time to do so. That laws existed to protect olive stumps also suggests that in both peace and war cutting was a common method of quicker extraction—but one that did not kill the tree outright. Thus even stumps were protected, on account of the olive's vigorous ability to regenerate.

A much easier method of destroying olive orchards would seem to be simply to set fire to, and burn, the trees where they stood.[39] Surprisingly, though, there is only scattered evidence that this method was attempted.[40] One example is again found in the seventh oration of Lysias, where olive stumps at one point are referred to as the *purkaïas*, "the charred" (7.24). This rare word suggests that the enemy burnt olive trees as well as cut them down (7.7). We know also that Agesilaos at one point chopped down and torched fruit trees near Lechaion (Xen. *Hell.* 4.5.10). Teleutias, too, in 382 B.C. was careful "neither to burn nor to cut down" trees so that he might be free of any fallen trees during his approach and withdrawal from Olynthos (Xen. *Hell.* 5.2.39).

But, in general, references to the burning of fruit trees are relatively rare. Usually any burning that does occur tends to be in conjunction with cutting the trees (as in these examples). No doubt ravagers first had to lop off branches and pile the brush in or near the tree or trunk in order to ignite the fire. This time-consuming, extra effort was necessary because an olive tree will not suddenly burst into flames and quickly be reduced to a worthless, charred stump, as sometimes believed. Green

39. As, for example, Zimmern (1931, 46) and Hardy (1926, 348 n. 4) believe.

40. In more modern times, we know that Saracen raiders during summer attacks were able to burn some olive trees on the French coast; cf. Standish 1961, 78. During the recent Greek civil war of the late 1940s the almond groves of the village of Koukourava were burnt by guerrillas; cf. G. Chandler, *The Divided Land* (Oxford, 1959), 199.

olive wood, it is true, could be made to burn (e.g., Ar. *Lys.* 255, 267), especially in summertime, but only if the flame is well fed by surrounding dry grain or brush. Since the trees did not grow densely together, there was no chance of flames dancing from olive tree to olive tree, like the forest fires that sweep over whole stands of timber. In California, large orchards of fruit trees—almond, plum, peach, olive, nectarine, walnut, citrus—are uprooted by large tractors or Caterpillars, and the dead trees are stacked in enormous piles, sometimes twenty feet high. Orchard removal is always undertaken in the summer, since such stacks of dead trees require months of summer heat to become dry and combustible. But even after months of drying, portable propane tanks are often rented to feed winter fires in order to obliterate the denuded piles.

Another, and more important, problem that limited this tactic of burning olive trees was simply the inability of fire to kill the tree: *oliva in totem ambusta revixit* ("an olive-tree, even after completely incinerated, rejuvenates") observes Pliny (*HN* 17.241). The best-known instance of such revival is the legendary olive tree on the Acropolis, which survived the burning of the citadel and purportedly sprouted new growth the next day (Hdt. 8.55; Paus. 1.27.2). Granted, the story may be exaggerated, but it holds some degree of truth in that it accurately illustrates the invincibility of the olive and the ancients' correct belief that the tree was not destroyed by fire. Indeed, those burned olive stumps called *purkaïai* in Lysias's seventh oration really seem to have been live trees that were only temporarily damaged by fire and had sent up new, wild shoots (cf. LSJ and Steph. Byz. s.v. purkaïa). These stumps needed only to be grafted onto the more productive domesticated varieties. In Attica today, especially in the northwest, brush fires often sweep the lower foothills in the late summer and early fall. In these areas it is not difficult to find blackened olive trees with substantial green growth shooting out from the trunk, in vivid contrast to the charred, lifeless, and dead evergreens around them. Even on the rarer occasions when the solitary olive was surrounded by dry brush or stood in a dry grainfield, and thus could be ignited and the flames constantly fueled, the tree, nevertheless, did not die:

> In the summer of 1948 a small grass fire worked its way into the hollow of an old olive-tree, part of an abandoned grove on my land. The hollow trunk acted like a chimney, creating a fierce up-draught. The tree was far from water, so I allowed it to burn to the ground, taking care lest it spread. For two days after the tree had ceased to exist it went on burning beneath, and it smoldered for long after that. But when spring came it began to send up healthy green shoots as though nothing had happened.[41]

Such shoots could be grafted onto domesticated cultivars, ensuring that the developed root system of the wild olive host would promote rapid growth and a crop within just a few years.

Burning olive trees was not always the most effective means of destruction and never became a widespread choice for devastation. The tactic was also practicable during the summer months, when dry brush and weeds surrounded the tree, and daytime heat and low humidity made wood more susceptible to combustion. But even after apparently severe burning, the olive was rarely killed outright. New shoots would always emerge. The best that could be said for this method was that it required less effort than cutting the tree and occasionally could cause temporary disruption in production, destroying perhaps the year's crop, should enough of the leaves ignite.

It should now be apparent that the best and most common way to devastate olive orchards in Greek warfare was neither uprooting nor burning but chopping down the individual trees.[42] Indeed, this practice

---

41. Standish 1961, 61; see, too, Gavrielides, "A Study in the Cultural Ecology of an Olive-Growing Community," 66.

42. See, for example, the numerous descriptions in which *temnô* or *koptô* (cut) is used with *dendra* (tree/fruit tree): Dem. 53.15–17; Lys. 14.33; Paus. 4.7.1; Poll. *Onom.* 1.174; Thuc 2.75.1, 4.69.2; Xen. *Mem.* 2.1.13; *Hell.* 4.5.10, 5.2.39, 5.2.43, 6.5.22, 6.5.30.

was so routine that the two verbs *koptô* and *temnô* (to cut) are used by ancient authors in a generic sense with "the land" to specify grain, tree, and vine ravaging: "cutting the land." Such nomenclature describes the devastation of the countryside where troops are understood to cut down standing grain, orchards, and vineyards. There are even more specialized words, such as *dendrotomeô* and *dendrokopeô* (to cut a tree), that refer only to the devastation of fruit trees by cutting. But just how speedily and effectively could ravagers cut down olive trees?

At the outset, we should note that the Greeks were hardly novices at tree felling.[43] There are plenty of wartime instances where troops cut timber rather quickly in order to make a path, build fortifications, or evade obstacles and roadblocks (e.g., Polyaen. *Strat.* 1.32.3, 1.38.5, 3.9.8, 18; Thuc. 2.75.2, 2.98.1, 4.69.2, 6.66.2, 6.99.3; Xen. *Anab.* 4.8.2, 4.8.8). Yet the systematic devastation of entire olive groves would not be the same thing as these other operations. For example, when timber is needed, the most accessible and best trees are chosen. When a road is to be cleared, a path can be directed to some degree free of especially troublesome obstacles such as large stumps and trees. Brush piles can be made from cutting trees at random, usually the nearest and easiest. But to destroy an entire olive orchard systematically, every tree must be chopped down, regardless of its size or location. Here is where some difficulty arises. Olive orchards in Greece were often on rugged, elevated, and isolated ground,[44] and troops would be forced to run up and down hillsides to reach many trees. As a result of the most common method of propagation—the grafting of the domesticated olive cutting

43. From what we know of Greek and Roman tools, the ancients seem to have developed quite efficient iron axes, single and double-headed, with stout, long hardwood handles. See D. Robinson et al., *Excavations at Olynthus* (Baltimore, 1952), 10: 341–342; Dar.-Sag. s.v. securis, 1165–1172; White 1967, 60–61.

44. See French 1964, 132; Gavrielides, "A Study in the Cultural Ecology of an Olive-Growing Community," 74–75; McDonald and Rapp 1972, 53.

onto preexisting wild olives—many trees could be found outside of uniform orchards, scattered randomly throughout the countryside—regardless of terrain or farming considerations. We should imagine that, as today in rural Greece, almost every country estate would have had various olive trees randomly planted around houses and buildings, in addition to those in the grove itself.

More important factors to be considered are the size and toughness of the olive itself—a tree famous for its longevity, strength, and expanse. The hardwood, gnarled trunk of the tree can reach enormous proportions, and the wild root system and lower trunk are especially tough and among the hardest of woods. Indeed, a trunk diameter of more than twenty feet for an olive tree is not uncommon in Greece today.[45] The thought of felling one of these monsters is ludicrous; thus we should not assume that troops who "cut" the olive always felled every tree at the trunk. They may have merely lopped off the larger and more accessible branches.[46] Delbrück had these characteristics of the olive in mind in his analysis of the damage done during the Peloponnesian devastation of Attica. He dismissed the idea of widespread destruction: "To cut down a moderate sized tree requires several hours even with the best of tools."[47] A. W. Gomme also denied that many olive trees were destroyed during these invasions, suggesting that only their expected fruit was lost.[48]

These inherent problems in chopping down the olive have led some to suggest that the tree could just as easily be killed by girdling the trunk (sometimes described in Greek as *phloios periairetheis kuklô,* "bark being

45. Gavrielides ("A Study in the Cultural Ecology of an Olive-Growing Community," 75) records that some olive trees in the Argolid have diameters measuring more than ten meters; he estimates they are more than 2,000 years old.

46. Cf. Modern Greek *kopsimo,* which signifies the pruning of large olive branches.

47. Delbrück 1890, 110.

48. Gomme 2: 289. Gomme may be too generous even in assigning damage to the fruit. It would be difficult to destroy green olives while on the tree, as they are hard and small.

stripped off in a circle").[49] To my knowledge, however, there are very few references in classical literature to this method of devastation. The occasional use of *ekkoptô* (cut from) and *katakopeô /katatemnô* (cut down) (e.g., Dem. 53.16; Lys. 7.7; Polyaen. *Strat.* 3.10.5; Polyb. 18.6.4; Xen. *Hell.* 4.1.33, 6.5.37) suggests that trees were felled or branches cut off, rather than that bark was stripped from the trunk. In a rare and metaphorical passage, Aristophanes at one point may be referring to tree girdling when he compares the whip scars on a slave's back to the incisions on fruit trees during wartime (*dendrotomêse to nôton:* "tree-cutting the back," *Pax* 746–747), but otherwise we have few references to such methods of tree or vine devastation.

Theophrastus, it should be said, remarks that if tree bark is stripped off in a continuous ring, trees usually perish (*Hist. Pl.* 4.15.1). But after making that statement, he names exceptions, listing varieties of trees that are not killed by girdling, and taking into consideration the depth and extent of the cutting. In fact, mature olive trees are rarely destroyed by girdling. In antiquity, mud or bark covering could be applied to the wound to protect it from heat and cold (e.g., *Hist. Pl.* 4.15.2), in much the same way as tree wax is used today on injured fruit-tree bark. I have girdled hundreds of vine stumps and peach and nectarine limbs in the spring to encourage the production of larger fruit. Even when the knife has gone too deep, beyond the cambium layer, and injured the tree, damage was limited to the loss of an individual tree limb or vine cane. Farmers in Greece today confirm that if the olive is effectively girdled— and by that they mean a deep, wide cut, completely encircling the trunk (a job entailing many feet of cutting and thus not much easier than simply felling the tree)—and left alone, the tree will not die. Rather, portions of the trunk above the cut may revert to a wild olive and need to be regrafted.

Girdling also brings up the topic of the olive tree's amazing characteristics of regeneration. A consideration of these properties is crucial to

49. As, for example, Hardy 1926, 348 n. 4.

any analysis of wartime destruction but, surprisingly, has been neglected by most scholars who have dealt with the subject. Yet the longevity, vigor, and particular sanctity of the olive are well documented in classical literature.[50] We can best begin by examining a few examples that illustrate the olive's imperviousness to even radical cutting.

During the first Peloponnesian invasion of Attica, Pericles downplayed the severity of the devastations by reminding the Athenians "that fruit trees, even if they are lopped or cut down, quickly grow again."[51] Eight years after the occupation of Dekeleia, in the midst of the Spartan plundering and ravaging, the chorus of Sophocles' *Oedipus at Colonus* could still call the olive tree a "a terror to the spears of enemies" (699). In 405 B.C. olives were still trees "that flourish most greatly in this land" (*OC* 700), a tree species impervious to any effort of young men or old to destroy it (702). The detailed references by the chorus at this time to the hardiness of the olive tree reflect the contemporary failure of Peloponnesian tree-cutting brigades.

The Attic laws limiting the uprooting of the olive (Dem. 43.71; Lys. 7.7, 7.25)—the only method that ensures its destruction—also illustrate the tree's invulnerability: olive stumps were not viewed as dead wood, but rather as live trees, temporarily dormant. Protection from uprooting may have been aimed at insuring that the stumps would be safe, and thus able to send up new vegetation quickly; that way the tree could once again become productive. Also, in some descriptions of wartime devastation, troops are mentioned as going over once-ravaged ground in order to recut wood that had grown up again or had been missed in earlier invasions. For example, in the fourth invasion of Attica during the Archidamian War (427 B.C.), Spartan troops ravaged areas that had

50. See the examples collected in Detienne 1973, 294–295.
51. Plut. *Per.* 33.4. On the effect of radical pruning, Columella (5.9.15) remarks: "He who plows the olive grove asks it for fruit; he who manures it begs it for fruit; he who lops it forces it to give fruit." In Greece today, heavy pruning of the olive tree is felt essential to ensure a good crop.

been devastated only a short time before, laying waste to whatever had sprung up or had been passed over (Thuc. 3.26.3). Olive trees, as well perhaps as other fruit trees and vines, must have already sent forth substantial growth since the prior ravaging campaign of 428 B.C., a mere year before, if the enemy had to repeat their devastations.[52] In modern times, Standish recalls an example of an old olive tree that had been cut down for forty years and paved over by a public road. When a trench was dug alongside the street, letting in air and water for the first time, the tree's root system immediately sent new growth out.[53]

It should be clear now that even the most favored method of olive orchard destruction, radically cutting the branches or chopping the tree down at the trunk, also did not always kill the tree.[54] The usual view that farmers in ancient Greece suffered losses of twenty to sixty years as they waited for newly planted replacement trees to reach production needs reexamination.[55]

In the cases where olives were completely cut down at the trunk, the stump would, nevertheless, not be removed; an entirely new replacement tree did not need to be planted.[56] Instead, fresh shoots would soon

---

52. In remarkably similar language Xenophon also describes land that needed to be ravaged again in order to destroy trees that were skipped or had grown back (e.g., *ei de ti ên loipon dendron, koptôn and kaôn*, "if any fruit tree was left, cutting and burning . . .," Xen. *Hell.* 4.5.10; *ei ti denron hypoloipon eiê . . . phtheiroi*, "if any fruit tree were left remaining, he would destroy . . . ," Xen. *Hell.* 5.3.3). Polybius (18.6.4) also mentions fruit trees that had been chopped down but were expected to replace their growth (*auxêseôs tôn ekkopentôn dendrôn*, "the growth of fruit trees that had been once cut down").

53. Standish 1961, 73.

54. Greek farmers today can stop the growth of the olive tree only by uprooting it or by chopping the trunk close to the ground and applying repeated doses of strong herbicide to the stump.

55. See, for example, French 1964, 109; Zimmern 1931, 46.

56. The method of propagation of the domestic olive tree is, in general, a confusing and complex question. To the best of my knowledge, there seem to be only three ways to propagate the olive: by seedlings, by cuttings, or by graft-

appear from the chopped tree. Such sprouting revealed that the stump was very much alive,[57] although this new growth could revert to the wild olive variety whether the tree had been originally propagated from cuttings or by grafting. The tree, then, would be immediately grafted again onto a domesticated olive variety. Because the farmer had this mature olive trunk intact, with its vigorous wild olive root system, the five-year wait for the pruning and preparation of a suitable new wild olive recipi-

---

ing. We can be sure that domestic olives were not propagated by seedlings in antiquity for a variety of reasons. Besides the fact that great care (see Bioletti and Oglesby, "Growing and Grafting Olive Seedlings," 305) and time are needed to keep the seedlings alive, the domesticated variety of olive tree planted in this way eventually reverts to the wild strain: that is, the domesticated olive tree seems to be self-sterile (see, for instance, Forbes and Foxhall, "The Queen of All Trees," 38). From ancient and modern evidence we know that a common method was to take cuttings or ovules from the mature domesticated olive tree, plant them in seedbeds, and after five years transplant the small trees to the orchard (White 1970, 225–227; McDonald and Rapp 1972, 54; Dem. 53.15–16), where they will reach production in another five or ten years. (Pliny's statement at *HN* 15.2 that olive trees "now bear while in the nursery and [their] fruit is picked seven years after planting" perhaps illustrates that carefully nurtured trees could produce fruit much sooner.) The third method of propagation, the grafting of shoots from the domesticated olive onto a wild olive trunk, was also practiced widely. This method is more important to our study because it was probably the primary way of replacing wartime losses if the trees had been cut down at the trunk. See Gavrielides, "A Study in the Cultural Ecology of an Olive-Growing Community," 68–91, on the process of grafting in the Argolid today.

57. Standish (1961, 73) gives a good example: "In the heart of this desolate region which had great beauty, there is the charred stump of what must have been a giant among the olives. From this stump has grown a small jungle of fresh green olive shoots which, miraculously, have escaped the marauding goats. The shoots go to a height of some fifteen feet now, the biggest of them as thick as my wrist and almost trees. The remarkable thing is that the shoots, with everything against them, produce in most years a fine quality black olive for pickling, which a woman I know gathers regularly."

ent trunk for grafting was eliminated. Farmers in Greece say that a cultivated olive graft on a preexisting mature trunk reaches production within six or seven years at the most.[58] In my own experience, I have chainsawed down large, mature plum and nectarine trees, grafted scions of new varieties onto the bare trunk (sometimes a single nurse limb of the prior species is left for a year), and had sizable crops of fruit in the third year. (See updated commentary, page 222 [Regeneration and Planting to Production].)

In conclusion, I have not meant to minimize the disruption caused by the devastation of olive trees. The countless references in our sources testify that most armies felt the tactic was successful. If olives were ubiquitous in the Greek countryside, and invading armies wished to prompt defenders to meet them in the pitched battle, then attacking their olive groves was an obvious incitement. But I would suggest that modern scholarly opinions of the wartime damage inflicted are greatly exaggerated. If ample time is devoted to cutting the tree down at the trunk, good production may be interrupted for up to seven years. Such a loss for the enemy might in some cases have been worth the effort. But the inherent difficulty and uncertainty of results in chopping down the trees ensured that entire olive orchards were not destroyed on a wide scale.

58. Scholars who quote a fifty-to-sixty year waiting period for replacement of lost olives ignore the possibility of grafting onto a mature preexisting olive trunk. And even when olives are propagated from cuttings, if the tree is well taken care of and well watered, it usually bears fruit in six to eight years, reaching good production sometime after its twelfth year. In California, young olives come into bearing at three to five years of age, reaching heavy production between their eighth and tenth years (Hartmann and Opitz, "Pruning Olive Trees in California," 4–5). Of course, young orchards that are dry-farmed, that is, not irrigated at all (which often must have been the case in antiquity), may take longer to reach full production—usually sometime between their tenth and fifteenth years, but by no means after their sixtieth year.

The tactic may have been most effective (and been so intended) in terrifying or inciting to battle the farmer-hoplites who were worried about enemy troops running loose among their livelihood, and threatening even a few trees. Given the centrality—religious, spiritual, cultural, and economic—of the olive tree in the life of the Greek agrarian population, it is understandable that any threat to olive trees might draw some sort of strong response from their hypersensitive owners.

VINES

There is very little specific information on the devastation of vineyards. Only a few details can be found, mostly in the comedies of Aristophanes. There we learn that enemy ravagers either trampled or cut down vines. The chorus of Acharnian farmers, for example, threatens to pierce with reeds the enemy ravagers who trample their vineyards (*Ach.* 232; cf. *Pax* 319–320). Ravagers were able to walk over vines because the plants were relatively small, grew close to the ground, and were trellised to flimsy reeds or occasionally were not supported at all.[59] But because the vines were already low-lying, it was difficult to smash the canes or break the trunk by pressing the plant closer to the ground. And since enemy ravaging often took place in the spring to early fall, the canes of the vines would be green and pliant, not stripped of their foliage and dry, as in winter. Consequently, they could not be easily broken off at the trunk by mere trampling.

59. For the evidence for propping (which must have been the regular practice in most areas of Greece, as it is today), see Michell 1957, 79–80. White (1970, 231–236) discusses the various ways of training or not training the vine in Roman practice. A few varieties of grapes in modern Greece are only supported in infancy, the mature vine not reaching the production capacity of stronger American vines, which are trellised on stout 2″ x 2″ stakes or metal poles and wired in long rows, usually reaching a height of five to seven feet or more.

A more common and destructive method was to cut the vine down.[60] In the *Acharnians* (182–183), for example, the chorus complains that Aphitheos has negotiated with the enemy who has cut down their vineyards. Later (512), Dikaiopolis tells the chorus that his vines had been chopped. Polyaenus (*Strat.* 2.1.26) reports that during the Spartan advance on Lampsakos, Agesilaos had his troops cut down the surrounding vineyards. In Demosthenes' fifty-third oration, the villain Nikostratos broke into a nearby farm and cut down the tree vines (53.15).[61]

Understandably, there is little indication that vineyards were ever torched or torn out by the roots. Green canes—in many locales present from April to November—cannot be ignited.[62] While uprooting is possible, the roots of vines cling stubbornly to the soil and require the effort of more than one person.

Trampling and more commonly cutting, then, were the usual methods of ravaging vineyards. Both could be done quickly and easily to the individual vine, but destroying an entire vineyard is a different matter altogether. In one acre alone there could be over 2,000 vines.[63] Even if an individual ravager could destroy an average of one vine per minute and keep up the constant pace unabated, each acre of vineyard could cost over thirty-three hours of labor. Paradoxically, vines, which are

60. Cf. the boast of Sargon I: "I cut down its splendid orchards, I cut down quantities of vines, I made an end of its drinking" (D. Luckenbill, *Ancient Records of Assyria and Babylonia* [New York, 1926], 2: 90, no. 164).

61. Cf. also Plut. *Mor.* 15E–F, where *ekkoptô* (cut out) is used again for vine destruction.

62. I verify this from personal experience. Even when a fire is constantly fed, the canes merely become scorched, with a few leaves curling up and blackening. The flame never ignites the vine.

63. White (1970, 246) gives a figure of 1,225 plants per *iugerum*, or about 1,960 per acre. Closely planted vines in Greece today can occupy as little as one square meter each (Kent 1948, 291 n. 173), or about 4,047 plants per acre. In California most table, raisin, and wine grapes usually average between 453 and 622 vines per acre, because substantial space is needed between rows for tractors and machinery.

rather easy to cut or trample, might be as difficult to eradicate as the more resistant olive tree on account of their sheer density per acre.[64]

Because vines were not uprooted in wartime, there was no guarantee of permanent destruction. Like the olive, should the grape trunk be pruned and denuded of all its canes, or even be cut down, new growth would sprout forth regardless the next spring—especially when domesticated varieties are grafted onto wild rootstocks.[65] The impression we get is that the devastation of vineyards was chiefly a question of destroying the year's crop by trampling and smashing the berries or cutting off the fruit-bearing canes. A good example is found at Thucydides 4.84.1, where we hear that Brasidas arrived at Akanthos in mid- or late August, right before the grape harvest. Because the Akanthians were afraid for the year's crop, that they would either lose access to their vineyards at harvesttime or have their grapes destroyed in the field, they—both the farmers and the urban dwellers at large—were forced to let the Spartans inside their city (Thuc. 4.84.2, 4.87.2, 4.88.1).

Similarly, the loss of the annual grape crop, more than permanent destruction of the vines themselves, seems to be a chief complaint in Aristophanes' plays. The Acharnians (*Ach.* 987) lament that the war has poured out the wine of their vines. In the *Knights* (1076–1077) ravagers are compared to small foxes who eat the grapes in the fields (cf. *Pax* 634). And while characters do mention vines that are trampled or cut, they nevertheless take for granted that their vineyards are still intact and will be productive when the invaders leave. The implication is that the damage to the vine is confined to only the year's crop. In short, the wartime ravaging of vines rarely, if ever, resulted in the permanent destruction of vineyards. (See updated commentary, page 223 [Vines].)

---

64. Gomme (2: 164) and Delbrück (1890, 110) rightly acknowledge the time and difficulty involved in the destruction of vineyards.

65. Thuc. 3.26.3 refers to both olive trees and vines that had sent out new growth after the Spartans' initial devastations. Cf. Hardy 1926, 351 n. 5. Normal autumn pruning takes 85 percent to 95 percent of the past year's growth.

Vines, it should be remembered, regenerate like olives but come into full production much earlier. In California, heavy production is often achieved in the third year after planting (through either cuttings or one-year rootings); indeed, most viticulturists worry about overcropping by vigorous young vines in their third year when excessive fruit production weakens the plant. Such young vineyards have a tendency to produce too heavy a crop, which stresses the vine and is often difficult to bring to maturity.

FARMHOUSES

Enemy ravagers out in the countryside routinely first plundered and then destroyed any homestead farmhouses or groups of rural dwellings that they encountered. The loss of these buildings would not only disrupt agriculture by denying farmers the use of barns, granaries, livestock shelters, and mill-houses,[66] but would also leave country people homeless and in general cause particular psychological distress and loss of morale.[67] Unlike the devastation of grain, olive trees, and vines, which is only rarely mentioned in detail in ancient literature, there are numerous, vivid descriptions of attacks on homesteads and rural villages. Thus

66. Of course, in preindustrial agriculture the need for large investments in storage and shelter is less than in modern farming. Nevertheless, we know of the existence of ancient farm outbuildings and must assume that they were important to production. See Boardman 1956, 50–51; Jones, Sackett, and Graham 1973, 369–370: Kent 1948, 295, 299; Pecírka 1970b, 471; and cf., too, *Hell. Oxy.* 12.5.

67. At Hdt. 1.17 the homes of the Milesians (*oikêmata ta epi tôn agrôn*) are spared in order that they might remain and continue to work their land—providing crops for the invaders to plunder each year. In the Boer War (1899–1902), the English destroyed Boer farmhouses as a matter of policy to weaken enemy resistance and erode civilian support. After the war, 63,000 separate claims for compensation were submitted. Cf. T. Pakenham, *The Boer War* (New York, 1979), 466–467, 608.

we can form a fairly clear picture of how this destruction was accomplished.

Construction of houses in and outside of cities could vary widely throughout the Mediterranean world, depending on the availability of building materials, the pattern of land tenure, and the custom and usage of the inhabitants. For example, one has only to reflect on the vast difference between the ponderous, solid rock houses at Dystos, which must have been as invulnerable in antiquity as they seem today,[68] and the flimsy reed dwellings at Sardis that Herodotus relates were engulfed in a vast fire when the Greeks took the city (5.101.1; cf. Xen. *Anab.* 5.2.24–25). But in general we can assume that most rural houses, especially in mainland Greece, were of a common type: stone foundations and socles, mud-brick walls with wooden frame supports, tiled roofs, and, in the larger dwellings, wooden columns on stone bases.[69]

When these farm buildings were attacked by ravagers, they were in almost all cases destroyed by fire.[70] This may seem surprising, since so much of the house was made up of noncombustible materials, such as mud brick and clay tiles. But the little wood that was used in these structures played a crucial role as the supporting framework for the entire house. If this could be burned, the whole building would quickly tumble down.

68. See T. Wiegand, "Dystos," *Mitteilungen des Deutschen Archäologischen Instituts, Athenische Abteilung* 24 (1899): 458, for a brief description of the ruins.

69. In Attica especially this seems to have been the common model, as the Dema, Vari, and Priest's houses, as well as the structures at Draphi, show. See Jones 1975, 63–61; and cf: Xenophon's well-known description of the ideal house (*Mem.* 3.1.7).

70. The evidence is unquestionable. See, for example, Arr. *Anab.* 1.12.10; Aeschin. 3.123; Dem. 29.3; Diod. 12.43.2, 12.45.1, 12.78.2, 14.58.3; Polyb. 9.6.8; Polyaen. *Strat.* 1.32.3; Xen. *Hell.* 6.5.28, 6.5.37; *Anab.* 4.2.19, 5.2.24–25, 7.4.1, 5.

In a rather strange article D. H. Gordon reviews the problem of torching such mud-brick houses.[71] He comes to the understandable conclusion that the woodwork of native mud-brick huts would not automatically ignite. Instead, it was essential that dry brushwood be stacked near the interior walls and roof beams to feed the flames. He adds that the whole operation could be easily thwarted by the simple absence of plentiful brush or other fuels.

We can assume that ravagers in Greece undertook a similar method of burning, although they might have been faced with somewhat less difficulty, because of both the hotter, drier climate and the abundance of scrub, maquis vegetation that could supply sufficient fuel.[72] Ravagers, then, first plundered the house, gathered brush from the surrounding area, and then set the interior woodwork and roof beams on fire. Thus when, at the end of Aristophanes' *Clouds* (1486–1500), Strepsiades begins to destroy the schoolhouse, he has his slave first climb up on the roof and rip off the roof tiles. He then torches the exposed roof beams.[73]

71. "Fire and Sword," *Antiquity* 27 (1953): 144–152. Gordon writes from his past experience as an British officer who torched a number of native villages in the Indo-Afghan borderlands.

72. Wood collected from the wild is still a chief, if increasingly scarce, source of fuel in Greece today. Brush fires, accidental and otherwise, are easily set and quite common. Cf. H. Forbes and H. Koster, "Fire, Ax, and Plow: Human Influence on Plant Communities in the Southern Argolid," in Dimen and Friedel 1976, 123. If enemy invasions took place during the harvest season, dry grain, of course, could be cut and used to ignite the fire.

73. Cf. also, again, the letter of Sargon (ca. 714 B.C.): "Shardurihurdu, their great stronghold, together with 57 cities of the neighborhood of the Sangibutu district, I destroyed them totally, leveled them to the ground. The beams of their roofs I set on fire and burned them up" (D. Luckenbill, *Ancient Records of Assyria and Babylonia* [New York, 1926], 2: 88, no. 161). See also J. D. S. Pendlebury, *Annual of the British School at Athens* 38 (1937–1938): 66–67, for a description of the flammable materials used in the construction of ancient and modern houses on Crete.

In the Greek civil war of the late 1940s such destruction was widespread, and hundreds of farmers were made homeless and forced into refugee centers. Concerning the latter devastation, L. Chandler remarks:

> It was a shock to see homeless and bewildered people again and to smell the stench of burnt dwellings. These old homes built of mud bricks on a frame of wood collapsed completely when the fire destroyed the framework and now their owners were searching for possessions in the hot ruins on which the hoses played.[74]

If country houses in Greece were able to be burnt down, they were probably also quickly rebuilt after the invaders departed. Since the roof's tiles were usually not robbed, it was simply a matter of reassembling the fallen mud-brick walls and putting the roof back on new frame supports.[75] The foundation and stone orthostates usually would have remained in situ and suffered no damage; doors, shutters, and other valuable, detachable woodwork were often removed and could be reattached as soon as the walls were up again. Gordon reports, for example, that the mud-brick houses in Waziristan, which were thoroughly burnt, usually were inhabited again after only a few months.[76]

Barns, pens, fences, and outbuildings would also have to be replaced, although many were built of stone or rubble, and so were not so vulnerable. Farm towers, for instance, which seem to have been an integral part of many ancient farms, roughly equivalent to the present-day barn, were constructed usually of stone, and so were impervious to fire. The best-known examples are the towers noted by John Young in the Laureion region of southern Attica.[77] Built usually from local limestone and

74. *The Divided Land* (Oxford, 1959), 172.

75. Wood, though, was scarce and expensive in many areas of Greece, and so a worry in reconstruction. Some mud bricks, of course, would be broken in the collapse, and thus new, replacement bricks would have to be made.

76. Gordon 1953, 149.

77. *Hesperia* 25 (1956): 122–145. Outside of Attica towers have been found on many of the islands and in both the Argolid and the Megarid—giving credence

even marble, they probably ranged as high as nearly ten meters originally, and their remains are still considerable today. Besides their great size, the solidness of their construction makes earlier, mistaken suggestions that all the towers were actually military garrisons or refugee centers seem understandable. In an anonymous speech attributed to Demosthenes (47), the speaker complains that three of his adversaries broke into his farm and looted his belongings. He remarks that some household furniture and his female slaves were not touched in this assault because they were safe up in the tower and had barred the door (47.56). Later, however, the attackers returned and carried off the remaining goods, which had unfortunately been brought down after their first attack (47.63). In this case, the tower served as a farm blockhouse of sorts or private fort, which could keep a farm's equipment safe from the attacks of small raiding parties. (See updated commentary, page 225 [Farm Towers].)

One wonders just how ravagers could destroy such well-built towers or any other rock structure, which would serve as the repository of agrarian infrastructure in unsettled times. The only possible way would be to pry out key stones in the lower wall with crowbars or shovels, and so undermine the entire building—a task much more difficult than burning a house down, and one replete with the danger to the attacker from falling blocks. In very rare instances, we do hear of such destruction by means other than fire, perhaps suggesting the devastation of farm outbuildings. For example, before the battle of Delion, Athenian troops tore down surrounding buildings to use their stones and bricks in the construction of a rampart (Thuc. 4.90.2). In Plato's *Republic* (5.471A–B) it is suggested at one point that Greeks should neither ravage each other's crops nor burn nor *overturn* (*oikias anatrepein*) houses. Similarly, during the Lydian invasions of the Milesian countryside, the invaders choose neither to *tear down* (*kateballe*) nor burn the farms (Hdt.

---

to Young's belief that "a Greek country estate comprised three basic structural elements: tower, court, and house."

1.17.3).[78] The implication in these cases is that either some dwellings (i.e., stone outbuildings) could not be torched and were destroyed by dismantling the walls or, to make destruction especially complete in the case of burned farmhouses, stone orthostates and foundations were also knocked down, and clay roof tiles smashed.

Attacks on farm buildings were as much a part of agricultural devastation as the ravaging of growing crops. Most Greek farmhouses could probably be burned down after carefully igniting their wooden supports. Long-term displacement of the rural community, however, did not occur simply because such houses of simple construction could relatively easily be rebuilt or replaced. Subsidiary outbuildings, barns, pens, and storage houses may have been only plundered (if there was anything left behind) and not destroyed, since many were built of rubble and were hardly combustible.

78. For other examples of houses or barns destroyed by means other than fire, see Paus. 4.7.1; Polyaen. *Strat.* 3.10.5; and especially Diod. 14.58.3, where Himilcon "ordered his soldiers to raze to the ground the houses, and to leave not a tile or timber or anything else, but either to burn or to smash (*suntripsai*) everything."

PART TWO

The Defense of Agriculture

THREE

Fortification

FIELD WALLS

Greek plans of defense in the classical period seldom incorporated either stockades built directly around cultivated fields or extensive frontier walls designed to stop invading armies from reaching the croplands of the interiors.[1] Although it is true that in a few early instances walls were constructed at key border passes to prevent entry into friendly territory,[2] the usual practice was to gather the country's population, valuables, and movable property into places of refuge (see chapter 4, "Evacuation"), and consequently either to prevent the enemy from ravaging the fields by pitched hoplite battle or to submit to terms and thereby save one's agricultural produce. The alternative was to stay fast inside

---

1. This is in contrast to some of the early walled systems of Egypt and the East. See Harmand 1973, 178.

2. The Phokian Wall at the pass of Thermopylai (Hdt. 7.176.4–5) and the fortifications at the Isthmus of Corinth during the Persian Wars and later (cf. Diod. 15.68.4; Hdt. 8.40.2, 8.71, 9.7; Lys. 2.44–45; Paus. 7.6.7) are two examples. There was also an earlier Mycenean wall on the Isthmus. See O. Broneer, "The Cyclopean Wall on the Isthmus of Corinth and Its Bearing on Late Bronze Age Chronology," *Hesperia* 35 (1966): 346–362.

the walls of the city and watch ravagers attack farmland—outside of Athens not a palatable choice among most Greek city-states.

If the open space within a city's walls that may have been used for small gardening during wartime is not considered real farmland,[3] the first (and only?) fifth-century reference to a true agricultural wall is not found in mainland Greece, but across the neck of the Thracian Chersonesos. There Miltiades originally built a wall across the peninsula to halt the incursions of the Apsinthians, who habitually ravaged the rich farmlands (Hdt. 6.36-37). Later, Pericles rebuilt the wall, and so protected the Greek homesteaders there against Thracian marauders (Plut. *Per.* 19.1–2). When Derkylidas arrived in 398 B.C. he complied with the requests of the inhabitants and once more reconstructed the wall to keep out the Thracians. By doing so "he brought inside the circuit of the wall eleven towns, many harbors, plentiful farmland ideal for both grain and fruit, and large tracts of excellent grazing land for all varieties of stock animals" (Xen. *Hell.* 3.2.10–11).[4]

3. There are numerous examples of open lands included within a city's walled circuit that were perhaps used for cultivation; see Kirsten 1952, 1002 (Athens); Martin 1973, 110 (Stratos). Thucydides speaks of *ta erêma tês poleôs*, which the refugees from Attica quickly filled during the war. Andocides (frag. 3.1 [Loeb]) laments that during the evacuation of Attica into the city the inhabitants were forced to eat wild greens, which suggests that some herbs in or near the walls could be eaten. A lengthy, rambling wall, closely following the terrain, which scholars refer to as a *Geländmauer*, fitted only loosely around a city and consequently offered substantial areas of open space (cf. Winter 1971, 110–114). Cities such as Messene and Megalopolis—the practice became especially popular in the fourth century B.C.—stood amid valuable cropland and were surrounded by large circuits, and hence, as Martin (1956, 192) points out, "une zone de cultures et de pasturages était ainsi protégée." The *Geländmauer*, however, was not intended primarily to protect agriculture. See also Plut. *Phil.* 13.1 for grain cultivated inside Megalopolis during a siege; in the summer of 1997 the entire site of the ancient city was under wheat, which nearly masked the ruined circuit of the walls.

4. Such a long field wall (in this case seven kilometers) required a well-disciplined and carefully deployed group of troops; the difficulty of its defense is

It is recognized that beginning sometime in the fourth century B.C. ongoing changes in military practice in general began to accelerate, lessening dependence on pitched hoplite battles. With improvements in both fortification and siegecraft, the development of artillery, specialization in troops, and the introduction of mercenary armies, more emphasis was given to passive defense strategy.[5] The exhaustive, offensive wars of the prior century no doubt also contributed to this turnabout in thinking.[6] In the case of Athens, the abandonment of the country under Pericles and his followers had proven unwise to many. Conservatives felt that a rejection of hoplite battle was shameful for the reputation of the community and injurious to the character of the individual citizen. Social tensions created among different groups of the Athenian citizenry—farmers, traders, small-business owners, and artisans—illustrated the need in the future for a policy that sought first to protect the lives and property of citizens more equitably. This emerging "pensée politique conservatice du IVe siècle"[7] in Greece turned attention toward border and interior defense as an alternative to both pitched battle and evacuation. It made more attractive the idea of coordinated protection, which, depending on the particular polis, could involve either

reflected by the continual need for reconstruction. Justinian also rebuilt the wall (Procop. *Aed.* 4.10.5). On the wall in general, see Merrit, Wade-Gery, and McGregor, *The Athenian Tribute Lists* (Cambridge, Mass., 1939–1953), 1: 563; and U. Kahrstedt, *Beitrage zur Geschichte der thrakischen Chersones* (Baden-Baden, 1954), 11–14, 24.

5. For the various developments in warfare in the fourth century B.C., see Adcock 1957, 22–24; Delbrück 1975, 149–157; Griffith 1935, 3–7; Grundy 1948, 258–266; Parke 1933, 20–22; Tarn 1930, 5–12, 101–112; Winter 1971, 308–324; and cf. Dem. 9.47–50.

6. Compare the similar defensive strategy of the French after their enormous losses in World War I: "Never again, he [Petain] promised, should such sacrifices be forced upon the youth of France. As early as 1922, he was calling for the creation of a 'Wall of France' that would protect her against the restive, traditional enemy" (A. Horne, *The Price of Glory* [New York, 1962], 338).

7. Garlan 1973, 154. Cf., too, Xen. *Oec.* 6.6–7.

urban, rural, or frontier fortification—or all three combined. And the growth of well-disciplined, if not professional, light-armed troops, who were more flexible in attack and more easily deployed for long periods of time, made the garrisoning and maintenance of stockades and field walls (often on mountain frontiers) practicable in a way not possible in the fifth century B.C. Students of the so-called Dema Wall in Athens have remarked:

> The elaborate defensive scheme implies a tight control of men and a confident ability to move from defense to attack and to re-vert again under pressure. Sorties are altogether risky: if success-ful they would be very successful, for they might well inflict heavy casualties on the enemy without the sallying party's incurring serious loss or being seriously impeded in its return; but if mis-managed or allowed to pursue too far, they might possibly be disastrous, the detachment being checked, counter-checked, cut off, and annihilated. To base the whole defense so largely on sor-ties suggests the battle drill either of a very well-trained levy, or perhaps rather a professional soldiery. As for the choice between heavy infantry in close formation or light-armed men in more fluid combinations, the presumption must be that the large num-ber of posterns and their narrowness, indicative of many local counter-attacks to be carried out by small detachments, favoured the adoption of light-infantry skirmishing tactics.[8]

It is, then, within these larger trends toward defense that occasional field walls, not surprisingly, begin to appear. (See updated commentary, page 226 [Field Walls].)

The first and most famous agricultural field wall that we hear of in Greece was the curious, elaborate stockade that surrounded the prime

8. Jones, Sackett, and Eliot 1957, 180. For the use of light-armed and merce-nary troops in guarding rural territory and the frontier, see Xen. *Hiero* 10.5–6; *Vect.* 4.52.

cropland of Thebes in the early fourth century B.C. When Agesilaos invaded Boiotia in 378 B.C. and proceeded customarily to ravage the land, "he found, however, that the plain and most valuable sections of their land had been enclosed with both a trench and surrounding palisade" (Xen. *Ages.* 2.22).[9] Agesilaos was baffled for a time as the mobile Thebans within the stockade matched his movements and prevented any possible breakthroughs.[10] They were aided by cavalry sorties that issued out of exits in the walls and harassed the surprised Spartans. Agesilaos, however, attacked at sunrise one morning, burst through the unguarded sections of the wall, and ravaged the plain. Again, on his return the next year, he once more caught the Theban defenders unawares inside the wall and entered through an unprotected section of the stockade, which was apparently left intact from the prior invasion and defended in the same way (Xen. *Hell.* 5.4.49).

Years later when the Thebans took the offensive and mounted one of their invasions against the Peloponnese, the Spartans and their allies fortified the passes near the Isthmus in an attempt to keep the enemy from even entering the Peloponnese (Diod. 15.68.2–5). The wall was rather hastily constructed of palisades and deep trenches. Although the Theban invaders purportedly challenged the Peloponnesian defenders to engage in pitched battle, they refused and remained fast behind their lines. After sharp fighting, Epameinondas led his army through the wall and forced his way into the Peloponnese. There he immediately began to ravage the croplands of the Argolid.

9. See also Xen. *Hell.* 5.4.38–42, 49. The stockade has become a favorite topic of scholars. See Anderson 1970, 132–138; Jones, Sackett, and Eliot 1957, 180–181; McCredie 1966, 96. The field wall may not really have been circular, as Xenophon implies, but rather linear—like other examples of agricultural field walls from the fourth century B.C. Cf. again Anderson 1970, 133.

10. The Theban defenders were probably amply supplied with light-armed troops, since the Athenian general Chabrias had been instrumental in organizing their defenses with his mercenaries (see Diod. 15.32.2–3; Xen. *Hell.* 5.4.54).

Archaeological investigation on occasion has revealed the remains of similar, though more permanent stone field walls. For example, sometime in the fourth century B.C. a long field wall (ca. 4,360 meters) was built in the interior of Attica across a gap in the mountains of Aigaleos and Parnes. Known as the Dema Wall, this strange fortification apparently was intended to cut off direct access to the Athenian Plain, and so protect the rich farmland around Acharnai and Dekeleia from any enemy force that had penetrated the Attic borders.[11] Not too far away, there was another longer rambling frontier wall, in this case eleven kilometers, on the inland slopes of the mountains separating the interior of Boiotia from the small coastal plain of Salganeos, opposite Chalkis. The Antiforitis Wall, as it is called, was aimed at guarding the cropland of this plain against incursions from the area around Tanagra in the interior. From Diodorus (19.77.4), we learn that the wall was most likely constructed by Polemaios in 313 B.C., making it another example of a fourth-century permanent field stockade.[12] (See updated commentary, page 227 [Dema Wall].)

11. The fullest treatment is found in Jones, Sackett, and Eliot 1957, 152–189. Cf. also McCredie 1966, 63–70, 114–115. Many questions regarding the Dema Wall remain unsolved. Besides the problem of its date (serious suggestions, published and otherwise, range from the early fourth century to mid-third century), the intent and practicality of the wall are not completely understood. There is, as yet, no firm evidence of any complementary forts or walls at the pass of Dafni or on the coastal route opposite Salamis, sites that one would expect to be guarded to prevent an enemy force from simply making an end run around the Dema. That the wall was built inside the borders of Attica between the Thriasian and Athenian plains, and not on the frontier, is also odd and also has not yet been adequately explained. It must have served as some type of secondary line of defense, like the Theban stockade of 379 B.C., which also protected only a part of the interior plain.

12. See S. C. Bakhuizen, *Salganeus and the Fortifications on Its Mountains* (Groningen, 1970), esp. chap. 2, "The Antiforitis Wall and the Adjacent Fortifications," 66–68; and for the date, pp. 105–111.

An even clearer example in this period of a field wall constructed to protect agriculture can be found in the Crimean Chersonesos. There excavations have brought to light a vast farming complex of more than 10,000 hectares. One segment of the area, a small peninsula three kilometers by two kilometers, known as Lighthouse Point, consists of a series of farmhouses and accompanying farm plots. This entire point was cut off at its isthmus by a double wall, which served alone to protect the unfortified farms behind. The date of the wall is uncertain, but suggestions of a late-fifth-century date are probably mistaken. It seems likely that the wall—like those in Attica and at Salganeos—was constructed in the later fourth century B.C.[13] The Kapikaya field wall in the Termessos region of southern Turkey seems also to have been designed to protect agricultural land. It was apparently constructed in the third or second century B.C. by Pergamene forces to stop attacks from Termessos against the plains to the east.[14]

Agricultural walls and stockades, then, appear first in number in the fourth century B.C. and continue to be incorporated into defense strategy in the Hellenistic period. While emphasis on this chronological development is necessary, it cannot be pressed too far, for no real universal trend emerges. For example, many cities in Hellenistic times turn their attention exclusively to the city proper and concentrate on strengthening and shortening their urban circuits in the face of new developments in siegecraft.[15] Even in the fourth century B.C., when these random field walls are found, the majority of cities do not opt to protect their cropland with such fortifications: as in the fifth century, pitched

13. The excavations are summarized in a series of articles by Jan Pecírka: "Country Estates of the Polis of the Chersonesos in the Crimea" (= Pecírka 1970a); "Homestead Farms in Classical and Hellenistic Hellas" (= Pecírka 1973); "Excavations of Farms and Farmhouses in the Chora of the Chersonesos in the Crimea" (= Pecírka 1970b, with M. Dufkova).

14. Winter 1966, 127–137.

15. Tarn 1930, 107ff.; McNicoll 1972, 789.

battles remain common.[16] Moreover, in the case of a city choosing to incorporate rural areas within its walls, the decision usually had little to do with agriculture and represented no new emphasis on protecting croplands. The rambling circuit of the wall more often followed the slope of the mountains, its course determined in large part by a desire to take advantage of the natural defensibility of the terrain, and the need to provide ample room for refugees from neighboring hamlets and villages in time of invasion. Even the great circuit constructed far beyond the limits of Syracuse by Dionysios "did absolutely nothing to assure the Syracusans of continuous access to their farmlands."[17] What, if anything, then, are we to make of the appearance of these walls?

No doubt social and military changes, and the natural reaction of exhausted states following the Peloponnesian War, caused a general rethinking of policy among all Greek city-states and gave greater flexibility and options in defense. Consequently, the employment of field walls to protect agriculture became in particular cases *one* possible alternative to pitched hoplite battles. But why their use remained haphazard and was never common during any period needs to be examined.

In the first place, the construction of any wall large enough to protect cropland adequately was costly, perhaps beyond the resources of all but a handful of Greek city-states. Few cities could muster the funds and labor of a Syracuse, which under Dionysios marshaled a workforce of 60,000 men and 6,000 oxen to build its vast circuit (Diod. 14.18ff.). The construction of walls, both in wood and in stone, by both Thebes and Athens, suggests that only larger poleis would have the labor and capital to undertake—and maintain—such projects.

Second, the maintenance of a wall after initial construction also was expensive, and the practicality of defense questionable—much more so than the increasingly popular frontier garrison or fort, which could be better fortified, offered less exposed, vulnerable points of attack, and re-

16. Cf. in general Anderson 1970, 1–12.
17. Winter 1971, 314.

quired fewer men and smaller expenditure. Although well-disciplined professional troops, largely made up of cavalry and light-armed contingents, were now more effective on such garrison duty than their citizen counterparts of the fifth century B.C., they could not be continually successful in difficult, sudden sorties or quick marches along all the many vulnerable points in a long stockade. Not surprisingly, then, Agesilaos had little problem penetrating the Theban stockade and brushing aside the defenders. Epameinondas likewise was not stopped for long by the palisade across the Isthmus. The frequent reconstruction of the Thracian Chersonesos wall, and the apparent abandonment of work on the northern section of the Dema, may also reflect these inherent difficulties of walled defense.[18]

Finally, to be effective, these walls required an almost ideal setting from a topographical standpoint, a location immune from possible encirclement in the rear and without alternate routes of entry and exit. Accordingly, it is on an isthmus (e.g., Corinth), across a peninsula (e.g., Crimean Chersonesos), in a mountain pass (e.g., the Dema), or around a small coastal plain (e.g., Salganeos)—places where a linear wall would usually suffice—that most of these field walls are found. Construction in an exposed, level valley or plain was impractical, if not impossible. Even the Theban stockade, which Xenophon suggests encircled the plain of Boiotia, was probably a linear wall incorporating natural points of defense offered by the terrain.[19]

In conclusion, for the construction of an effective wall to protect their croplands, Greek cities needed sufficient labor and money, natural

18. For the Dema, see again Jones, Sackett, and Eliot 1957, 189.

19. On this point, see Anderson 1970, 133. Xenophon remarks at *Hell.* 5.4.49 that Agesilaos, during his second campaign against the stockade (377 B.C.), made his way through the rampart at Skolos—a site now located by W. K. Pritchett (1965, 107–109) on the northern bank of the Asopos River. Similarly, Mardonios benefited from the protection offered by the river for the construction of his square fort (Hdt. 9.15).

sites for fortification, a commitment to passive defense strategy, and specialized troops. While some of these obstacles could be more easily overcome during the fourth century and later, field walls and stockades were rare even then.

BORDER FORTS AND GARRISONS

Agricultural land could also be defended by placing troops at border forts and mountain passes, in theory to stop enemy forces from entering the interior of a country. Since the terrain of Greece in many places is characterized by numerous fertile plains ringed by mountains, this should have been a common strategy, as the enemy ideally could be cut off at the frontier with little effort and the croplands thereby saved. Yet it is generally acknowledged that, at least in the fifth century B.C., mountain passes were rarely successfully guarded or fortified. The paradox has troubled scholars for years.

G. B. Grundy suggested that the cause was economic.[20] Because the food-producing plains were so vital to a city-state's livelihood, enemy invaders sought a decisive victory there in pitched battle, so they could proceed to ravage the defeated's crops and then return quickly to harvest their own land. Gomme rightly pointed out, though, that such an explanation "does not answer the question 'why were not the strategy and the tactics of mountain warfare by light-armed troops developed in order to prevent the invasion reaching the plains?'" He thinks the reason was rather "social and political."[21] The citizen-soldiers in each state frowned upon lengthy, professional training and were suspicious of a permanent military force and centralized control of arms— prerequisites for the creation of light-armed troops fit to occupy the frontier passes. Gomme's theory has generally been accepted and often

20. Grundy 1948, 244–250.
21. Gomme 1945, 1: 12.

elaborated on. F. E. Adcock, for example, in pointing out the strategic problems of mountain defense, remarked that "mountains often defend nothing but themselves"—eventually conflict must center on the valuable land where the majority of the people reside and the locus of food production is found.[22] J. K. Anderson noted the lack of a properly organized commissariat and accumulated capital to maintain and pay standing troops.[23] The traditional view, then, is that border forts and garrisons were not used in the fifth century as real points of frontier defense. When they did appear they usually served as bases for sorties and small raids.

The best example of fifth-century border fortifications can be found along the Attic frontier.[24] On the eastern end of the Attic-Boiotian border, the Athenians held a garrison somewhere in the Oropia during most of the Peloponnesian War. It was betrayed to the Boiotians in 412 B.C., and so ceased to serve as a base for securing Euboia (Thuc. 8.60, 8.95.1–3; see also 4.96.7, 7.28.1).[25] Westward from Oropos was the crucial garrison at Panakton, guarding the Athens-Thebes route via Phyle.

22. Adcock 1957, 68–69.

23. Anderson 1970, 5.

24. The date, location, and function of the major Attic forts are disputed, and given the evidence available, questions will probably always remain. See the sensible article of Chandler (1926), whose identifications of Oinoe with Myoupolis, Panakton with Kavasala (Prasino), and Eleutherai with Gyphtokastro have endured later criticism (e.g., Oinoe: Kahrstedt 1932, 25–26; Philippson 1950, 1: 525–526; Wallace 1952, 82–84; Hammond 1954, 121–122; Gomme 2: 66–68; Panakton: Kahrstedt 1932, 10ff.; Hammond 1954, 121; Gomme 3: 632–633; Eleutherai: Kahrstedt 1932, 10ff.; Wallace 1952, 81) and are probably correct.

25. The remains and location of this fortification (?) have not been identified. Three miles north of Varnava on a big hill near the small, isolated church of Hagia Paraskevi, there are traces of what must have been an extensive fort. But the site seems to me too removed and inaccessible from the sea to be this important and effective maritime base in the Oropia.

It, too, was taken through treachery by the Boiotians (in 422 B.C.) and was not handed back intact as agreed upon during the peace negotiations of 420 but rather was destroyed.[26] The next fifth-century fort was still farther west, at Oinoe. Here the Athenians successfully held out against Archidamos's invasion forces of 431 B.C. The base was not captured until 411, once more by treachery.[27] Eleusis, controlling major routes between the Peloponnese, Attica, and Boiotia, was also fortified by this time in the fifth century and could serve as a frontier base for raids against any army entering Attica from the south.[28] On the coast, Sounion,[29] Thorikos,[30] and Rhamnous[31] were all garrisoned and strengthened with fortifications around 412 B.C. to keep grain ships coming from Euboia (e.g., Thuc. 8.95) and to prevent maritime enemy

26. Thuc. 5.3.5, 5.39–46; and cf. Plut. *Alc.* 14.1. J. Wiesner (*RE* 36 [1949] 449–450, s.v. Panakton) is wrong on the location—and thus in his description of the remains of Panakton. See Chandler 1926, 6–8.

27. Thuc. 2.18.2, 8.98; Xen. *Hell.* 1.7.28; and cf., too, *RE* Supp. 8 (1956) 370–372, s.v. Oinoe (J. Wiesner); Chandler 1926, 8–9.

28. On the walls and fortifications at Eleusis, see G. E. Mylonas, *Eleusis and the Eleusinian Mysteries* (Princeton, 1961), 124–128; F. Noack, *Die baugeschichtliche Entwicklung des Heiligtums* (Berlin, 1927), 183ff.; J. Travlos, "The Topography of Eleusis," *Hesperia* 18 (1949): 140ff.

29. Thuc. 8.4; and see H. Mussche, "Notes sur les fortifications du Sounion," *Bulletin de Correspondance Hellénique* 88 (1964): 423–432.

30. Xen. *Hell.* 1.2.1. The actual date of the fortification of Thorikos is disputed (Xenophon says it occurred in 409 B.C.); but the disagreement is over only a few years. Cf. the two articles by H. Mussche (who argues for a date of 412 B.C.): "La fortresse maritime de Thorikos," *Bulletin de Correspondance Hellénique* 85 (1961): 176–205; "Recent Excavations at Thorikos," *L'Antiquité Classique* 13 (1970): 128–129. See also C. A. van Rooy, "Fortifications in South Attica and the Date of Thorikos," *Acta Classica* 12 (1969): 171–180, which supports 410/409 B.C. as the date of construction.

31. For a description of the walls and other remains at Rhamnous, and their date of construction, see Pouilloux 1954, 43–66.

raiding against the Attic coastal demes. Salamis, too, had been fortified by at least 429/8 B.C., when the Spartans attacked the garrison there by night.[32] (See updated commentary, page 227 [Forts].)

Pericles was referring, at least in part, to this system of border fortifications when he mentioned troops stationed in garrisons during his review of Athenian military strength at the outbreak of the war.[33] Similarly, Lysias charged that among the other damage done by the Thirty, the Attic border forts were also dismantled (12.40). And in his speech against Alcibiades the Younger, the defendant's father is criticized for having given information to the enemy about Athenian garrisons that were poorly guarded, and revealing areas in Attica that were naturally strong positions (14.35).

The garrisoning of these Attic border forts in the fifth century was probably made easier by the deployment of a mobile force called the *peripoloi* who were especially organized for this purpose. Made up in part of foreigners, they seem to have been the fifth-century forerunners of the later fourth-century ephebes, who likewise were often stationed on the border.[34]

It is clear, then, that Attica had some sort of organized system of frontier defense with numerous forts and sufficient men to garrison them as early as the fifth century B.C. However, from the evidence of the

32. Thuc. 2.93–94. See W. E. McLeod, "BOUDORON, An Athenian Fort on Salamis," *Hesperia* 29 (1960): 316–323. Eliot, in an overly critical note (1962, 132 n. 1), disputes McLeod's location of the fort—wrongly, I think.

33. Thuc. 2.13.6. See Gomme 2: 33–34. See also Thuc. 2.24.1 and Diod. 12.42.6 for other references to Athenian forts at this time.

34. The composition and date of organization of the *peripoloi* are not really known. But it is apparent that they were troops organized (though much more loosely than the later ephebes) in the fifth century to serve in border forts; cf. Eupolis F341 (Kock); Griffith 1935, 86–88; Gomme 3: 529; Kent 1941, 346–349; Pélékidis 1962, 35–49.

Peloponnesian War, these forts were apparently not able to stop full-scale invasions and were not intended to do so.[35] Rather, as mentioned earlier, they served mostly to delay and harass enemy invasions, interrupt communications, and prevent smaller ravaging and plundering parties from entering Attica. Apparently, they were useful in thwarting small incursions, against which a full muster of hoplite infantry would have been unnecessary.

We hear, for example, of an enemy force that was waylaid on its return from Dekeleia by the Athenian garrison at Oinoe (Thuc. 8.98.2). In Aristophanes' *Acharnians* (1071ff.), Lamachos is sent off to the snowy Boiotian-Attica border to engage a marauding band of Boiotian plunderers. And during the first Peloponnesian invasion of 431 B.C., Athenian cavalry sorties from Eleusis attacked enemy ravagers, presumably in hopes of hampering the progress of devastation (Thuc. 2.19.2).

Yet the universal consensus on the ineffectiveness of such forts and frontier garrisons of the fifth century B.C. in completely stopping enemy forces at the border may be somewhat exaggerated. Their role in Attica during the Peloponnesian War seems in large part determined by the Periclean policy of not seriously challenging the enemy with sustained and combined attacks of land-based troops, rather than by any intrinsic weakness. At times during the war the forts do seem capable of a potentially stronger role. Oinoe repelled numerous Peloponnesian attempts at seizure. It stalled the entire enemy invasion force of 431 B.C., allowing additional time for the Athenian evacuation (Thuc. 2.18). Thucydides relates that while a garrison was stationed in the Oropia, the Athenians could determine events and harm both Eretria and parts of Euboia (Thuc. 8.60.1). The possession of Panakton became a key point in negotiations of the Peace of Nikias (Thuc. 5.18.7). The Boiotians reluc-

---

35. The limited role of these fifth-century garrisons is nearly universally accepted. See Adcock 1957, 69; Anderson 1970, 5–6; Kahrstedt 1932, 8–28; Kent 1941, 346–347; McCredie 1966, 88–89. Henderson (1927, 56–59) faulted Pericles for not using these garrisons as major points of defense.

tantly returned the garrison only after destroying the fortifications—again underlining the fort's importance (Plut. *Alc.* 14.4). The Athenian fortifications at the sanctuary of Delium near the Attic border with Boiotia were of grave concern to the Thebans, who marshaled an entire Boiotian army in order to take the site and attack the invaders who had built it (Thuc. 4.76).

Well-fortified border forts in the fifth century, it should be remembered, could not really be taken by storm, given the ineffectiveness of siegecraft during this period.[36] And if states did not invest heavily in such fortifications, it may not have been because they were vulnerable to sieges. Oinoe, the Oropian garrison, and Panakton were all captured only through treachery. The fall of the Athenian outpost at Delium—not properly a permanent border fortification—seems to have been the result of its recent ad hoc construction, and the small garrison posted for its defense.

Moreover, G. E. M. de Ste. Croix has recently pointed out that for fourteen years of the first Peloponnesian War (460–446 B.C.), no Peloponnesian invasion even attempted to make its way into Attica.[37] The reason, he thinks, is that the Athenians were able to occupy the passes in the Megarid over Geraneia and station garrisons in Pagai and Megara itself. Accordingly, during the expedition to Doris in 457 B.C., the Peloponnesians were forced to travel by sea into northern Greece. On their way home they were again prevented from going overland, since the route through Geraneia was not safe (Thuc. 1.107.3) while the Athenians held Megara and Pagai. Only after the Athenians marched out and were defeated at Tanagra, could the Peloponnesians make their way home by land. Peloponnesian success, then, at entering northern Greece by an overland route apparently depended on easy entry through the Megarid during these years. When Megara returned to the Peloponnesian alliance in 446 B.C., and the Athenians thus lost access to

36. See Garlan 1974, 106–147.
37. De Ste. Croix 1972, 190–195.

these forward posts, the Peloponnesians naturally quickly mounted an overland invasion from the Isthmus. And during the second Peloponnesian War (431–404 B.C.), when Megara was hostile, and Boiotia, too, became a formidable enemy, a variety of routes were opened up into Attica from both its borders. Consequently, the Athenians simply must have despaired of keeping the enemy out of Attica at the frontier as had been possible before, since now so many points of entry were available. Border forts were more effective when a polis was concerned only with one border and a single enemy, not two. Thus we can understand that there were more than just political, economic, and cultural reasons why hoplite warfare remained prevalent so long: very pragmatic difficulties were inherent in successfully garrisoning the porous circumferences that characterized so many Greek states.

In the fourth century B.C. the picture seems to change somewhat. Mountain passes and routes of entry that were often ineffectually guarded by fifth-century garrisons could now in theory be turned into veritable points of resistance thanks to fundamental changes in warfare and strategy. The idea of keeping the enemy out at the border if at all possible grew increasingly popular, especially since fifth-century garrisons and forts had proved to be surprisingly effective loci of resistance during the Peloponnesian War.

We catch glimpses of this new emphasis on border defense already in the very last years of the fifth century and the early decades of the fourth century B.C.[38] In Xenophon's *Memorabilia* (dramatic date of ca. 406 B.C.) Socrates advises the newly elected general, Pericles, to deploy more light-armed young Athenians on the mountain frontier between Attica and Boiotia, and so provide a strong defense for the Attic countryside (*Mem.* 3.5.25–27). Before the battle at the Nemea (394 B.C.), light-armed contingents of troops who were allied against Sparta greatly harmed the Peloponnesians crossing over into Corinth from

38. Cf. de Ste. Croix 1972, 191–194; Garlan 1974, 66–79.

Sikyon by hurling missiles and shooting arrows from the heights of Epieikeia (Xen. *Hell.* 4.2.14–16). Had more efficient, professional peltasts or other well-trained light-armed troops been available at this time to supplement this loosely organized force, the Spartans might have been stopped before they ravaged the coastal plain beyond. Later that same year Spartan troops were forced to go by sea to join Agesilaos in northern Greece, since garrisons in the Corinthia effectively blocked the land route through the Isthmus (Xen. *Hell.* 4.3.15, 4.4.1; Lys. 16.16). Of course, in the more remote and rugged areas of Greece, light-armed troops had long been successful in hampering and even blocking the approach of enemy hoplites (e.g., Akarnania [Xen. *Hell.* 4.6.7–11]; Aitolia [Xen. *Hell.* 4.6.14; cf. esp. Thuc. 3.97.2–3, 3.98.4]; along the route of the retreating Ten Thousand [Xen. *Anab.* 1.3.14, 3.4.24–29, 3.4.37–49, 4.1.20, 4.8.8–19, 5.6.7]).

By the third decade of the fourth century B.C. especially, the growing popularity of mercenaries, the standardization of light-armed forces, and the emergence of particularly innovative and aggressive commanders made the effective occupation and garrisoning of mountain passes even more desirable.[39] Some states began at this time to rely often on their border defense to keep the enemy out, rather than on pitched hoplite battles in the interior plains.

The best example of this strategy is found in the 370s B.C. when the passes over Mt. Kithairon into Boiotia became the site of repeated struggles between Spartan invaders and Theban defensive troops. For example, in winter 379 B.C. Kleomenes was not able to enter Boiotia via Attica because the pass at Eleutherai was guarded by Athenian peltasts under Chabrias (Xen. *Hell.* 5.4.14). He was therefore forced instead to go over Kithairon and descend into Boiotia near Plataia; moreover, the Peloponnesians were forced to return home that same year via the treacherous path through Aigosthena—once more kept from passing

---

39. For this period of expansion in the use of light-armed troops and mercenaries, see Parke 1933, 73–132; Pritchett 1974, 59–125.

through Attica. There they met with near disaster, losing their stock and baggage, which fell from the high cliffs into the sea. The next year (378 B.C.) Agesilaos realized that "unless one gained hold of Mt. Kithairon first, it would not be an easy thing to invade Theban territory" (Xen. *Hell.* 5.4.35–37). He hired a mercenary army to occupy the pass in advance. After Agesilaos successfully made his way down into Boiotia, he encountered the famous Theban stockade that served as a secondary line of defense. In the third invasion (377 B.C.), Agesilaos once more successfully occupied the Kithairon border passes ahead of time. He then entered the Boiotian plain unexpectedly at Erythyrai, not Thespiai, where a second Theban border garrison waited in vain (Xen. *Hell.* 5.4.47–49). But in 376 B.C. the Thebans, with aid from Athenian troops, finally secured Kithairon first. The Spartan general Kleomenes consequently simply turned back and disbanded his army, "since then he thought it impossible to cross over into the country of the Thebans" (Xen. *Hell.* 5.4.59). The Spartans were able to pass the Boiotian defenses in 371 B.C. only by "unexpectedly" slipping through their frontier at Thisbe (Xen. *Hell.* 6.4.4–5) and thus making their way on to Leuktra.[40]

Other examples of serious attempts at border defense are numerous in this period and need not be cited, though it should be noted that the Thebans for their own part were hesitant (although not for long) to invade Sparta in 370 B.C. because "Lakonia was said to be especially difficult to invade, and they thought garrisons were stationed at the routes of easiest entry" (Xen. *Hell.* 6.5.24; cf. Polyb. 2.65.6 for a later example).

This new emphasis on border fortification is reflected, too, in the nonhistorical writing of the fourth century B.C. In Xenophon's *Hiero* the poet Simonides is made to advise the Syracusan king to enlist an elite force of trained mercenaries. Among their other tasks, these troops were to provide safety for country workers and stock by guarding the

---

40. See also in general Xen. *Hell.* 5.4.63, 6.4.4–5; for the Spartan difficulty in invading Boiotia in this period, see Kent 1941, 346–349, and Pélékidis 1962, 35–49.

key points of the countryside (*Hiero* 10.5). Cyrus, in Xenophon's *Cyropaedia*, often talks about the necessity of capturing enemy border forts, constructing additional fortifications, and garrisoning mountain passes to keep enemy troops out of friendly territory (e.g., *Cyr.* 3.2.4, 6.1.14). And in his *Poroi* (written about 355 B.C.) Xenophon carefully outlined a theoretical system of rural fortifications aimed at protecting the mining district around Laureion: the existing forts at Anaphlystos and Thorikos were to be joined together by a stronghold atop Mt. Besa to form a line of rural defensive bases where citizens could flee to keep safe (Xen. *Vect.* 4.43–49; cf. 4.52).[41] His contemporary, the strategist Aeneas Tacticus, argued that the rural areas of a country be occupied and guarded so that the enemy could be engaged right at the border (Aen. Tact. 9.1, 16.16–19). Aristotle in the *Politics* suggested the ideal state be situated in such a way that natural points of terrain make it "difficult for enemies to invade" (*Pol.* 7.5.2, 7.10.2). The ideal orator in his *Rhetoric* was supposed to know the nature of a city-state's rural defenses so that weak bases could be strengthened and unnecessary garrisons disbanded—something impossible for a statesman to understand, he adds, unless he was familiar with the terrain of the country districts (*Rh.* 1.4.10).[42]

Outside of Utopia, there is more reason to believe that in the second quarter of the fourth century agricultural land and property were often protected by garrisons of well-trained, light-armed troops at the border. Archaeological evidence, for instance, mainly consisting of the remains of ancient forts and towers in Attica and elsewhere, seems to predominate in the fourth century. At this time new fortifications were apparently being constructed, and old ones strengthened in an unparalleled effort to create serious lines of border defense.

41. Eliot 1962, 117–119.

42. The contemporary Demosthenes, it should be remembered, urged the Athenians to keep Philip as far away as possible by preventing his access to Attica—a departure from their previous strategy, in the Peloponnesian War, of allowing the enemy to cross their borders.

Sometime in the fourth century a series of blockhouses, fortresses, and pyramids was constructed inside the Argolid near Argos, Mycenae, and Nauplion. Usually found at important local roads and passes, they seem to have been intended to house small garrisons that could patrol the neighboring countryside, and so protect farms from enemy invasion and attack.[43] On Mt. Oneion in the Corinthia a permanent fortification was built in the mid-fourth century to serve as a strong point in the defense of the Isthmus.[44]

Attica's existing line of older, fifth-century border forts seems also to have been greatly expanded and strengthened in the early and mid-fourth century B.C. The natural stronghold of Phyle was for the first time fortified at this time. Along with Panakton, it helped to guard the short, but arduous pass into Boiotia.[45] Eleutherai (modern Gyph-

43. See the series of articles by L. E. Lord: *Hesperia* 7 (1938): 482–527; *American Journal of Archaeology* 43 (1939): 78–84; *Hesperia* 10 (1941): 93–112. There was also some system of forts on the border of the Argolid (at Hysiai, Katzingri, Karsarma, and Asine). See Winter 1971, 42–43.

44. R. S. Stroud, "An Ancient Fort on Mt. Oneion," *Hesperia* 40 (1971): 127–145.

45. See Wrede's excavation report: "Phyle," *Mitteilungen des Deutschen Archäologischen Instituts, Athenische Abteilung* 49 (1924): 220–224. G. Säflund ("The Dating of Ancient Fortifications in Southern Italy and Greece," *Opuscula Archaeologica* 1 [1935]) wrongly dated the present remains to around 300 B.C. From the style of the masonry and the architecture, together with finds uncovered by Wrede, it is clear that the existing fort dates from the early fourth century but could not have existed when Thrasyboulos sought refuge there. We need not, however, as Wrede does, consequently locate Thrasyboulos's stronghold to the northeast, near the ancient deme site of Phyle itself: the land there is hardly defensible, and there are few remains. Xenophon's description of Phyle as a *chôrion ischuron* (*Hell.* 2.4.2) could easily suggest the naturally strong fortress of Phyle—which would have been quite defensible even without its later extensive fortifications. In the fourth century B.C., when emphasis turned toward border defense and efforts were made to create new fortifications and beef up old ones, the "historic" (but unwalled) site of Phyle would have been an ideal candidate for a model border fort. Later, Phyle, along with Panakton and Eleusis,

tokastro) protected the road connecting Thebes with Eleusis and Athens and was used successfully as a border fortification for the first time in this period: its walls appear to have only one stage of construction and belong solely to the fourth century B.C., when it was under Athenian control.[46] Less is known about the purpose and date of the considerable fortifications at Aigosthena.[47] But they may well have been a supplementary outpost in Attica's plan of border defense—perhaps aimed at limiting enemy seaborne invasions of northwest Attica, as well as serving as an Athenian maritime base on the Corinthian Gulf.

In the fourth century, the walls of Oinoe also seem to have been rebuilt. Regular coursework blocks of conglomerate appear to replace the limestone trapezoidal stones (still visible) of the fifth-century fort attacked by Archidamos. Panakton, which was destroyed by the Boiotians at the close of the fifth century, was likewise reconstructed in such a standardized isodomic ashlar style, similar to that seen at Oinoe and Eleutherai. Besides this main line of border fortifications, there were numerous other smaller towers and forts built in the fourth century. They are found throughout Attica (e.g., at Aphidna, Mazi, Plakoto, Varnava) and probably served as additional bases for defense, shelter, and communications especially.[48] On the eve of Philip's descent into Attica, if we can believe a decree inserted into the text of Demosthenes' *De Corona*, Athenians were to leave the country and flee to the city and the

---

seems to form part of an important triad command (see, for example, *IG* II².1299; *IG* II².1303–1305; *IG* II².2971).

46. See Vanderpool 1978, 242–243. Chabrias and his peltasts guarded the pass at Eleutherai successfully in 379 B.C., and so forced Kleombrotos and his Spartans to go over Kithairon by way of Plataia (Xen. *Hell.* 5.4.14). On the fort itself, see Hammond 1954, 121; and Chandler 1926, 11–12.

47. E. F. Benson, "Aegosthena," *Journal of Hellenic Studies* 15 (1895): 314–324, has a brief description of the fortifications.

48. Sec Chandler 1926, 13–17; McCredie 1966, 58–61, 81–83, 89–91; Wrede 1933, 24–25, 32. Most of the hilltop towers are situated within view of major fortresses and thus probably served well as signal or courier stations.

Piraeus. These border garrisons were to be manned day and night, and property in the more remote countryside was to be removed to Eleusis, Phyle, Aphidna, Rhamnous, or Sounion.[49]

This fourth-century emphasis on serious border defense, in the case of Attica, may have paid off by establishing a clear deterrent to armed invasion, for until the closing years of the fourth century no foreign army entered Attic territory.[50] The only exception was apparently the very brief raid of Sphodrias in 378 B.C. But he slipped in at night and with only a small number of troops, who merely stole cattle, plundered houses, and then quickly retreated (Xen. *Hell.* 5.4.20–21).

This trend toward border fortification, of course, was not universally followed. Some states were not well suited topographically or were simply too small or poor to maintain the necessarily expensive border fortifications. Contemporary literature also reveals that this growing movement toward border defense and fortification was often strongly opposed by many reactionaries, who recalled fondly the more dramatic, honorable, and decisive pitched hoplite battles of the earlier fifth century. Plato, for example, in his *Laws*, complains of young Athenians who each year passively dug trenches and built walls in the country in the hope of keeping the enemy at the border (*Leg.* 778D; see also Xen. *Oec.* 6.6–7). Indeed, in the fourth century B.C. major hoplite battles were still commonly used in Greece to stop the approach of enemy armies (e.g., Nemea [394 B.C.], Koroneia [394 B.C.], Leuktra [371 B.C.], Mantineia [362 B.C.], Chaironeia [338 B.C.]). We should not, then, imagine a fourth-century military revolution that displaced altogether the hoplite option of decisive battle—in many ways it was still the cheapest and most decisive method of keeping the enemy out of friendly territory. One reason perhaps for the rise of defensivism in many Greek states in

49. Dem. 18.37–38; cf. also McCredie 1966, 92–93, and 95.

50. On Spodrias's raid, see now J. Ober, *Fortress Attica: Defense of the Athenian Land Frontier, 404–322 B.C.*, Mnemosyne Supp. 84 (Leiden, 1985), 211–212.

the three decades after the Peloponnesian War was the sheer battlefield superiority of the Spartan phalanx, which after the war proved to be far more willing and adept in projecting its influence outside of Lakonia. Its imposing presence in Attica during the Archidamian invasions and the string of successes at Mantineia (418 B.C.), Nemea (394 B.C.), and Koroneia (394 B.C.) made a profound impression on Greek thinkers: the best way to combat such a formidable force was not necessarily any longer to meet it head to head with hoplites, as the Spartan debacle at the hands of peltasts at Corinth (390 B.C.) and the Spartan kings' problems in entering Boiotia in the 370s demonstrated. Until Leuktra (371 B.C.) and the rise of the ferocious phalanx of Thebans under Epameinondas, it may have been assumed that to meet the Peloponnesian army in hoplite battle meant sure defeat, and thus alternative strategies were necessary that incorporated light-armed troops who could manipulate terrain and fortifications.

To summarize: field walls and stockades were rarely built to protect farmland in classical Greece. When they did appear occasionally, it was usually during the fourth century B.C. and afterward, when changes in warfare and military strategy made their use possible. But even then the inherent impracticality of keeping the enemy out of valuable farmland by a wall limited their success, and the idea understandably never really became widespread. A more popular and successful alternative were border forts and frontier garrisons. Troops stationed at such bases could ideally prevent enemy invaders from descending from the mountains into the valuable, fertile plains. But, as in the case of field walls, the lack of well-trained, if not professional, light-armed soldiers in the fifth century B.C. made the use of forts and garrisons at that time only haphazard. Scholars consequently interpret the fifth-century forts we know of as intended for raids, sorties, and sudden, brief attacks on larger invasion forces, rather than serving as true lines of absolute frontier defense.

Yet we also see Attica relatively well protected at its border in the first Peloponnesian War. From the little information we possess, then, we cannot say for sure that lightly armed and equipped hoplites, stationed in mountain garrisons or border forts, did not successfully at times limit enemy entry and exit at the frontier.[51] By the turn of the century, however, there were unquestionable signs that more serious defensive strategy was on the rise. And in the second quarter of the century, border forts and the garrisoning of mountain passes appear from both archaeological and literary evidence to have been more and more common. Unlike their fifth-century counterparts, these bases were now able to halt or at least delay large enemy forces at the frontier and thereby limit destruction of cropland—as the Theban and Spartan struggles over Kithairon in the 370s, and the lack of any real invasion into Attica may suggest. Particular states did not have to submit automatically to enemy terms or engage in pitched battle (although this was often the case). There was at least the option now in the fourth century, under certain circumstances, of successfully protecting farmland by engaging and halting an enemy's advance right at the frontier.

51. Consider, for instance, Mardonios's anxiety about being cut off in Attica and forced to retreat over its treacherous border mountain passes into Boiotia, where "a very few enemy troops might stop all his army" (Hdt. 9.13.3).

FOUR

Evacuation

The most effective method of "defense" was evacuation from the countryside. From descriptions in ancient literature it seems to have been a commonplace activity. Rural residents routinely gathered their possessions together and trekked to places of refuge, regardless of whether their own forces chose to fight in pitched battle or border skirmishes. A wealth of fascinating detail surrounds this process of rural evacuation—most of it unnoticed or passed over—which makes careful study desirable. Many questions come to mind. For example, where did refugees go in times of invasion? What crops and valuables were taken along or had to be left behind? Were special measures followed for the protection of livestock, slaves, women, children, and older people? And were traps and obstacles erected to sabotage enemy progress, or was property simply destroyed to prevent it from falling into the hands of the enemy?

THE REMOVAL OF PROPERTY

Unfortunately, little reference is made to specific articles that were removed from farms in times of invasion. Instead, stock, almost formulaic, descriptions are used in our sources for the evacuation of movable property (e.g., Aeschin. 3.80; see also sch. on Ar. *Pax* 631; Arr. *Anab.* 1.10.2).

Besides the verb *skeuagôgeô* (drive in property), *eiskomizô* (carry in) and *anaskeuazô* (take up property) in a very general sense also commonly denote the transference of household furniture or any other article that was readily removable.

What should we understand by "movable property"?[1] Besides livestock and slaves, the most important items of personal wealth, there are at least three general categories: food and crops, farm implements, and household furnishings. Of the three, food was the most essential, and residents must have given priority to emptying their storage bins and hastily removing any ripe crops from the field (e.g., Diod. 12.50.5, 13.81.3; Hdt. 5.34.1; Thuc. 5.115.4; Xen. *Anab.* 4.7.1, 4.7.17). And because food, unlike other movable property, was crucial to the survival of both rural refugees and urban residents—that is, the entire citizenry of the state—the government usually intervened and made arrangements first of all for the safe evacuation of crops. (See updated commentary, page 229 [Movable Property].)

From various inscriptions, mostly honorific decrees from the third century B.C., we learn that military commanders often had their men protect and aid harvesters gathering their crops before the city was cut off. So, for example, among the other services provided Athens by one Kallias of Sphettos, he is thanked by the demos because "he marched his troops into the countryside and made every effort to protect the harvest of the grain so that as much grain as possible could be brought into the city."[2] Indeed, from numerous other examples, it is clear that the state often sent troops out to make sure the harvest progressed and the crops

1. The Greek words *kataskeuê*, *ktêmata*, *ktêsis*, *paraskeuê*, *skeuê*, and *chrêmata* can all be used to denote "movable property" taken from the farm. Cf., for example, *Hell. Oxy.* 12.4; *SEG* 21 (1966) 644.16; Thuc. 1.89.3, 2.5.4, 2.14.2, 6.49.3; and also *Hesperia* 19 (1960): 213.

2. Shear 1978, 2–3 (1.23–27). Kallias seems to have been in charge of protecting the harvesters, while another officer, Zenon, organized troops and other laborers to do the actual gathering of the grain (*IG* II². 650.16–19; Shear 1978, 21).

were brought in behind the city's walls. The brother of Kallias, Phaidros, was also praised "for bringing in the grain and the other crops from the countryside" a little earlier, before an aborted invasion of Attica by Ptolemaic forces (*IG* II².682.35–36). During the Chremonidean War, an Epichares was honored by the citizens of Rhamnous because "he gathered both the tree-fruit and cereal crops into his camp, as far as thirty stades, after establishing concealed watching posts, which he and his soldiers garrisoned so that the crops could safely be harvested by the farmers" (*SEG* 24 [1969] 154.8–11). The general in charge of the Eleusis command in 235 B.C., Aristophanes, likewise was honored because "he took care that the grain was brought in from the field in safety" (*IG* II².1299.66ff.). Four years later, we hear that the Athenians were to raise funds "for the protection of the countryside" in order that "the crops for the remainder of the year can be harvested with safety" (*IG* II².334.10–13).

To these Attic decrees an interesting inscription from Istros, a Greek city in Thrace, should be added. The decree (ca. 200 B.C.) records the service provided the city at a time of crisis by one Agathokles, son of Antiphilos. He tirelessly took troops out into the field to defend the surrounding farmland. Soldiers under his command again and again provided protection from Thracian raiders so that citizens could bring in the harvest. As "general with absolute powers over the countryside" (*stratêgos epi tês chôras autokratôr*), Agathokles "kept the countryside free of danger, and the stock and the crops safe." Cavalry, it should be noted, were an integral part of his defense strategy: Agathokles at one point is honored for obtaining a special force of 500 horses from Phradmos, son of King Rhemaxos.[3] These honorific decrees come to us after the age of classical hoplite battle and suggest that warfare in the Hellenistic Age often consisted of constant undeclared plundering and raiding, to the extent that communities often delegated permanent officers to oversee

---

3. See H. Bengston, "Neues zur Geschichte des Hellenismus in Thrakien und in der Dobrudscha," *Historia* 11 (1962): 21–22 (lines 15, 25–33, 41–45, 53–56).

rural protective forces that were entrusted with the protection of harvests. Incidentally, the majority of these inscriptions deal with the grain harvest, an emphasis that again indicates that enemy ravagers must have timed their arrival to coincide with wheat and barley ripening, in hopes of denying an entire year's work to the invaded (whose stocks right before harvest would be at the lowest level of the year), catching cereals at their combustible stage, when firing would be easy, and ensuring supplementary supplies of food and fodder for their own troops.

In Aeneas Tacticus's treatise *On the Defense of Fortified Positions*, much attention is paid to the state's responsibility for procuring food from the countryside. (See updated commentary, page 229 [Aeneas Tacticus].) Aeneas advises that proclamations be issued telling the free population to come into the city with their crops—any who hold out are liable to have their property seized with impunity (10.3). Likewise, he lists signals to be given as a warning to farmers who linger outside the walls attempting to get all their crops inside (7.1). Special care is to be taken that the nearest and most accessible gates of the city are kept open for men or wagons carrying shipments of grain, oil, and wine from the countryside (28.3). Xenophon, in his *Hipparchus*, pointed out that even a small cavalry force could help remove inside the walls all the property that needed saving (7.6).

Less detail is provided concerning the evacuation of farm tools. Yet we must assume that they were almost always saved and comprised a chief part of the "movable property" taken into the city. Mattocks, hoes, pruning hooks, pitchforks, ladders, harrows, plows, axes, saws, and threshing equipment were all relatively light, easily carried—and expensive to replace.[4] In Aristophanes' *Peace*, for example, Trygaios looks over his fellow farmers in refuge inside Athens and remarks on the shiny shovels and pitchforks they have with them (566–567). He later urges them to return to their farms with their "farming implements" (*ta*

---

4. See Pritchett 1956, 287.

geôrgika skeuê), which apparently they brought inside the walls during their initial evacuation.[5]

More is known about household articles. Anyone who has read the plays of Aristophanes or glanced at the *Attic Stelai*—the formal inventories of confiscated property of those Athenians accused of profaning religious rites and symbols—is aware of the vast assortment of pots, pans, chairs, couches, lamp stands, tables, rugs, mats, and various other furniture used in the supposedly "sparse" Greek household. These items were obviously prized by their owners and must be assumed to have been removed in an evacuation. Thucydides remarks in his famous account of the first Athenian evacuation that farmers were obliged to remove "the rest of the property that was employed in the household" (2.14.1). Any personal property left on an estate was probably taken by ravagers; in nearly all cases where troops destroy farmhouses, they first ransack the place in hopes of finding such booty left behind (e.g., Diod. 12.78.2, 14.97.5; Polyb. 9.6.8; Xen. *Hell.* 6.5.15, 6.5.27–28, 6.5.30). So, too, in an oration attributed to Demosthenes (47.53–56), one Euergos raids a neighbor's farm and carries off all the furniture and household articles he can get his hands on. Utensils of bronze or iron were especially highly prized.[6] Xenophon thought it worthwhile to mention that when the Ten Thousand overran the village of the Karduchians, they found plentiful provisions and numerous bronze vessels still in the houses (*Anab.* 4.1.8). After the fall of Plataia, the victorious Spartans gathered together all the bronze and iron from the city and made couches that they dedicated to Hera (Thuc. 3.68.3). J. Roux has argued convincingly that in a disputed passage in Euripides' *Bacchae*, the "bronze and iron" carried off from the villages of Kithairon by the frenzied

5. See also line 1318: "And it is necessary now to bring all the equipment back onto the farm" (*kai ta skeuê palin eis ton agron nuni chrê panta komizein*). Thucydides mentions farm implements (*kataskeuê*) evacuated from the farms before the first invasion of Archidamos. Cf. Gomme 2: 48.

6. See again Pritchett 1956, 287ff.

bacchants were actually precious utensils that were commonly stolen in raids and plundering expeditions.[7]

Doors and woodwork were also valuable movable property and must have been taken along whenever possible.[8] The Athenians, for example, stripped even the woodwork from their houses (Thuc. 2.14.1) before the initial Peloponnesian invasion of the Archidamian War to prevent theft or destruction by the enemy.[9] And in a speech of Lysias (19.31), doors, along with household furniture, are taken out of a house to prevent seizure. In an oration of Demosthenes (29.3), we hear of a defendant who ransacked his house and, before leaving the premises, gathered up all the furniture and tore off the door (see also Dem. 24.197).

On the other hand, because doors were cumbersome and not so easily removed and carried away in an emergency as other personal property, they sometimes fell into the hands of the enemy. The Ten Thousand, for example, encamped in a native village whose houses had been stripped of all their woodwork by the Persians (Xen. *Anab.* 2.2.16). Aly-

7. J. Roux, "Pillage en Béotie (Euripide, *Bacchantes*, vers 751–758)," *Revue des Etudes Grecques* 76 (1963): 34–38.

8. Anything composed of wood was costly in many areas of Greece (especially Attica) and often had to be imported. Cf. Guiraud 1893, 503–506; Michell 1957, 82–83; and again Pritchett 1956, 297 nn. 80, 81. Doors were usually considered separate from the house: in rental agreements, for example, the door was sometimes to be supplied by the tenant. See Kent 1948, 293; Pritchett 1956, 239.

9. Gomme (2: 47–48) rightly includes wooden fixtures such as doors and window shutters under "woodwork" (*xulôsis*) but, curiously, suggests barns as well. Barns, however, were more often towers constructed of stone, and thus hardly collapsible. The Oxyrhynchus Historian relates (12.4) that during the Dekeleian plundering raids, the Boiotians stripped the woodwork from the farmhouses of Attica. Apparently, these farms by this time had been resettled and refurbished with their woodwork after the Archidamian War and subsequently were not reevacuated during the renewed hostilities—perhaps because of the small size of the enemy garrison at Dekeleia.

attes, during the invasions of Miletus, chose not to destroy the vacant farmhouses or to tear away the doors, which presumably had not been removed to safety (Hdt. 1.17.2). In the midst of the siege of Syracuse, the Athenians captured the enemy stockade by putting doors and planks down over a marsh and thereby crossing over the mud (Thuc. 6.101.3). These doors must have been torn from the surrounding abandoned Syracusan homesteads.

Obviously, there were also other items of wealth that were always too bulky and heavy to be brought to safety: they had to be left to the enemy to be either plundered or destroyed. Wine vats and roof tiles are the best examples. When the mercenary forces of Mnasippos overran the Corcyraean countryside, they plundered and destroyed all the rural homesteads that had been abandoned with their wine cellars intact. The story then got around that these soldiers became so luxurious that they would not drink any wine unless it had a fine bouquet (Xen. *Hell.* 6.2.6). Similarly, during the retreat of the Ten Thousand, the Greeks were able to quarter themselves in a Karduchian village whose houses were well supplied with provisions and wine stored in stone cisterns (Xen. *Anab.* 4.2.22). And again in Demosthenes' twenty-ninth oration, when the accused stripped his house of all the valuable furniture, slaves, and doors, we hear also that he destroyed the wine vat—suggesting that he wrecked all that could not be evacuated (29.3). Roof tiles, too, were always left behind intact on the farmhouse during evacuation before enemy invasion. Not only were they heavy and somewhat difficult to remove, but they were also relatively inexpensive.[10] Being made from native clay, they were much easier to replace than other personal property and may not have been worth the effort of enemy ravagers to destroy. We must imagine that should the farmhouse go up in flames, the roof tiles would be left scattered around the site and reused in later reconstruction.

10. Pritchett 1956, 281–286. Even today, there are numerous very well preserved, if not intact, roof tiles scattered around the site of the houses from the fourth century B.C. at Draphi.

The sole exception occurred in Attica during the Dekeleian depredations, when both the woodwork and the roof tiles were carried off from the farms of Attica.[11] But then the Boiotian plunderers were given a very rare, and probably unparalleled, opportunity in Greek warfare: free access year in and out to the rich croplands right across their border, making the transference of even heavy, marginally valuable booty desirable and profitable.

OBSTACLES AND TRAPS

As the country people left their farms, some measures could be taken to protect their abandoned fields and make conditions as difficult as possible for enemy ravagers. Roads and access to croplands could be obstructed, with special attention paid to hampering enemy cavalry patrols.[12] Herodotus relates how the Phokians, on the eve of an invasion from Thessaly, dug a broad trench, filled the void with empty wine jars, and smoothed over the area with loose dirt. They then awaited the enemy cavalry, who rode on through—only to be overthrown as their horses broke their legs (8.28). Unfortunately, Aeneas Tacticus's monograph *Military Preparations* is lost, but he mentions that it contained, along with other interesting information, instructions on making native territory unfit for invading cavalry (8.4.; see also Polyaen. *Strat.* 1.39.2).

Obstacles were not aimed at cavalry alone. To hamper the retreat of the Ten Thousand, the Persians had ditches and canals filled with water, requiring the Greeks to engage in the time-consuming construction of temporary bridges (Xen. *Anab.* 2.3.10). And during the last desperate march of the Athenians in Sicily, the Syracusans hindered

---

11. *Hell. Oxy.* 12.4; and see, too, Jones, Sackett, and Graham 1962, 107.

12. Cavalry, it should be noted, were always vulnerable in rough terrain; the horses lacked shoes, the riders stirrups and good saddles. Cf., for example, Hdt. 5.63.4, 6.102, 9.13.3; Plut. *Cleom.* 6.3; Thuc. 7.27.5; Xen. *Hipp.* 8.3.

their progress by placing barricades across roads and rivers (Thuc. 7.73.1, 7.74.2, 7.78.5; see also Polyb. 10.30.2). Invading armies, for their own part, were aware of the potential trouble and inconvenience caused by these obstacles. Teleutias, for instance, in his march on Olynthos in 382 B.C., was careful neither to burn nor to cut down any trees so that he could ensure free and easy movement during his approach to the city. On his retreat, however, his own troops chopped down the surrounding orchards to obstruct any attack on his rear (Xen. *Hell.* 5.2.39).

Besides barricades on routes of entry and exit, we occasionally hear of impediments and traps scattered throughout the fields to make systematic ravaging difficult. The chorus of farmers in Aristophanes' *Acharnians* vows to keep out the Peloponnesian ravagers with concealed stakes:

> I shall not let up until I stick a reed (*schoinos*) in them,
> A sharp one, a painful one, that goes in deep, so that
> Never more will they walk over my vines.   230

Schoinos here is a sharpened reed implanted among the vines to cripple unsuspecting Spartan ravagers. Consequently, the scholiast on the passage connects *schoinos* with the word *skolops* (sharpened stake), stating that "it was the custom to hide some pointed stakes (*skolopas*) among the vines so that no one could suddenly and with ease inflict damage" (sch. on Ar. *Ach.* 232).[13] Likewise, Pollux (10.131) lists among other farming equipment the "reed," "bramble," "barrier," "thorn hedge," "fleabane," "prickly teasel," and "all the other spiked objects placed among the crops for their protection." In fact, this practice of planting stakes and thorns in vineyards to ward off intruders was apparently quite common

---

13. See also Suda s.v. skolops. At Ar. *Ach.* 1178, Lamachos returns from the Boiotian frontier pierced by a stake (*tetrôtai charaki*). The *charax* here, though, probably refers to part of a palisade of a fortification or wall, and not necessarily a stake hidden in croplands.

(e.g., Plut. *Mor.* 94E; Poll. 1.225; Strato [*Anth.Pal.*] 12.205.4) even in peacetime and would only be intensified during evacuation.

PLACES OF REFUGE

After they had gathered up their property and forsaken their farms, where did residents of small country villages and isolated farmhouses flee? In the great majority of cases the obvious place of refuge was inside the fortifications of a central polis, whose modest walls, until the later part of the fourth century B.C., were still virtually impregnable from outside assault—given the primitive state of Greek siegecraft.[14] (See updated commentary, page 230 [Places of Refuge].)

In some instances, however, evacuation to the city was just not possible. This was especially true in more backward areas where there was no real centralized political organization, and rural residents were not citizens of some larger, walled polis. In these cases one alternative was isolated strongholds (*phouria, ischuria, chôria, erumna*), often incorporating natural places of defense. Crudely fortified and distant from strategic points of potential conflict, these redoubts could be used effectively as refugee centers (what German scholars call *Fluchtburgen*).[15] The semibarbarous Taochians, for example, were able to keep themselves and their property safe from the advancing Ten Thousand by retreating into a system of such fortified refugee camps (Xen. *Anab.* 4.7.1). Likewise, the Macedonians in 428 B.C. saved their goods by fleeing to refugee centers before the advance of a large Thracian army (Diod. 12.50.5). Polybius relates how the rural citizens of Elis—some of whom

14. See Garlan 1974, 106–146. The evidence for evacuation to a city or large hamlet is overwhelming. A random sampling of examples includes Arr. *Anab.* 1.26.6; Diod. 12.42.2, 13.81.3; Hdt. 5.34; Aen. Tact. 10.3; Lycurg. *Leoc.* 14–16; Plut. *Phil.* 13.1; Thuc. 2.5.4, 4.25.8; Xen. *Anab.* 6.2.8; *Cyr.* 5.2.2; *Hell.* 4.6.4; and, of course, the various references in Thucydides and Aristophanes to Attica during the Peloponnesian War.

15. See McCredie 1966, 92–93.

had not ventured into town and taken part in civic affairs for two and three generations—fled into scattered country villages and strongholds in time of invasion, and so saved both themselves and their property (4.73ff.). But even in more organized countries, where the majority of the citizens usually fled to the poleis in time of danger, not all farmers could always make their way in with their property. This was especially true of those yeomen in larger city-state territories like Attica, who might live thirty or forty miles distant. Xenophon suggested in the *Poroi*, for example, that a stronghold be built on Mt. Besa in southern Attica and be linked with the forts at Thorikos and Anaphlystos; in that way residents of the mining region would have but a short distance to flee from invasion and not have to trek all the way to Athens (4.43–48). A decree mentioned earlier, which was inserted into the text of Demosthenes' *De Corona*, specified

> That no Athenian upon any pretext be permitted to spend the
> night in the countryside, but only in Athens or the Piraeus, except
> those assigned to the garrisons; that these troops maintain their
> assigned positions, neither leaving them day nor night. . . . That
> all property from the farms as quickly as possible be removed, if
> within 120 stades, to Athens and the Piraeus; if outside 120
> stades, to Eleusis, Phyle, Aphidna, Rhamnous, and Sounion.[16]

Whatever the authenticity of this document, its presence in the Demosthenic corpus suggests credibility and might at least confirm that the idea was prevalent in Attica in the fourth century, and later that preexisting forts could also double as rural strongholds for property (if not in some instances people).[17]

16. Dem. 18.37–38. It is impossible to determine the degree of the authenticity of this decree; it may represent the essence of genuine legislation in the time of Demosthenes.

17. Since border forts and garrisons were to be manned by troops and thus situated at key roads and border passes, they were hardly suitable places for refugees. Not only would large groups of people interfere with defense, but

The mountains, sea, and neighboring friendly, or neutral, countries also always offered safe refuge. This alternative was especially useful in the face of unusually large invading armies, which were liable to over-whelm rural strongholds and eventually win over even walled cities. The best-known example is the abandonment of Attica before the great Persian advances of Xerxes and Mardonios. In those instances, the Athenians—rural and city residents alike—forsook their homeland and sailed across to Salamis, Aigina, and Troizen.[18] At the same time, in more mountainous regions like Delphi, residents were said to have climbed Parnassos and sent some of their population over to Achaia and nearby Amphissa (Hdt. 8.36; see also 8.33). During the first Persian invasion of Greece, the Eretrians considered leaving their city and hiding out in the mountains of Euboia.[19]

So far we have assumed that all citizens alike left their farms and re-treated in mass to the same place of refuge. In reality, however, women, children, and older people must have received special treatment, as they would today, and there must have been different treatment for slaves and stock. It was always preferable also to drive stock (e.g., draft animals, cattle, sheep, goats, and pigs) up into the mountains or onto some nearby land rather than inside the city walls where they would compete for scarce space and provisions. Aeneas Tacticus, for example, flatly states that "those citizens who own stock or slaves must be notified to deposit them among neighbors, since they cannot drive them into the

---

conditions there were probably even more dangerous than they would have been back on the farms the farmers had left behind.

18. Hdt. 8.41, 8.60; and see Michael Jameson's editio princeps of the Themistocles Decree in *Hesperia* 29 (1960): 211–212. For other cases where ships are able to transport entire peoples, property, even livestock, across the water to safety, see Hdt. 1.164, 1.166.

19. Hdt. 6.100; and cf., too, Thuc. 8.41.2; Xen. *Anab.* 4.1.8; *Hell.* 4.6.4–5; and Tod, *Greek Historical Inscriptions* (Oxford, 1948), 2: 189–190 (=*SIG*³ 229), where the city of Erythrai and the tyrant Hermias agree to deposit property in each other's territory for safekeeping in time of crisis.

city" (10.1). Thus during the evacuation of Attica before the first invasion of Archidamos, the Athenians sent most of their sheep and draft animals over to Euboia rather than bringing them inside the walls (Thuc.
2.14.1). The Akarnanians drove their herds up into the hills to keep
them away from Agesilaos's ravagers, who had overrun the countryside
(Xen. *Hell.* 4.6.4). Perhaps the ideal situation was a mountain refuge in
close proximity to the city, a place where stock could be kept safe and
yet available to residents under siege. Such was nearly the case in 390
B.C., when the Corinthians were able to drive their cattle to the nearby
mountainous peninsula of Piraion, and so continued to be supplied with
beef (Xen. *Ages.* 2.18; *Hell.* 4.5.1).

In some cases, it is true, we do hear of cattle and other livestock that
were brought behind the walls—implying that during a possible siege at
least a few animals were taken in to be slaughtered and thereby provide
fresh provisions as needed. But this was possible only in a very few cities
with larger open areas within the circuit walls, where stock would not
overly crowd residents and might even be able to graze for a few days on
scrub brush. Andocides complained that during the Peloponnesian War
(most probably the Dekeleian occupation), Athens was unbearably
crowded with refugees, sheep, cattle, and wagons (frag. 3.1 [Loeb]). Demades, in somewhat rhetorical language, recalled that after the battle of
Chaironeia, "the enemy was encamped near Attica, and the country was
being confined in town, and the city . . . was being fitted like a stable
with oxen, sheep, and flocks, and there was no hope from any quarter"
(14; cf. Xen. *Cyr.* 5.2.2).

Slaves, as Aeneas pointed out, were best not brought into the city if it
could be helped. Not only would they draw on precious stores of food,
but more important they were liable, whatever the immediate prospects,
to desert to the enemy and so aid the besiegers.[20] Ideally, rural slaves,

20. The flight of 20,000 slaves to Dekeleia during the Peloponnesian War
comes quickly to mind (Thuc. 7.27.5). Cf. also *Hell. Oxy.* 12.4. The majority of

like livestock, should be taken to the mountains and guarded. The Euboians begged Eurybiades to stall the Persian forces of Xerxes so that they could get their household servants (*oiketai*, that is—most likely slaves) to places of safety (Hdt. 8.4; and see also the examples at Hdt. 8.41, Plut. *Them.* 10.4, and Xen. *Anab.* 6.6.7).

In many societies special consideration is given to women and children in times of danger; this was also often the case in classical Greece. Women and children were the first to be evacuated and were directed to the safest refuge possible (e.g., Hdt. 1.164, 1.166, 8.4, 8.36, 8.41, 8.60; Lycurg. *Leoc.* 16; Thuc. 2.6.4; Xen. *Anab.* 4.1.8; *Hell.* 7.2.18). One would logically expect such preferential treatment to extend to the elderly— that is, old men unfit for military service. In the Decree of Themistokles, for example, elderly males are to be sent, along with movable property, to Salamis, and so are kept out of the fighting.[21] The same was true during the siege of Plataia, when the older men were evacuated along with the women and children to Athens (Thuc. 2.6.4). And yet if we can believe an anecdote in Plutarch's *Themistocles*, some citizens of advanced age were simply left behind in Attica when the Athenians fled before Xerxes (10.5). Nor was this necessarily an isolated occurrence. During the Carthaginian invasions of Sicily, the older residents of both Kamarina and Akragas were left to fend for themselves, and so fell into the hands of the enemy (Diod. 13.89.2–3, 13.111.3). In all of these cases, there was no real time for careful and orderly withdrawal. The actual evacuation probably resembled a mad free-for-all for safety. Such panic alone can explain their abandonment, for under normal plans of retreat, older people, apart from humanitarian considerations, could provide a valuable service watching and protecting children, slaves, and stock.

---

slaves left Chios and went over to the Athenians once they had established secure fortifications (Thuc. 8.40.2). See, too, Ar. *Eq.* 20ff.; *Nub.* 7; *Pax* 451.

21. *Hesperia* 29 (1960): p. 199, 1.10.

SCORCHED EARTH POLICY

Finally, as residents left their homes and farms, one drastic method of impeding the advance of the enemy was to burn one's own crops, houses, and anything else of any potential value. But such a "scorched earth" policy—so common in modern warfare[22]—was not widespread in classical Greece, and we hear of only a few isolated examples. The Thebans, for instance, left Lakonia in 370 B.C. in part because their potential supply of local provisions was in part wasted or burned up (Xen. *Hell.* 6.5.50). Aeneas Tacticus, once again in reference to his lost *Military Preparations*, alludes to ways of "making useless the material voluntarily left behind in the country that might be helpful to the enemy—for example, that for building walls or huts or any other project" (8.3–4; and cf. 21.1).

There are a variety of reasons why the concept of "total warfare" was not prevalent in mainland Greece during the classical period. Citizen armies usually campaigned only seasonally and for relatively short distances, rarely, if ever, embarking on any great march or *anabasis* into the interior of a large enemy country. And because of the unique Hellenic concept of a citizen as landowner-hoplite, troops would essentially have to vote on destroying their own property—in most other contemporary societies, autocracy preempted such discussions, and the idea of a citizenry with certain rights based on a freeholding land tenure was absent.

22. The Russian retreats before Napoleon (see, for instance, R. F. Delderfield, *The Retreat from Moscow* [New York, 1967], 34, 37), and the Germans in the Second World War are well-known examples. Sherman, in his autobiography, quotes appeals of the Southern press in the wake of his march to the sea: "Let everyone fly to arms! Remove your negroes, horses, cattle, and provisions from Sherman's army and burn what you cannot carry. Burn all bridges and block up the roads in his route" (*Memoirs of General William T. Sherman* [Chicago, 1875], 2: 189–190).

In addition, a good deal of the provisions of hoplite armies was brought along—lessening somewhat absolute dependence on local produce, and thus vulnerability to its possible destruction.

Also, up until the early fourth century B.C., much of the activity of these city-state armies was aimed primarily at the devastation of the cropland to draw the enemy out to battle. Massive plundering and pirate expeditions in search of provisions and booty were not so frequent. A polis's destruction, then, of its own crops and other capital investments during evacuation would not really hinder the enemy in any great degree. Rather, such destruction contributed to the ravaging of its own lands, making resettlement after the typically short stay of an invader even more difficult. Indeed, Pericles remarked to the Athenians at the outset of the Archidamian War: "If I had thought that I could persuade you, I would have had you go out and lay them [houses and crops] waste with your own hands" (Thuc. 1.143.5).[23] The contrary-to-fact sentence illustrates that, whatever his own wishes, this was not the policy of the citizens of Attica, and it would have been nearly impossible to convince a free citizenry to vote to destroy its own property.

Where a "scorched earth" strategy could be more effective was to the East, outside of mainland Greece, in the wider expanses of Asia Minor, where warfare often transcended local borders, and autocrats governed defense policy. There massive expeditions were also often dependent on local produce, and thus vulnerable to its destruction. An early classic example is Darios's ill-fated Skythian invasion of 514 B.C. After the Skythians refused open pitched battle with the vastly superior Persian forces, they retired, "driving off their herds, choking up their own wells and springs, destroying the fodder of the entire countryside" (Hdt. 4.

23. Of course, Pericles most likely urged the Athenians to destroy their farms not so much to hinder the Peloponnesian ravagers as to make his unpopular policy of forced evacuation more absolute and final.

120.1).[24] The Persians were drawn farther and farther into the interior in futile pursuit. After much loss, and in want of provisions, they retreated hastily to the Ister River,closely followed by the Skythians. (See updated commentary, page 230 [Pollution of Waters].) Similarly, many tribes destroyed their own property and crops before the approach of the Ten Thousand through Asia Minor. The Drilai, for example, torched all their vulnerable strongholds, leaving the Greeks only "an occasional pig, ox, or other animal that had escaped the fire" (Xen. *Anab.* 5.2.3). Earlier, on the initial Greek march with Cyrus, the retreating Persians burned all the dry fodder and anything else that might have been of use to the Ten Thousand (Xen. *Anab.* 1.6.1).[25] We hear,

[24] Herodotus brings out nicely the advantages in mobility enjoyed by a nomadic people. The Skythian strategy was much easier for them than it would have been for a city-state in Greece: as the Skythian king put it, "We have neither cities nor cultivated lands for which we have fear lest they should be taken and ravaged, and therefore quickly offer you battle" (Hdt. 4.127). Herodotus seems to remark favorably: "How can such a people not be invincible and impossible to meet in battle?" (4.46)—surely contrasting the traditional practice in Greek poleis of pitched battles fought for the protection of crops and homes (see, among others, Garlan 1974, 28–29; Grundy 1948, 85). And yet the inherent problems accounting for the unpopularity of a "scorched earth" policy are obvious: while the destruction of one's own resources harms the enemy, it, nonetheless, leaves nothing to return to. Even the nomadic Skythians, who boast about their self-sufficiency and readiness to ravage their own land, do not get off without some injurious effects. When they reversed their course and assumed the role of the pursuer, "it would have been possible for them to find the Persians easily, if only they had not destroyed all the grazing land of the country and choked up all the wells" (Hdt. 4.140).

[25] We should imagine that the polluting of water was also a key part of any "scorched earth" policy, since during the summer months in the middle of the campaigning season it was often scarce (e.g., Dem. 14.30, 50.61; Thuc. 3.88.1). Both troops and their horses could be stopped completely, or at least be disorganized, should their supplies of water be cut off (e.g., Aen. *Tact.* 8.4; Aeschin. 2.115; Frontin. *Str.* 3.7; Hdt. 4.120; Thuc. 7.78.4, 7.84.2ff.).

too, of numerous proposals to destroy friendly property before the advance of Alexander the Great through Asia—a tactic that was often effective when actually carried out (e.g., Arr. *Anab.* 1.12.9, 3.28.8; Diod. 17.18.2).[26]

CONCLUSION

Before armies reached the territory of their adversaries, most rural residents had already gathered up well in advance a great deal of property and moved inside fortification walls or some other place of refuge. Absolute surprise by large invading forces was rare, then, in Greek warfare. Furthermore, in the majority of cases, evacuation seems to have been carefully organized. For example, the removal of stores and crops was the responsibility of the state, as soldiers were ordered to go out and protect the harvesters while they brought in the ripe crops. Their success may help to explain the surprising difficulty in Greek warfare of starving out a besieged city, whose rural citizenry had voted on a variety of state mechanisms for their protection. While we should imagine that there were always property and provisions left behind, citizens could be quite thorough in stripping their houses clean, taking along farm implements, and often even the doors and woodwork. Stock and slaves were ideally sent to more distant, safer areas of sanctuary, along with women, children, and, perhaps less regularly, older people. Therefore, raping, kidnapping, and random killing of civilians out in the field were not routine acts during most invasions. The destruction of one's own property and provisions was also rare in mainland Greece, but a frequent tactic in the East, especially in Asia Minor, where a variety of circumstances made the practice more effective.

In short, we should imagine that the total losses to ravagers and plunderers were reduced by careful evacuation. Agriculture would especially benefit, as tools, and, in some cases, slaves and livestock, were not

[26] See also Engels 1978, 30.

harmed at all. It is no wonder, then, that Thucydides gives an especially thorough description of the Dekeleian depredations (7.27ff.), and Xenophon similarly goes to great length to recount how the Lakedaimonians overran Corcyra (*Hell.* 6.2.5ff.): such unrestricted devastation and plundering of abandoned property in the countryside were rare in Greek warfare and worthy of record. Most invaders had to be content with much less.

FIVE

Sorties

Once rural citizens had been evacuated to a place of refuge, and the enemy was in control of the countryside, as a result of either victory in hoplite battle or default, the invaded still had one last—and very good—chance of impeding ravagers. Well-organized, sudden sorties, usually made up of cavalry troops,[1] could issue forth from the city, not only forcing the enemy hoplites to remain in formation, but also going after light-armed ravaging patrols who were dispersed throughout the countryside. (See updated commentary, page 230 [Cavalry against Ravagers].)

Theoretical treatises about military tactics and strategy give much attention to such sorties and express confidence that even a small, closely disciplined mounted force could successfully keep the enemy on their

---

1. Cavalry in Greece during much of the classical age played a subservient role to infantry. Lack of good pasturage, poor breeding, difficult terrain, and the absence of stirrups and strong saddles all in varying degrees made the independent use of a shock cavalry corps impossible (cf. Adcock 1957, 48–50; Anderson 1970, 57–58; Gomme 1: 15; Grundy 1948, 277–279; Kromayer and Veith 1928, 53–54). But mounted troops could be effective against isolated bands of ravagers; we rarely hear of hoplites alone on such patrols. They were, of course, cumbersome, slow, and vulnerable to counterattack.

guard and protect property and some farmland outside the walls. Xenophon, in his essay on the cavalry commander, outlines the general operation of such patrols:

> It seems to me that the commander's job is to keep his men always prepared for action, and yet out of sight, watching for any mistake the enemy might make. There is a tendency that the more numerous the soldiers, the more numerous are the mistakes they make. For either they scatter out of a need for provisions or in utter disorder some march too far ahead while others lag way behind. All these mistakes the cavalry commander must capitalize on; if he doesn't, the entire country will fall into enemy hands. And once he decides to strike, he must be very careful to retreat well before the main enemy reinforcements arrive. (*Hipp.* 7.7–10)

Aeneas Tacticus suggested a rather elaborate, if not idealized plan to check ravagers:

> Meanwhile, some of the enemy troops break up into small patrols to ravage the countryside; others lie in wait, hoping to ambush some of your relief forces who arrive in disorder. Therefore, there is no need to rouse the invaders with an immediate engagement. Instead, allow them first to feel secure, and, in utter contempt of you, to rush after booty and loot. At this time, they will be gorged with food and sated with drink; in their drunkenness,[2] they will soon be in no shape to fight and will retreat if you can catch them at the right moment. For when you've assembled your relief sortie at the announced place, then you must immediately attack, cut off their retreat with your horse, set up ambushes with your special forces, engage them with your light-armed troops, and, next, bring up your heavy infantry in close formation right after. (16.4–7)

---

2. Wine stored in vats was difficult to remove, and so often left behind. Also, abandoned alcohol might sometimes have the (intentional?) effect of undermining discipline among enemy ravagers (see Xen. *Hell.* 6.2.6).

Such theorists were not postulating these ideas out of thin air. Rather, they derived their thoughts from the experience of Greek warfare, where the vulnerability of ravagers to well-organized cavalry sorties was an established fact. A classic example occurred in 381 B.C., when an Olynthian raiding party descended on Apollonia and pillaged the countryside. At that point, Derdas, who was in charge of a squadron of defensive troops at Apollonia,

> kept quiet, keeping his horses ready for action and their riders armed. But when the Olynthians carelessly drove on, not only into the suburbs, but even to the very gates of the city, then in good order he rode out to the attack. As soon as the enemy saw him, they broke and ran. But Derdas, when once the rout had begun, did not cease pursuing and killing for ninety stadia, until he chased them right up to the city walls of Olynthos. (Xen. *Hell.* 5.3.1–2)

Similarly, a very small Phliasian cavalry patrol (sixty in number) was able to sally forth from their city and put to flight an entire Argive army of invasion, which was slowly retreating after ravaging the countryside (Xen. *Hell.* 7.2.4). To combat Athenian seaborne ravaging raids against the coast of the Peloponnese, the Spartans needed defensive forces who could effectively match the quickness and mobility of these light-armed parties. "In contrast to their usual practice," they created a special detachment of 400 cavalrymen assisted by archers (Thuc. 4.55.2). And a large Athenian army that invaded and overran Thessaly nevertheless failed to take Pharsalos, or "to achieve any of the objects of their expedition." One of the reasons, Thucydides tells us, was the continual presence of the cavalry, which never permitted the Athenians to leave their formation. That is, light-armed ravagers could neither go forth from the hoplite ranks to destroy cropland nor forage (Thuc. 1.111). The cavalry sent by Dionysios to aid the Spartans in 369 B.C. was also extremely effective against ravagers. By constant sorties against the Theban troops who were in the Corinthian Plain, they forced the entire army to withdraw (Xen. *Hell.* 7.1.20–22). Other examples need not be cited, since we hear of countless instances in Greek history where ravagers and plunderers are cut to pieces by sudden, well-led cavalry attacks, or even by organized sorties of light-armed infantry.[3]

Perhaps the best-known instance of effective counterattacks was the Athenian experience during the Peloponnesian War. It may seem a strange example, since the Athenians give the general impression that they had utterly forsaken the traditional strategy of defense and chosen to remain fast behind their walls as Spartan ravagers destroyed their croplands right before their eyes. Actually, the Athenian cavalry was constantly active and kept the enemy always on their guard.[4] In the first invasion of the Archidamian War (431 B.C.), when the Peloponnesians had barely begun to devastate the Thriasian Plain, we hear of an Athenian cavalry patrol—which must have been some sort of advance detachment stationed at Eleusis—attacking and then retreating before the enemy near the streams called Rheitoi (Thuc. 2.19.2). A few days later Pericles sent out constant cavalry sorties (*hippeas exepempen aei*) to keep enemy ravagers away from the rich farmland near the city (Thuc. 2.22.2). In one of these engagements near Phrygia a combined force of Athenian and allied Thessalian cavalry fought the Boiotian horse to a standstill until the enemy was reinforced by hoplites.[5] During the third

3. E.g., Arr. *Anab.* 3.30.10; Thuc. 2.25.2 (and Gomme 2: 83), 6.37.2 (Athenagoras's prediction that the Syracusan cavalry would confine the Athenian army of invasion to their camp); Xen. *Ages.* 1.30; *Anab.* 6.1.1, 6.4.24–25; *Hell.* 1.1.33, 3.4.22, 4.1.17, 4.8.18–19, 5.4.39; *Vect.* 4.48.

4. We know that at the outbreak of the war the cavalry was quite large. Pericles, in his effort to encourage the citizen body, pointed out (Thuc. 2.13.8) that there were 1,200 cavalry troops, including mounted bowmen (that is, 1,000 regular riders [e.g., Ar. *Eq.* 225; Xen. *Hipp.* 9.3] and 200 horse-archers).

5. Thuc. 2.22.2–3. The Athenians apparently considered this relatively minor skirmish a morale booster and made much of it in later times. The Thessalian cavalry who died there were buried on the road to the Academy (Paus. 1.29.6). For the Athenian dead in the battle, see again Paus. 1.29.6; *Anth. Pal.* 7.254; A.

invasion of Attica of 428 B.C., the Athenian cavalry "as usual"[6] attacked the enemy in the countryside "wherever possible" and prevented the main body of light-armed ravagers from roaming beyond the protective hoplite ranks. Once again, the fields near the city were not touched (Thuc. 3.1.1–3). And throughout the Dekeleian War, when there was a Spartan force always present, the Athenian cavalry patrolled the countryside and made daily (*hosêmerai*) raids against Dekeleia itself—so much so that some horses were lamed by the rough terrain and constant action, others wounded by the enemy (7.27.5). Understandably, King Agis could never approach the walls of the city and was repulsed decisively in all three of his attempts at advancing on Athens.[7] Years later, Xenophon in his *Hipparchus* recalled the vital role of the Athenian cavalry at this time, remarking how they had been expected alone to protect the countryside outside the city's walls (7.4). And in his *Poroi*, with their service during the Peloponnesian War no doubt again on his mind, he pointed out that any contemporary army advancing toward the mines of southern Attica must pass near Athens, and so take their chances with Athenian cavalry and garrison troops (4.47).

It is not hard to see why ravagers were so vulnerable to mounted sorties. Troops had to lay down their weapons, leave ranks, and search out crops and farmhouses. In this way they were almost helpless from sud-

---

Wilhelm, *Beiträge zur griechischen Inschriftenkunde* (Vienna, 1909), 35–37; Gomme 2: 77–78, 86, 101–102.

[6] Perhaps we cannot assume (as, for example, Kagan [1974, 17] does for the second invasion of Attica, and Busolt [1904, 3:2: 944 n. 6, 1021] does for the fourth) that when Thucydides does not specifically mention cavalry attacks within his brief yearly notices, they were therefore absent. See Gomme 2: 289–290.

[7] Thuc. 8.71.1-3; Xen. *Hell.* 1.1.33; and cf., too, Diod. 13.72ff. Similarly, during the civil war of 403 B.C., the cavalry of the Thirty often inflicted losses on foragers whom they encountered outside the walls of the city (Xen. *Hell.* 2.4.26).

den, concentrated attacks by horsemen, who could pick off individual soldiers at will. Also, all invading armies have the universal disadvantage of unfamiliarity with the local terrain. This would be especially true of ravagers who must wander through the countryside among orchards and vineyards and are liable to become lost, or, worse yet, trapped in an unfavorable position. There are many instances in Greek warfare where invading troops meet with disaster because of their ignorance of local topography (e.g., Aen. Tact. 2.6, 16.20; Diod. 13.108.7; Thuc. 1.106.1, 3.112.6; and cf. Xen. *Hipp.* 4.6, 8.3)—understandable in light of the often remote nature and difficult terrain of many Greek orchards and vineyards.

Also, in purely ravaging expeditions where troops mostly seek to destroy, not plunder, the countryside, we still cannot rule out the occasional collection of booty. Provisions in almost all campaigns were expected to be augmented from local produce: some ravagers would carry crops they did not destroy back to camp. Likewise, ravagers who torched farm buildings might first ransack the house in hopes of finding some precious article left behind (e.g., bronze and iron utensils). Consequently, the mobility of the invading force as a whole, and individual troops in particular, would be diminished somewhat by even haphazard foraging—giving another advantage to unencumbered mounted sorties from the city (e.g., Aen. Tact. 16.5–7).

Besides making widespread devastation difficult, sorties could also protect choice farmland near the city and enable some residents to take their chances outside the walls. The Akarnanians, for example, initially were able to work the greater portion of their cropland, although Agesilaos was present with a large army. The reason, Xenophon tells us, was that the enemy was advancing very slowly, intent on methodically ravaging one section of land after another. But we should also imagine that the expert force of Akarnanian peltasts kept the enemy in one body and prevented parties of ravagers from roaming or advancing too far from the slow-moving main army. The Akarnanian farmers, then, were given a sense of security—a false sense as events later turned out—and continued to work their holdings as long as possible (Xen. *Hell.* 4.6.4–14). In general, we often hear of farmers who choose to remain on their farms in the hope that the enemy might not actually reach their land, or at least that friendly patrols would cover any eventual evacuation later on (e.g., Xen. *Hell* 7.5.14; Thuc. 6.49.3). During the Archidamian and Dekeleian wars, all the farmland near the walls of Athens, and other parcels in more remote areas, were saved and cultivated continuously (see chapter 6). The honorific decrees mentioned earlier (see chapter 4) give the impression that a great deal of farming continued in time of crisis—the rural residents placing their confidence in organized sorties and patrols from the city to keep ravagers away from their cropland. In short, after most enemies had arrived, and the local population had evacuated to nearby fortifications, the countryside was still not the unquestioned domain of the invading party. There must have been continual sorties and patrols as the defenders attempted to catch overconfident or lost ravagers away from the main body of hoplites; in this manner, ravaging must have had severe restraints put upon it, as cropland was never quite securely in the hands of the enemy.

PART THREE

The Effectiveness of Agricultural Devastation

The Devastation of Attica during the Peloponnesian War

The Spartan annual invasions and eventual occupation of Attica during the course of the Peloponnesian War are the best-known and best-documented examples of wartime destruction of agriculture in classical antiquity. So far I have emphasized the pragmatic difficulties of crop devastation in warfare and suggested that permanent destruction of farmland was often not achieved. Nowhere can the validity of these conclusions be better determined than in the countryside around Athens during the Peloponnesian War, when for over a generation the Spartans engaged in an unparalleled effort to ruin the agriculture of the Athenians.

The contemporary works of Thucydides and Aristophanes both contain vivid and often moving accounts of the damage to the fields of Attica. The devastations, consequently, have usually been regarded by scholars as catastrophic: annual crops completely lost, orchards and vineyards permanently destroyed, farms looted and ruined. Often the entire history of fourth-century Athens is seen through the lens of agricultural ruin as a result of the war with Sparta, the destruction purportedly explaining the "decline" of Athenian power, an ensuing class struggle, and the rise of a defeatist mentality. That the agriculture of Attica suffered during the Peloponnesian War cannot be doubted, but more needs to be known about the degree—and nature—of the damage. The devastations are often referred to and yet have been little studied. A wider sampling of evidence must be collected, and both Thucydides and Aristophanes should be reexamined in light of what each says, or does not say, about the actual destruction. Practical questions too can be asked about the Peloponnesian ravaging:

1. How much time was available to the Peloponnesian invaders?

2. How much territory in Attica was or *could be* covered?

3. Was the damage temporary (e.g., annual cereal crops), or more long lasting (e.g., olives and vines)?

4. Was rural productivity imperiled by damage to agriculture itself—trees, vines, and cereals—or by damage to infrastructure (buildings, fences, houses), the flight of rural slaves, and the evacuation and general dislocation of agrarian populations?

5. How effective were Athenian countermeasures?

The inherent differences between the five temporary Peloponnesian invasions of the Archidamian War and the later constant Peloponnesian occupation of Dekeleia make separate studies of the agricultural damage desirable.

THE ARCHIDAMIAN WAR (431–421 B.C.)

The Five Enemy Invasions

The Peloponnesians first invaded Attica in the early summer of 431 B.C. under the command of the Spartan king Archidamos (Thuc. 2.19.1).[1] They did not come directly to Eleusis through Megara, the

---

1. Thucydides says "summer and the grain harvest coming on" (*therous kai sitou akmazontos*). For this and other similar expressions, see Gomme 2: 145, 252, 288; 3: 437. Garlan 1974, 23 n. 1, contains a brief bibliography.

shortest and most direct route,[2] but rather descended from Oinoe.[3] There Archidamos wasted precious time in a fruitless attempt to take the garrison, giving the Athenians ample opportunity in the process to evacuate Attica (2.18.4). He also apparently still refrained from harming the countryside, and so bypassed the rich Mazi Plain around Oinoe. On arriving at Eleusis and the Thriasian Plain, the Peloponnesians first began to ravage the countryside seriously (2.19.2). After a short cavalry skirmish there, they hastened on through the Parnes-Aigaleos gap[4] to Acharnai, where they remained "some time" (2.20), devastating the land in hopes of drawing out the Athenian hoplite force. They had not, and would not, enter the fertile plain around the city itself. Instead, after another cavalry skirmish, this time at Phrygia, they left through the Kephissos Valley, ravaging "some other demes between Mt. Parnes and Mt. Brilessos [Pentelikos]" (2.23.1), but apparently leaving Dekeleia untouched (Hdt. 9.73). Graike was also ravaged as the enemy exited Attica through Oropos on their way to Boiotia (Thuc. 2.23.3). They had not been in Attica long, perhaps as little as twenty-five days, leaving when their provisions gave out.[5] Of the actual details of the devastations Thucydides tells us little, using only characteristically

2. Pleistoanax must have led the Spartans this way in 445 B.C. (Thuc. 1.114.2; cf. also Hdt. 5.74.2). On the route used by Archidamos that year, see Gomme 2: 66–69; Hammond 1954, 112; Vanderpool 1978, 232.

3. The site of ancient Oinoe has been the source of continuous debate. Chandler (1926, 8ff.) opted (rightly) for modern Myoupolis; see also Hammond 1954, 120ff., for Villia (which cannot be correct); C. Edmondson, "The Topography of Northwest Attica" (Ph.D. diss., University of California, Berkeley, 1966), for Agios Georgios. There exists a fine ancient road from Oinoe to Eleusis that would have made Archidamos's descent rather easy. The road is described in detail by Vanderpool 1978, 227–245.

4. This is the site of the later fourth-century Dema Wall. See Jones, Sackett, and Eliot 1957, 152–189.

5. The second invasion, of 430 B.C., was the longest—40 days (Thuc. 2.57.2), the fifth, of 425, the shortest—15 days (4.6.2). Busolt (1904, 3:2: 913, 931) suggests this first expedition lasted around 25–30 days; Gomme (2: 79) 30–35 days.

vague terminology for destruction, such as *diaphthê rô* (destroy: 2.20.4), *kakourgô* (inflict harm: 2.22.2), and *dêoô* (ravage: 2.23.1, 3). The frequent appearance of *temnô* (cut: 2.19.2; 2.20.1, 2, 4; 2.21.2, 3) within his description, however, suggests that much of the Spartan destruction was aimed at croplands.[6]

In early May of 430 B.C. Archidamos once again led the Peloponnesians into Attica. This second invasion was both the longest (Thuc. 2.57.2) and the most destructive (3.26.3) of the five, its severity no doubt heightened by the simultaneous outbreak of the plague inside the city walls (2.47, 2.57.1). The Spartans probably entered from Eleusis, although Thucydides does not say, and ravaged the rich Kephissos Basin for the first time (2.55.1). Later, they penetrated the Paralos all the way to Laureion, devastating the small but fertile valleys on the west coast from Aixone to Sounion, and on the east from Sounion to Rhamnous (2.55.1).[7] The extent of Archidamos's second invasion led Thucydides to state that "the entire countryside was ravaged" (2.57.2), although the tetrapolis in the Marathonian Plain seems to have been spared, and his own description of the depredations does not suggest Attica was blanketed with ravagers.[8] There is again no specific reference to the type of damage inflicted, although agriculture should be assumed to have been the primary target.[9] After these first two invasions the Athenians inside the walls were described as being deprived of the use of their houses and fields (2.62.3). The poorer, Thucydides says, lost what little they had to begin with, the rich their fine estates with lavish furnishings (2.65.2).

The following year, 429 B.C., the Peloponnesians bypassed Attica altogether and went directly to Plataia, presumably because of the plague

6. Cf. Hardy 1926, 349 n. 2.

7. See Gomme 2: 162.

8. Diod. 12.45.1; Istros *FGrH* 334F30.

9. *Temnô* (to cut) appears frequently in Thucydides' brief description of this invasion (e.g., 2.55.1, 2.57.2). Diodorus (12.45.1) states that fruit trees were cut down and farm buildings torched.

at Athens.[10] They did not return until 428, and thus two years went by in which the agriculture of Attica went undisturbed by the enemy. Thucydides' description of this third invasion is quite short; he states only that the Peloponnesians came around mid-May and "ravaged the land" (3.1.2). Athenian cavalry "as usual" kept the light-armed ravagers from harming the fields near the city walls. The Peloponnesians left Attica when their provisions gave out (3.1.3). Later that summer they considered a rare second invasion in conjunction with a sea attack, but by then the allies were busy with their harvests in the Peloponnese and "in no mood for war"; the plan was tabled (3.15.1, 3.16.1–2). Throughout the Archidamian War, the Peloponnesians and their allies never returned to Attica twice in the same year—a tendency that was soon well understood by Attic farmers themselves.

King Kleomenes[11] commanded the fourth invasion, in 427 B.C., the most destructive of the five except for the second (3.26.3). The enemy during this inroad, Thucydides reports, "devastated both what had grown up again in the parts previously ravaged[12] and the territory that had been skipped over in the prior invasions." He adds that they "covered a great deal of territory in their devastation," departing when their grain gave out and they heard nothing from the fleet (3.26.4).

Fear of earthquakes stopped the invasion of 426 B.C. at the Isthmus. No attack took place (Thuc. 3.89.1). The fifth and last expedition was led by Agis, the son of Archidamos, in 425 B.C. (4.2.1). Nothing specific is mentioned about the Peloponnesians' activity during this invasion, only that they encamped and "ravaged the countryside." Damage to Attica this year must have been negligible, though, since the enemy left

10. Thuc. 2.71.1. Cf., too, Adcock 1947, 3.

11. See Gomme 2: 289 for the question of command.

12. *Ei ti ebeblastêkei,* "if anything had grown back out." This phrase makes no sense in reference to annual crops, such as wheat, and must refer to fruit-trees, vines, or both, which were only partly damaged in earlier devastations. Cf. again Hardy 1926, 351 n. 5; Zimmern 1931, 46 n. 2.

immediately on hearing that Pylos had been taken, after staying only fifteen days (4.6.2). They were eager to leave anyway, since they had entered Attica a little too early that year, when it was still cold and when the grain was still green (4.6.1). One gets the impression that after seven years of haphazard mustering and invasions, the Spartans and their allies were by 425 B.C. no longer zealous believers in the idea that Attica could be ravaged to the extent that the Athenians would either starve or yield.

In addition to the testimony offered by Thucydides, the comedies of Aristophanes contain numerous references to damage inflicted by the Spartans during the five invasions of the Archidamian War. The evidence falls roughly into two groups. First, there is a very general picture of the delights of peace contrasted with the hardships of the ongoing war.[13] A repeated theme here is the unhappiness of forced evacuation into the unpleasant confines of the city (*Ach.* 32–39, 71–72; *Eq.* 792–794; *Pax* 632–640). Rural characters dream constantly of being free of war and military service (*Ach.* 247–251; *Pax* 335–336, 439–453) so that they can renew their interrupted festivals and enjoy country food once again (*Ach.* 1049–1054; *Pax* 520–526, 636ff., 774, 990–995, 1127–1139). They yearn to see their fields again and farm their crops (*Ach.* 994–99; *Pax* 550–581, 596–597, 706–708).[14]

Second, there are more direct, specific references to actual agricultural damage inflicted during the Archidamian devastations. For example, at one point, the chorus of Acharnian farmers accuses Amphitheos: "Villain, you dare bring treaties when our vineyards are cut down?" (*Ach.* 182–183). Later, they vow that the heels of the Spartan ravagers shall be impaled on stakes so that "they cannot trample down [our] vines" (231–232). Dikaiopolis, the hero of the play, admits to the chorus: "I, like you, have had my vines cut down" (512). Trygaios, the vine

---

13. See Busolt 1904, 3:2: 925; Ehrenberg 1951, 308; Hardy 1926, 350.
14. Cf. also especially Ar. frags. 107, 109, 363, 364, and 400 (Kock).

dresser in the *Peace*, remarks that the Spartans had cut down the fig tree that he had planted and raised (*Pax* 628–629); in the same play, the whip scars on a slave's back are compared to the cuts on fruit trees during wartime (746–747).[15]

This combined evidence from Thucydides and Aristophanes has led most scholars to believe that the invasions of the Archidamian War seriously damaged the agriculture of Attica.[16] Donald Kagan, for instance, remarks on the condition of Athens after the first two invasions: "They had permitted their fields and houses to be destroyed without offering battle. Now that all of Attica had been devastated . . ."[17] P. A. Brunt seems to agree with the picture of considerable ruin: "But even without establishing a fort in Attica the Spartans could and did do the Athenians much harm by annual devastations. In a war of attrition the side that does all the damage must win in the end."[18] B. W. Henderson flatly states:

> When war came invading armies marched into Attica, driving the
> scared peasants and landowners to take refuge behind the city
> walls, living on the produce of the countryside, destroying the
> olive-trees, cutting down the vines, plundering farm and house,
> and carrying the spoils in triumph home.[19]

This current consensus, however, exaggerates the severity of the agricultural damage to Attica somewhat, since it assumes that most, if not all, crops were destroyed, with permanent consequences for decades after. (See updated commentary, page 231 [Periclean Strategy].)

---

15. There are other references to damaged crops at *Ach.* 986 (vine crops); *Eq.* 1076–1077 (grapes); *Pax* 612–614 (vines), 1326 ("all the good things").

16. Hardy's sensible article is often ignored or not understood.

17. Kagan 1974, 99.

18. Brunt 1965, 270.

19. Henderson 1927, 15–16.

The Evidence of Thucydides and Aristophanes Reexamined

At times Thucydides' account of the devastations seems inconsistent, contradictory, and overstated. (See updated commentary, page 233 [Thucydides and Archidamian War].) His declaration that during the second invasion *all* of Attica was ravaged (*kai tên gên pasan etemon*, 2.57.2) is a good example—for later he seems to contradict himself twice on that point. In the first place, at 2.55 he has just described the extent of the Spartan devastations that year: the enemy laid waste to the Attic Plain and marched into the Paralos. But even if we understand that the Thriasian Plain was ravaged on their entry into Attica, the entire tetrapolis, as well as the small though rich valleys around Mazi, Aphidnai, and Oropos, was apparently left untouched. Second, in his description of the fourth invasion, Thucydides in fact surprisingly alludes to areas of Attica that had not been ravaged in earlier devastations (*kai hosa en tais prin eisbolais pareleipto*, 3.26.3). All of Attica, then, was not ravaged during the second invasion of 430 B.C., as Thucydides had earlier reported.

Another apparent discrepancy appears at Thucydides 2.65.2. Pericles there is made to state that after two invasions the rich had lost their fine possessions in the country consisting of lavish houses and furnishings. Yet, during the initial evacuation of 431 B.C., the year before, the Athenians had evacuated their household furniture into Athens, going so far as to save even the woodwork of their homes (2.14.1; cf. 2.18.4)—an unusual evacuation that aimed at saving the interior structural furnishings of the houses themselves. These contradictions are puzzling and cast some doubt on the bleak picture presented in Thucydides' year-by-year descriptions of the devastations. Nevertheless, they are minor in comparison with a later summary statement that seems to contradict the very essence of Thucydides' earlier, contemporary accounts of the Archidamian ravaging.

In the description of the Dekeleian depredations in the seventh book of his *History*, Thucydides remarks that the Athenians earlier, during the "short" Archidamian invasions (*bracheia gignomenai hai eisbolai*), had *not* been prevented "from making full use of the land during the rest of the year" (7.27.4). After the fortification of Dekeleia, however, he says in contrast, the Athenians suffered from loss of supplies, stock, and slaves. Apparently, Thucydides' initial statements about the Archidamian ravaging were written earlier and left unrevised; later, the damage wrought by the later Dekeleian occupation proved that, in comparison, these brief, yearly invasions had been, in fact, mild.[20]

Thucydides' conclusions are supported by the *Hellenica Oxyrhynchia*. At one point, the unknown author of this fourth-century history explains how Thebes had grown so prosperous in the early fourth century B.C. He suggests that after the fortification of Dekeleia, the Thebans received slaves and war spoils at a small price and plundered Attica, carrying back all their rural infrastructure, "beginning with the wood and tile of their houses" (*Hell. Oxy.* 12.4). This was possible, he adds, because "the country of the Athenians at that time had been the most lavishly furnished in Greece, for it had suffered but slight injury (*epeponthei gar mikra kakôs*) from the Lakedaimonians in the former invasions and had been elaborated with so much extravagance that . . ." (12.5). Both Thucydides and the Oxyrhynchus Historian, then, come to the same conclusion: in comparison with the Dekeleian occupation, the Archidamian invasions did little damage to Attica. With this in mind, some other evidence from Aristophanes' plays must also be re-examined.

20. See Brunt 1965, 266–267; Grundy 1948, 472–474; Hardy 1926, 347; Jacoby 1940, vol. 3b, pt. 2: 136–137. See also Thucydides' remarks on the armistice of the Archidamian War (5.14.1–4). He cites several reasons why the Athenians were tired of the war; conspicuously absent in his list is Athenian remorse or despair over the agricultural losses suffered in Attica. Similarly, the Spartans were eager for peace then, "since the war had gone contrary to their expectation. For they had thought that within a few years they could destroy the power of the Athenians by ravaging their land."

It should be noted first of all that, contrary to what we are led to believe, Aristophanes' comedies do not really offer vivid, contemporary documentation of the Archidamian devastations.. (See updated commentary, page 233 [Aristophanes and the Ravaging of Attica].) The earliest surviving play, the *Acharnians*, was brought out in the winter of 425 B.C., twenty-two months *after* the fourth invasion of May 427, and nearly *six years* after the first enemy invasion of Attica. The *Knights* was produced the next February, 424 B.C. True, in the preceding summer of 425 B.C. there had been an enemy invasion, but it was the shortest (fifteen days) and hardly destructive. By the time of the production of the *Wasps* (422 B.C.), nearly five years had passed since the Peloponnesians had last seriously ravaged Attica (in 427 B.C.). And when the *Peace* was presented—the comedy that more than any other of Aristophanes' plays alludes to destroyed crops—it had been nearly six years since the Peloponnesians had done any real damage in Attica. By this time it seems that the farmer railing on at the loss of his vines or trees had become an almost stock figure of comedy in this period, successfully illustrating the poet's own views about the futility of continual intrapolis warfare, but probably not representing good evidence for ongoing, contemporary ravaging of the Attic countryside by enemy invaders. In short, the allusions to damaged crops in Aristophanes' comedies were composed at a time of relative peace in Attica, long after Spartan ravagers had left the countryside.

There are also numerous passages in Aristophanes' comedies that suggest that the agriculture of Attica either was left untouched or at least was not severely damaged by the Archidamian inroads. There is, for example, constant mention of available fruits, vegetables, and food in general within the city and out in the countryside. If the Peloponnesian devastations had caused as much permanent damage as is usually assumed, could Aristophanes have joked and alluded so often to the eating of cakes and fruits? Dikaiopolis, for instance, is invited to feast on whole meal, cheese, and sesame honey cakes (*Ach.* 1089–1093). In the *Knights*, Demos will regain his strength when he returns to the country and feeds on rural dishes (806). Amynias is described in the *Wasps* at one point as dining on an apple and a pomegranate (1268).

It would seem unlikely that the passages in the *Wasps* (252) and the *Clouds* (56–59) attesting to a lack of oil in each case imply ongoing, contemporary destruction of olive trees in Attica.[21] In the *Wasps* passage, the poet simply wants to highlight the general poverty of the chorus, who cannot afford much of anything at any time, even staples like oil— not to comment on the decline in agricultural production.[22] The *Clouds* passage is similar. Strepsiades has just (39–54) been complaining of his own poverty and thriftiness compared to the spendthrift habits of his city-bred wife. At that point, the servant suddenly enters in comic fashion out of oil, providing a timely example of unnecessary waste (he has placed a needlessly thick wick in the lamp)—not evidence of a country-wide shortage and consequently the exorbitant price of olive oil. A similar passage in the *Birds* (1589) has no outside allusion to any such "scarcity" and cannot be proof of destroyed olive trees. Indeed, in the *Acharnians* (1128), the play closest to the time of the invasions, olive oil could not be too expensive, for it is poured on a shield as polish! Socrates, at some time, was said to have taken a friend complaining of high prices to the food market, where he pointed out that olives sold for the cheap price of two *chalkoi* per *choinix* (Plut. *Mor.* 470F).

21. As McDowell (Aristophanes' *Wasps* [Oxford, 1971], 167) and Brunt (1965, 267) seem to think.

22. I would explain *Wasps* 302 in this same way. There, figs are thought to be dear because the jurors are especially impoverished, not because of wartime destruction of fig trees. Figs actually seem to have been plentiful both during and after the Archidamian War; see *Plut.* 798; Pritchett 1956, 190–191. (Figs are especially large trees and would be very difficult to chop down.) At *Wasps* 274 an especially poor juror can afford only one pair of shoes: surely no one would suggest on the basis of this that all the shoe stores or sources of leather in Attica had been destroyed in the war, and consequently footwear was scarce and high-priced. Mention of general poverty, or even scarcity, cannot be automatically equated with devastation of crops and property by enemy ravagers.

Farms with both fruit trees and vines are also referred to in these plays and can only be assumed to be intact and healthy. The cloud chorus explains that they will protect the crops and vineyards of Attica—apparently very much alive in 423 B.C.—though they can, if they should desire, destroy the produce by killing the blossoms of the olive and vine (*Nub.* 1119–1125). The chorus of Attica farmers in the *Peace* is eager to return to their fields and see the vines and figs that they planted in their youth (557–563). Later (570), Trygaios is ready to regain his farm and cultivate his vineyard. At the end of the comedy, the farmer chorus prays to the gods that their fields may produce abundant wheat, wine, and figs, implying once more that fruit trees and vines were not all chopped down by 421 B.C. (1320–1325). Likewise, in the lost *Farmers* (frag. 109 Kock), a similar desire to return to the farm and work the soil is expressed.

All these passages, with their frequent references to produce and healthy vineyards and orchards, suggest that the agriculture of Attica was in good condition after the Archidamian invasions.[23] In this respect they are at odds with the other references to farmers complaining of lost crops, fruit trees, and vines. This apparent discrepancy, however, can be explained. The sight of Peloponnesian invaders out in the fields of Attica must have been a traumatic experience for most farmers inside the city (e.g., Thuc. 2.21.2–5). Naturally, frequent references by the poet to enemy ravaging would draw the wished-for, sharp response from any audience made up in some part by farmers, for they especially would be extremely sensitive to the slightest damage to farms and crops. Yet at the same time the actual, permanent destruction to the agriculture of Attica was minimal and mostly a thing of the past. This accounts for the almost unconscious assumption of Aristophanes that orchards, vineyards, and farms in the countryside of Attica stand pretty much intact. Consequently, loud complaints concerning devastated

23. See also *Ach.* 544–554; *Vesp.* 264–265, 450; *Pax* 590ff., 999–1002, 1249.

agriculture can often appear in close proximity (a few lines away) and strange juxtaposition to mention of healthy crops.[24] This is more evidence that neither Aristophanes nor his audience assumed that the Peloponnesians had extensively damaged the agriculture of Attica in the Archidamian War.

Other literary references to the Archidamian invasions are not especially helpful, because, for the most part, they are very general. Most are brief statements to the effect that "Attica was ravaged" during the war.[25] An interesting tradition that Athenian counterattacks on the Peloponnese did more damage than did Archidamos's invasions of Attica is probably mistaken, although it suggests that later commentators felt more damage could be accomplished by small marine parties of plunderers than by enormous hoplite armies of enemy crop ravagers.[26]

The Survival of Olive Trees and Vines

References to specific types of agriculture that remained intact during and after the Archidamian War are found in a variety of both contemporary and later sources and can also be additional proof that many orchards and vineyards were not destroyed by the Peloponnesian ravagers. Olive trees, for example, which should have been the prime target of any enemy whose aim was to destroy crops in Attica, for the most part survived the war.[27] There is no mention at all of their destruction in Aristophanes'

---

24. In the *Peace* (557–563), for example, the chorus sings of their return to the vines and figs they had planted in their youth, and a little later (628–629) Trygaios complains that the fig tree he planted and raised has been cut down.

25. E.g., Andoc. 3.8; Diod. 12.42 ff.; Paus. 3.7.10; Plut. *Per.* 33.3.

26. Westlake 1945, 81. Cf. Just. *Epit.* 3.7.5–6; Polyaen. *Strat.* 1.36.1.

27. Brunt (1965, 266), Ehrenberg (1951, 306 n. 6), and Hardy (1926, 351) seem to acknowledge this. Kagan (1974, 68) believes that olive trees were destroyed in the Archidamian War, citing Lys. 7.6. This probably cannot be used as sure evidence, since the destruction mentioned in this speech of the 390s more likely took place solely in the Dekeleian War.

comedies of this period. In fact, there are many references in the plays that reflect the olive's usual ubiquity (e.g., *Ach.* 35, 550, 1128; *Vesp.* 450; *Av.* 617; *Ran.* 988, 995). And even after the further depredations of the Dekeleian occupation, olive orchards were still standing—survivors of both wars (see below). Olives, along with grapes and figs, are included in the confiscation lists of the profaners of the mysteries and mutilators of the Herms (415/414 B.C.) and were to be sold unharvested right off the tree and vine.[28] These orchards (and perhaps vineyards, too) may well have survived the invasions of the prior decade.[29] In an Athenian decree of 422 (?) B.C. regulating the offering of firstfruits at Eleusis, reference is made to the collection of olive oil. (See updated commentary, page 236 [The Inscription from Eleusis].) This suggests that three years after the last Peloponnesian invasion olive trees in Attica were naturally

---

28. Pritchett 1953, 233; 1956, 190–191. The *Attic Stelai* yields much insight into the aftereffects of the Archidamian War. References to improved land, country houses, and produce are plentiful in these lists, and the abundance of such references suggests that much must have survived the invasions of ten years earlier. In this respect, the inventories seem to support the remarks of the Oxyrhynchus Historian concerning rural productivity and the fine state of affairs in Attica at about this time (12.4–5); improved landscapes, replete with terraces, ditches, fences, buildings, orchards, vineyards, and threshing floors and dotted with watchtowers, fortified farms, and border garrisons, are not the same as empty fields—as a general rule, the more developed the countryside, the more difficult it is to ruin it completely.

The somewhat low prices given for land on the *Stelai* (see Lewis 1966, 186) may reflect either the general unsettled conditions of the war year 414 B.C. (i.e., the threat of renewed hostilities in Attica) or the sale of the land by auction. They do not suggest that the well-stocked and furnished pieces of property on the lists are selling for reduced rates because of wartime damage from the prior invasions of 431–425 B.C.

29. Even if destroyed olive orchards had been immediately replanted after the last invasion of the Archidamian War (425 B.C.), they would just be at the point of reaching good production and would not yet have extensive crops, as suggested by the lists.

assumed to be alive and productive, and their fruit was available and harvested.[30]

From three of the Atthidographers—lost local historians of Attica— we learn that the sacred olive trees (*moriai*) of Attica were spared altogether by the Peloponnesians (Androtion *FGrH* 324F39; Philochorus *FGrH* 328F125; Istros *FGrH* 334F30).[31] (See updated commentary, page 236 [Sacred Olives and Atthidographers].) Besides this sure indication that a great number of olive trees were not even attacked during the Archidamian War, some scholars have speculated that the Peloponnesians' pious avoidance of the sacred olives (*moriai*) also extended to the ordinary domesticated variety (*elaiai*), and thus explains the surprising silence about their devastation as well.[32] There is, however, good

30. *IG* I2.76.59–61. For the problem of the date of the inscription, see Meiggs-Lewis, *GHI*, 220–223. The decree begins with requirements of grain and barley from Athenian farmers (lines 4–10), who apparently were doing well enough in this war year, and planting their cereal crops as usual. Allied cities were obliged (14–20), and other Greek poleis (30–36) "invited," also to offer firstfruits. Where the olive oil is to come from is not specifically stated, but it should be assumed that it (like grain and barley) would come first of all from Attic farmers (on the olive oil clause, see Guillon, *Bulletin de Correspondance Hellénique* 86 [1962]: 473; olives grew better and were more common in Attica than anywhere else: see *RE* 17.2 [1937] 2002, line 50, s.v. Olbaum [A. Pease]; Zimmern 1931, 53). Guillon (pp. 469–474), I think, misinterprets somewhat the spirit of the decree. The abundant mention of crops and agriculture at this time does not reflect serious Athenian concern that Attic farmers continue cultivation and overcome widespread wartime losses; rather, it illustrates Attica's well-being right after the last invasion. If farms had been destroyed, as we are usually led to believe, such a decree, requiring extensive harvest offerings that year, would have been ridiculous, if not cruel. Indeed, the crops mentioned in the inscription have led some scholars to date the decree before the war. There is no need to do so on those grounds, however, if we remember how little damage the Spartans actually inflicted in the first five invasions.

31. So not surprisingly in the *Clouds* (produced in 423 B.C.) the sacred olives (*moriai*) of the Academy are still standing (*Nub.* 1005).

32. Eg., Hardy 1926, 351–352.

reason to believe that the *moriai* were always thought of as distinct and separate from the ordinary *elaiai*.[33] And the point of the Atthidographers' tale is to reveal the traditional sanctity accorded these sacred olives—at a time when the enemy was attacking all other orchards at random. We never hear that *elaiai*, despite their prominence in myth, were ever accorded a sacrosanct status by warring armies. Besides, there is reason to believe that in the Archidamian War all the ordinary olive trees were the target of attack by ravagers. In his description of the Spartan invasions, Diodorus (12.45.1) uses the verb *dendrotomeô* (to cut a tree), which usually implies the ravaging of fruit trees. A reference in Thucydides may also refer to their cutting.[34]

We receive, therefore, the paradoxical impression that olive orchards in Attica were not spared but were attacked during these invasions and yet, at the same time, suffered little damage at all. The best explanation is the inherent difficulty in destroying olive trees—a task that we have seen requires a considerable amount of time and effort. Under the conditions of these yearly invasions, the enemy was simply unable to make the destruction of the common olive tree widespread—and avoided random (and apparently fenced and marked?) sacred olive trees altogether.[35]

Vines, also, may not have been seriously affected in the Archidamian War. If they were, vine props, which were usually favored for their cultivation,[36] should also have been destroyed (e.g., *Ach.* 985–986) and

33. Arist. *Ath. Pol.* 60.2; Lys. 7.7, 7.26; *RE* 16.1 (1933) 302, s.v. Moria (K. Latte).

34. The expression *ei ti ebeblastêkei*, "if anything had grown back out," found at Thuc. 3.26.3 can refer to olive trees, vines, or fig trees.

35. Some of the olive trees in Attica were probably planted on marginal, hilly ground where access would have been troublesome, compounding the difficulty of their destruction. Cf. French 1964, 21–22; Jardé 1925, 101–105.

36. The props (*charakes*) seemed to have been used extensively and prized: e.g., *Vesp.* 1200; Thuc. 3.70.4.

consequently have been scarce and high-priced both during and after the war. But in the *Peace* (1263), they were apparently selling for the cheap price of not more than one drachma per hundred. The price seems confirmed by the confiscation lists of a few years later. There, used props were only three and a half obols per hundred.[37]

Much of the evidence, then, for agricultural damage during the war (especially the evidence in the comedies of Aristophanes) is contradictory, alluding both to enemy ravaging activity and to crops and produce left untouched. But the combined testimony of Thucydides' later statements, the Oxyrhynchus Historian, and the many independent references elsewhere to healthy agriculture (olive trees and vines) suggests little long-term harm was done to the countryside during the Archidamian War. This conclusion seems logical if some practical considerations are kept in mind.

The Problems of Devastating Attica

The total length of the five invasions should not be forgotten. During the entire 11 years of the Archidamian War, the Peloponnesians were in Attica not more than 150 days, perhaps less than 5 months.[38] Like the rest of Greece, Attica is land characterized by rough terrain and isolated valleys;[39] it was scarcely possible, then, that in such a brief period most

37. Pritchett 1956, 305–306.

38. The second invasion was the longest—40 days; the fourth, the shortest—only 15 days. The other three lasted somewhere between 25 and 35 days.

39. Jardé (1925, 72) identifies four separate, great plains of Attica: the Thriasian Plain (95 km²), the Athenian Plain (130 km²), the Mesogeian Plain (75 km²), and the Plain of Marathon (15 km²). There was also much farming going on, as today, in small, upland valleys and on hillsides—the rocky, marginal, hard-to-reach *eschatiai*—which were even less accessible. See Langdon and Watrous 1977, 175; Lewis 1973, 210–212; Zimmern 1931, 53.

of the territory could even be reached, much less systematically devastated by enemy ravaging parties.[40] Also, we should remember the physical difficulty of devastation; cutting down olive trees and vines is a time-consuming process, entailing the chopping down of thousands of individual stock under conditions of war.

The time of year the Peloponnesians came is also important. They usually planned to enter Attica in mid- or late May while the ripe grain was still standing in the fields, not yet cut and stored inside the walls. Al-

40. Some rough calculations illustrate the problem of devastating all the agriculture of Attica in the Archidamian War. If the Peloponnesians numbered (say) 23,000 troops (to take a lower estimate [see Busolt 1904, 3:2: 860; but cf. Gomme 2: 13 and Jacoby 1940, vol. 3b, pt. 1: 150, for a higher number]) and were in Attica a total of 150 days, we obtain a figure of ca. 3,450,000 "work-days" spent inside the borders of Attica. The entire acreage under cultivation in the country may have been around 890 km² (Cooper 1977, 171; cf. Jardé 1925, 49–50, 78–79), or about 219,923 acres. This would require each soldier to ravage almost 1/15 of an acre a day to cover just the agricultural land of Attica one time. When engaged in destroying capital crops and not cereals, each infantryman would have to destroy around 118 vines (see White 1970, 246) or about 2 1/2 olive trees (see Jardé 1925, 186, for density; also McDonald and Rapp 1972, 54) a day to keep up the pace. These figures, of course, may be highly questionable, since wide fluctuations and inaccuracies can be assumed at each level of computation, but they do illustrate what an immense task the destruction of all the cropland of Attica one time would be—just barely possible for such a large force even under these theoretical conditions, no doubt impossible in reality. We should remember that not all the enemy could be assigned to crop devastation: a great many troops were needed for supply, command, and especially for protection against enemy cavalry attacks. That is, most hoplites had to be kept ready for the expected Athenian response and were not free to join the light-armed ravaging parties. Nor were all 150 days in Attica spent ravaging crops. Many were simply wasted (see Thuc. 2.18) in skirmishes with Athenian sorties or on the move. Many, then, of the 3,450,000 "workdays" in Attica do not represent actual time engaged in devastation. Nor was all the acreage of Attica even covered; many areas were skipped, and others were ravaged more than once. Terrain, as mentioned, would also pose a problem, since even the chief areas of cultivation are separated by high mountains.

though some of the grain crop might be burned, or the harvest interrupted and left in the field, as the Athenians in many instances could not gain access to any grainfields that were not destroyed, grape-, olive-, and fig picking would be unaffected. In fact, the Peloponnesians, mostly farmers themselves, had to return home to their own crops and could not in any case stay through the summer for lack of provisions (e.g., Thuc. 1.141.3, 2.10.1, 2.23.3, 3.1.3, 3.15.2, 3.26.4). The Athenians, then, were free to produce their wine and oil—the valuable cash crops—in the late summer and fall.[41]

Nor was the enemy able to invade Attica in consecutive years when the cumulative effect of their invasions could take their toll. In 429 B.C. the Peloponnesians bypassed Attica, probably out of fear of the plague (Thuc. 2.57.1, 2.71.1). Fear of earthquakes kept them away in 426 B.C. (3.89.1). They left Attica in 425 B.C. after a few days on hearing of the capture of Pylos (4.6.2) and did not return again because the Athenians held the Sphakterian prisoners captive (4.41.1)—apparently the entire strategy of attacking the rural productivity of Attica was not worth the lives of a few hundred captured hoplites. Not only were ravaged areas of Attica able to recover between invasions, but, more important, Athenians were left the hope that they might not be invaded in any one year or their lands might be passed over. Consequently, they kept busy and always planted their annual grain crops as usual.[42]

41. Hardy (1926, 351) is certainly right in saying that there "would be an opportunity to gather and enjoy the olive" in the autumn. But he is wrong to suggest that grapes and figs would be lost to the mere presence of the Peloponnesians. The enemy would be gone before the first of July or sooner (staying on the average of thirty days past mid- or late May), giving the Athenians ample time (July and August) to pick at least one crop of most varieties of figs; grapes in Attica would be harvested when the enemy was long gone (August and September). In fact, the grape, olive, and fig harvests would all be mostly unaffected.

42. The Athenians, it is clear, never ceased planting their grain during the Archidamian War (cf. Thuc. 2.22.2, 3.1.2, 7.27.4, and esp. 4.6.1, where the Attic

The actual policy of the Peloponnesians may help to explain why so many Attic farms survived the war. Their invasions were not designed so much to destroy completely the agriculture of Attica and thereby force the city into starvation as to do enough damage to incite the Athenians to rush out to battle (see, for example, Thuc. 1.82.3–6, 2.11.6–8, 2.18.5, 2.20.2, 2.21.2). Consequently, areas of Attica were temporarily held hostage, as it were (1.82.4), in hopes of drawing out Athenian peace feelers. Others were bypassed altogether or were ravaged unnecessarily severely (e.g., 2.20). The intention was to create tension among the owners within the walls (see, for instance, [Xen.] 2.14) in hopes of perhaps triggering some kind of reckless military response (e.g., Thuc. 2.21.3). Archidamos, therefore, delayed at the Isthmus (2.11–12) and lingered unnecessarily at Oinoe (2.18ff.), giving the Athenians the opportunity in the meantime either to yield or to attack before he began devastating the countryside. Pericles suspected that his own fields might be spared either out of friendship with Archidamos or, more likely, from a desire on the part of the Peloponnesians to embarrass and cast suspicion upon the Athenian leader.[43] Large fertile areas such as the entire tetrapolis, the land around Dekeleia, and the Academy were left completely untouched, apparently out of religious piety.[44] For a variety of

grain is described as still being green; cf., too, Diod. 12.58.4). Gomme (3: 441) wrongly thought that this was a reference to Boiotian grain, but see Pritchett 1971, 39 n. 43. Likewise, during the two prior Persian invasions of 480 and 479 B.C., the Athenians, nevertheless, planted their grain both years (Hdt. 8.109, 8. 142). Farmers are traditionally resourceful: given even a slight chance of success, they will always gamble to continue their livelihood.

43. Thuc. 2.13.1; Polyaen. *Strat.* 1.36.2; and cf. other instances that suggest that this was a common tactic of invading armies (e.g., Polyaen. *Strat.* 4.3.15; Garlan 1974, 25 n. 2).

44. Gomme (2: 162) did not accept the evidence of Diodorus (12.45.1), who says the tetrapolis was spared. Yet he failed to mention that Diodorus is corroborated by Istros *FGrH* 334F30, which may or may not have been his ultimate source. For Dekeleia, see Hdt. 9.73 and Adcock 1947, 2–7. On the Academy, see Plut. *Thes.* 32.3, which states that the Spartans spared the spot because of an

reasons the enemy did not, nor did it intend to, methodically ravage every acre of Attic farmland, as there were so many personal, political, and religious agendas that were in conflict with the idea of simply ruining the Athenian countryside. Indeed, F. Jacoby has suggested that Istros, the Atthidographer, may have compiled a special book just on places spared by the Spartans during the Archidamian War, "and his treatment must have been very detailed"[45]—such a work suggests not that there was severe damage to the Attica countryside, but that numerous areas were left untouched at a time when the *chôra* of Athens was purportedly under siege.

Finally, the residents of Attica were not idle. Evacuation must have saved much valuable stock, household furnishings, and even the woodwork from their homes (Thuc. 2.13.2, 2.14.1, 2.18.4). Farm implements and tools were also removed and kept safely within the walls (Ar. *Pax* 552, 1318). Once the Peloponnesians did enter Attica, frequent Athenian cavalry attacks kept the enemy on their guard and hampered ravaging parties. In this manner the rich farmland around the walls of Athens was patrolled, and the crops planted there protected (e.g., Thuc. 2.22.2, 3.1.2). Attic garrisons on the frontier, such as at Eleusis, Oinoe, and Panakton, served as bases for sudden, scattered attacks that also could cause distress to the enemy.[46]

Conclusion

The five Peloponnesian invasions of Attica during the Archidamian War did no widespread or lasting damage to the agriculture of Attica.

---

ancestral reverence for Akadamos (cf. Thuc. 2.71.4: an appeal of the Plataians to the Spartans on similar grounds, to save their land in 429 B.C.). The Academy, however, may have been skipped simply because of its famous sacred olive trees—trees which in general were not harmed in the Archidamian War.

45. Jacoby 1940, vol. 3b, pt. 1: 645.

46. Thuc. 2.13.6, 2.18.1, 2.19.2 (Eleusis), 5.3.3; Chandler 1926, 1–21; McCredie 1966, 88–91.

Thucydides' brief, contemporary descriptions of the devastations contain minor inconsistencies. They also appear to be contradicted by his later statements. Thucydides came to realize that, in comparison with the Dekeleian depredations, this earlier Archidamian ravaging was relatively ineffective. This view is supported by the anonymous Oxyrhynchus Historian, who flatly declared that Attica suffered little during the Archidamian War. The evidence for agricultural damage offered by the comedies of Aristophanes has never been properly examined. It is often forgotten that there are as many indications of healthy crops as destroyed ones. Aristophanes apparently uses vivid descriptions of devastation to highlight widespread dissatisfaction with the current war, especially the free movement of foreign troops in the Attic countryside. Yet it is always clear in his plays that farms and crops outside the walls are not destroyed, but ready for reoccupation. Other literary and epigraphic evidence suggests that olive trees, vines, and other crops were plentiful during and after the war.

The picture presented by our sources is understandable when we consider some practical limitations facing the Spartans. The invasions were too short to devastate or simply cover all the territory of Attica. Nor was that the prime intention of the enemy; we hear of many districts that were intentionally skipped, and the sacred olives were bypassed altogether. The invaders also did not come in consecutive years. There was no cumulative damage, nor was access to summer and autumn harvests even prevented; the Athenians could do necessary terracing, fencing, replanting, and other assorted farm tasks during the eleven months after the enemy left, and then still have very reasonable hopes that the Spartans might not return the next year. Forts and cavalry kept the enemy on their guard, while initial evacuation seems to have saved much of their property. The real damage—and it was severe—to Attica during these five invasions was not the loss of agriculture, but the physical and psychological problems caused by moving a great number of people off their lands into cramped and depressing conditions within the walls (Thuc. 2.17ff., 2.52.1; Diod. 12.45.2; Ar. *Eq.* 792–793), and the outbreak of the plague: for, as Thucydides admits, "nothing was more ruinous to the power of Athens" (3.87.2). The Athenians did suffer severely from Spartan invaders during the Archidamian War, but it was not as a result of damaged trees, vines, and cereal land.

THE DEKELEIAN WAR (413–404/403 B.C.)

The Damage to Attica

In early spring of 413 B.C., the Peloponnesians invaded Attica and began to fortify Dekeleia.[47] They had come equipped with iron and tools for the construction of the fortification (Thuc. 7.18.4), and large contingents of allies to help defend the garrison (7.27.3, 8.98.2; *Hell. Oxy.* 12.4; Xen. *Hell.* 2.3.3). From this base at Dekeleia—within sight of Athens—they planned to plunder the territory of Attica continuously, and cut off the Athenians completely from farming their crops.[48] The intent of these depredations was apparently different from their earlier, yearly invasions. These were not temporary incursions with large numbers of hoplites designed to incite the citizens to battle. The Peloponnesians were in Attica now year in and year out until the end of the war. It must be remembered that at the time Attica had been untouched for twelve years, since the very brief invasion of 425 B.C. The early devastations had been mild anyway and not destructive, and so recovery had been complete. Attica was at this time "the most lavishly furnished area in Greece" (*Hell. Oxy.* 12.5) and should have offered good opportunity

47. Thuc. 7.10.1. For the delay in fortifying Dekeleia, see Adcock 1947, 2–7; Brunt 1965, 268–270; Salmon 1946, 13–14.

48. Dekeleia was about 120 stades from Attica (Thuc. 7.19.2)—that is, about 18 kilometers by the shortest route. The Peloponnesians could view Athens from Dekeleia and vice versa, (see, for example, Thuc. 7.19.2; Xen. *Hell:* 1.1.35).

for plunder and destruction. (See updated commentary, page 237 [*Hellenica Oxyrhynchia* and Countryside of Attica].)

Thucydides vividly describes the effects of Dekeleia (7.27ff.), as part of his excursus on the general decline of Athens that began with the defection of Alcibiades and the catastrophic losses at Sicily. Regular enemy incursions from the base resulted in damage to property and loss of life, "which did as much as anything to ruin the city." Unlike the earlier Archidamian invasions, the Peloponnesians were now able to stop many citizens from farming while they overran the countryside, plundering and gathering supplies. "The sufferings of the Athenians," Thucydides says at this time, "were terrible." In addition to the loss of their land, more than 20,000 slaves deserted to the enemy.[49] (See updated commentary, page 238 [Flight of 20,000 Slaves].) All their sheep and cattle perished, and their horses suffered from constant sorties on the rough terrain. For the first time the Athenians were forced to import nearly all their foodstuffs, primarily from Euboia, and the cost was substantial.[50] Citizens were constantly on duty on the walls, or held ready in reserve for any expected attack. They did this day and night, summer and winter, "until they were quite worn out" (Thuc. 7.28.2, 8.69.1; and see Ar. *Lys.* 555; *Thesm.* 495; and Arist. *Ath. Pol.* 27.2). Prisoners, political outcasts, and opportunists made their way to Dekeleia and helped the garrison with their plundering (e.g., Andoc. 1.101; Dem. 24.128; Diod. 13.103.2; Lycurg. *Leoc.* 120; Lys. 18.9; Thuc. 8.98.1; Xen. *Hell.* 1.2.14, 1.3.22). Besides the physical damage, Dekeleia, as haven for dissidents and potential revolutionaries, caused particular psychological distress among the suspicious Athenian demos.

49. 7.27.5; cf. Xen. *Vect.* 4.25. There has always been some question as to where these 20,000 were employed: cf. Gomme 4: 405–406; Jameson 1978, 136–137.

50. Thuc. 7.28.1, 8.95.3; Arist. *Ath. Pol.* 33.7; and esp. Westlake 1948, 2ff.

As mentioned above, the anonymous Oxyrhynchus Historian (12.4) relates that after the fortification of Dekeleia, the Boiotians got slaves and other war spoils at a "small price" and stole all the furnishings, beginning with the wood and tiles, of the houses of Attica. The excavation of a large farmhouse between the Thriasian and Attic plains may confirm these Theban depredations. The excavators suggest that the so-called Dema House was constructed during the Peace of Nikias but was abandoned, and perhaps then destroyed, after 413 B.C. There were few surface finds (i.e., *pythoi*, loom weights, household items, roof tiles) around the site, which is possibly indicative of Theban plundering during the period.[51] Also, the speaker in Lysias's seventh oration at one point reminds his audience that among the other calamities caused by the war "the outlying districts (*ta porrô*) were ravaged (*temneto*) by the Lakedaimonians, while the nearer were plundered (*diêrpazeto*) by our friends" (7.6). The plundering by friends here is probably another reference to the comprehensive plundering done by the Boiotians—at the time of delivery of the oration in 397 B.C. the Boiotians were quasi-allies of Athens—during the past Dekeleian War.[52] Notice that the speaker assumes that the Peloponnesian ravaging was confined largely to the outlying districts (*ta porrô*, 7.6).

Isocrates recalled of Dekeleia that the Athenians were living in a state of siege during this time and, "in place of farming the lands of other states, for many years [413–404 B.C.] were denied the opportunity of even seeing their own fields" (8.92). There are also abundant other references containing only general, isolated mention of the calamity caused by the war and its aftermath.[53]

51. Jones, Sackett, and Graham 1962, 101.

52. For further Boiotian references, see Isoc. 14.31; Just. *Epit.* 5.10.12; Plut. *Lys.* 27; Xen. *Hell.* 3.5.5; *Mem.* 3.5.4; and Parke 1932, 42ff.

53. E.g., Aeschin. 2.147; Andoc. 1.101; Dem. 18.31; Diod. 13.72.2ff.; Isoc. 8.83ff., 14.31; Lys. 20.33, 31.18; Paus. 3.8.6; Pl. *Men.* 242C.

Finally, it has been argued that Aristophanes' later comedies, composed during and after this period, reflect widespread poverty throughout the countryside caused by the Dekeleian War. "The country districts were, of course, the worst affected by these operations. All contemporary texts refer to the distress of Athens in the immediate post-war period. Perhaps the most striking of these are Aristophanes' last two comedies, the *Ecclesiazusae* and the *Plutus*."[54] Numerous passages, it is true, do reflect poverty and depressed conditions. There is mention of a shortage of food (*Lys.* 1203–1204; *Plut.* 219). Hard work and a lack of material possessions are also evident (*Plut.* 262–263, 535ff.), and a fantasyland of socialistic reform frames both plays. Nevertheless, there is little reference in these comedies to actual Spartan ravaging (only at *Lys.* 1146).

It is difficult, then, to ascertain whether the passages in Aristophanes' later plays reflecting poverty are sure evidence of agricultural devastation. Extensive labor-losses from the war, loss of ships, forced taxes and contributions, the plague, decline in trade, loss of tribute and overseas territory, and property confiscations under the Thirty could just as well be responsible for these allusions to general impoverishment.

All these sources illustrate the great variety of ways in which the occupation of Dekeleia harmed Athens. The question must now be asked whether this anecdotal evidence implies total and absolute agricultural catastrophe in Attica, resulting in years of rural poverty and lost production, or rather severe but only temporary damage—mostly to movable property, with little actual permanent destruction of agriculture. This distinction, I think, has too rarely occurred to most scholars. A. French states, for example: "We must assume that the physical damage on the rural stock of Attica during the Peloponnesian War affected its farm income for at least half a century to come." G. Audring agrees: "Erst um die Mitte des 4. Jahrhunderts kann Attica den alten stand

54. Mossé 1973a, 13.

seiner landwirtschaftlichen Kulturen wieder erreicht haben." H. Michell offers an especially lurid analysis of the war damage: "There is reason to suppose that the soil of Attica never wholly regained its former fertility, and it has also been suggested that owing to neglect of the land and proper drainage, malaria, hitherto unknown in Greece, began to sap the vitality of the people."[55]

The Survival of Olive Trees and Vines

The olive trees of Attica, however, do not seem to have all been cut down by the Peloponnesians. Lysias's seventh oration, concerning the uprooting of a sacred olive stump, is usually alone cited as evidence of their destruction, since the speaker declares at one point: "Many plots at that time were thick with private and sacred olive trees, which now have for the most part been cut down, so that the land has now become bare" (7.7; and cf. 7.6). But besides the personal interest of the speaker in exaggerating the destruction caused by the war,[56] there are other reasons to believe that the speech does not really illustrate widespread devastation of olive trees. Later he remarks: "You know that in the plain there are many sacred olives (*pollas morias*) and burned stumps on my other plots" (24). And he adds: "You find me taking considerable care of the many olive trees (*tas men pollas elaias*) upon which I could more freely commit the offense" (26; cf., too, 7.25).

The speaker, then, naturally alludes to widespread destruction of olive trees in the war when he suggests that the stump in question was,

---

55. French 1964, 169; Audring 1974, 115; Michell 1957, 85. For views similar to these, see Glotz 1927, 253; Parke 1933, 230; C. D. Hamilton, *Sparta's Bitter Victories* (Ithaca, N.Y., 1978), 165. Most scholars apparently arrive at a fifty-year recovery on the mistaken assumption that all the olive trees in Attica were cut down and lost, and that replacement seedlings were then planted and did not reach full production for fifty or more years.

56. E.g., Brunt 1965, 266 n. 41: "Lysias 7.6ff. need not be veracious on their destruction."

of course, only one of the "many" losses from the Spartan attack. On the other hand, he asserts the existence of many perfectly healthy olive trees when he points out that he had greater opportunity to uproot olive trees elsewhere had he wished. Since the events of the speech took place around 397 B.C., the reference to both sacred and ordinary healthy olive trees implies that they survived the war intact.[57] (See updated commentary, page 238 [Lysias's Seventh Oration].)

The speaker in an oration that has come down under the name of Demosthenes (Dem. 43) also refers to olive trees that are alive and well in the fourth century B.C.—in this case an entire orchard, consisting of over 1,000 trees, the glory of the late Hagnias's estate (43.69–70). This orchard must have been bypassed by the enemy, too, for it was not destroyed until the heirs uprooted it years later.[58] (See updated commentary, page 240 [Demosthenes' Forty-Third Oration].) Olive trees are again alluded to in another Demosthenic speech (55). The exact date of this oration is unknown, though it is usually assumed to have been one of Demosthenes' earliest.[59] The speaker refers to a wall on the family property that had been constructed years earlier (55.26) by his father, about the time of his own birth (3). But even before the wall was built, there were olive trees on the property (14). Thus the orchard was planted sometime before the speaker's own birth and may well have survived the war.[60]

But what may be the best evidence that olive trees were not extensively destroyed during the Dekeleian War is found in Sophocles' con-

---

57. See Hardy 1926, 352 n. 3.
58. See Cooper 1977, 168 n. 30, which has further details on this passage.
59. Cf. A. Schaefer, *Demosthenes und seine Zeit* (Leipzig, 1858), 3 B; 256 n. 3.
60. The olive trees could antedate the speech by anywhere from thirty to fifty years or more—depending on both the age of the speaker and how many years before the building of the wall the olive trees were already there. If the speech was delivered in the 360s, there is a good chance that the olives were alive during and right after the Dekeleian occupation.

temporary *Oedipus Colonus*. In 405 B.C., eight years *after* the initial enemy occupation of Dekeleia, the chorus could still sing in the midst of the war:

> And there is something I have not heard to have grown
> in the land of Asia, or in the great Dorian island of
> Pelops, a tree not planted by men's hands, but self-created,
> a terror to the spears of enemies, that flourishes most
> greatly in this land, the leaf of the gray-green nurturer
> of children, the olive. This shall no young man nor any that
> dwells with old age destroy and bring to nothing; for it is
> looked upon by the ever-seeing eye of Zeus Morios and by
> gray-eyed Athena.[61]   (694ff.)

The chorus could hardly have sung praise of the olive tree's ubiquitousness, indestructibility, and immortality ("self-created," "a terror to the spears of enemies," "that flourishes most greatly in this land") if all the orchards had been cut down. The chorus's song is a hymn of proud defiance, not lamentation, and attests to the survival of the olive in Attica during the war years, a tree that "no young man nor any that dwells with old age shall destroy and bring to nothing." (See updated commentary, page 241 [Chorus of the *Oedipus at Colonus*].)

In Aristophanes' later plays there are no references either to lost olive-trees or to the destruction of other capital crops. Indeed, both

---

61. The translation is that of Hugh Lloyd-Jones in the Loeb edition of Sophocles (London, 1994), 2: 495. This passage (whose scholia are the source of the fragments of Atthidographers concerning the Archidamian ravaging) naturally has caused problems for scholars who assumed widespread devastation of olive trees in Attica during the Dekeleian War. Zimmern (1931, 46), for example, is at a loss and can comment only that "the farmers who heard him knew the hollowness of the words." Brunt's suggestion that "perhaps Sophocles had only the sacred olives in mind" is natural, given the reference to Zeus Morios (*Moriou Dios*, 705), but seems to be weakened somewhat by the additional reference to *elaiai* (*elaias*), not *moriai*, in line 701.

vines and green olive boughs are used for torches (*Lys.* 255, 308) and are mentioned in festivities (*Eccl.* 743). Olives and olive oil are likewise still consumed and apparently in good supply (e.g., *Eccl.* 308, 744; *Ran.* 988; *Thesm.* 420). And the famous passage in the *Ecclesiazusae* (817) concerning the farmer who sells his grapes to buy barley reveals that some vineyards were bypassed by the enemy or at least were very quickly replaced at the close of the war. In the *Plutus* (798), throwing figs to the audience is still described as a way of obtaining laughs (cf., too, Dem. 18.262).

It is surprising that even in Thucydides' very careful assessment of the damage done to Athens by the enemy at Dekeleia (7.27ff., quoted above), there is no reference at all to the destruction of agriculture, such as fruit trees and vines. In that summary of the effects of Dekeleia, the loss of slaves, stock, property, and men is described in vivid terms, as are the lack of access to fields, the importation of foodstuffs, and the Spartan plundering parties. But there is no direct mention here or in Alcibiades' earlier list of advantages to be had from the occupation of Dekeleia (6.91ff.) of the actual destruction of agriculture.[62] Possibly, Thucydides' allusion to the inability of Athenians to reach their fields suggests as much, but such destruction would affect only annual cereal crops, which could not be planted or harvested. Fruit trees and vines, on the other hand, would survive even without regular pruning and cultivation.

The only serious agricultural loss to the Athenians as a result of Dekeleia would be their annual harvests, if farmers were unable to reach their cereal crops. What little devastation of fruit trees and vines that did take place must have been overshadowed by, or been incidental to, the enemy's prime aims of keeping the Athenians cooped up inside the walls (e.g., Xen. *Hell.* 1.1.35), allowing subversives and troublemakers to come over to their side, robbing Attica of valuable rural slaves, and ac-

---

62. At 7.19.2 Thucydides says only that the fort was built to "damage" the countryside (*es to kakourgein*), which may or may not imply agricultural destruction. For the term *kakourgein*, see the appendix.

quiring booty and provisions from the countryside. The enemy ravagers, then, were always more interested in collecting food and supplies (Thuc. 7.27.4), gathering livestock or slaves (*Hell. Oxy.* 12.4; Thuc. 7.27.5), looting farmhouses (7.27.3; *Hell. Oxy.* 12.4), and keeping farmers away from their fields (Thuc. 7.27.5) than engaging in the less rewarding and more difficult task of systematically cutting down fruit trees and vines.[63] These constant references to enemy plundering, but not ravaging, seem understandable, since there was now endless opportunity to get booty, not as before, during the Archidamian War, when it was crucial to provoke some type of military response, and loot could not easily be carried all the way back to the Peloponnese anyway.[64] Indeed, Xenophon thought one reason that the Spartans and Boiotians had a falling out in the 390s B.C. was that they could not agree about the distribution of the booty collected from Dekeleia (*Hell.* 3.5.5).

Farmland Untouched by Enemy Ravagers

As in the Archidamian War, areas near the city walls consisting of some of the richest land in Attica, were surely patrolled and protected by Athenian defensive forces. Athenian cavalry were constantly active in the countryside. They finally wore themselves out by daily attacks, even against Dekeleia itself.[65] The Peloponnesians had to be constantly on their guard and for the duration of the Dekeleian War were never able to mount a successful attack in the Athenian Plain.[66] In 411 B.C., for

63. See chapter 3 for similar activity of troops garrisoned at an *epiteichismos*.

64. On the difference in the enemy strategy and activity during the two wars, see Garlan 1974, 36–40; Hardy 1926, 348–349.

65. Thuc. 7.27.5. Cf. Lys. 20.28; Xen. *Hipp.* 7.4. The infamous Thracian mercenaries who later attacked Mykalessos were originally brought to Attica in hopes of using them against Dekeleia (Thuc. 7.27.2).

66. Thucydides says only that right *before* the Peloponnesians began to fortify Dekeleia, when they were in Attica in full force, they ravaged the plain (7.19.1).

example, Agis hoped that he could take advantage of the instability inside the walls and march on Athens. He gathered large reinforcements from the Peloponnese to supplement his Dekeleian garrison and set out against the city. His troops were met by a strong Athenian response in the form of cavalry, archers, and heavy and light infantry. After a brief skirmish, the Peloponnesians hastily retreated (Thuc. 8.71ff.). A similar attack the next year (Xen. *Hell* 1.1.33), and a later expedition (Diod. 13.72.2ff.), had little success, and the enemy was forced each time to return to Dekeleia.

Besides sorties from the city, Athenian infantry on patrols and stationed in garrisons were active even in the more remote countryside. For example, an enemy plundering party on its way home from Dekeleia was waylaid by troops from Oinoe (Thuc. 8.98.2). Indeed, well after the occupation of Attica by the Spartans, there must have been open and frequent communications between Athens and the countryside. The forts at Oinoe and Oropos (8.60.1) both held out for some time. Other more extensive, coastal garrisons at Rhamnous[67] and to the south at Sounion, Thorikos, and Anaphlystos[68] were probably fortified *after* the enemy occupation of Dekeleia and were furnished with troops continuously until the end of the war. Eleusis, of course, had been walled earlier and was well protected at this time.[69]

Not only did these garrisons deny the Spartans access to many parts of Attica, but some demes, relying either on protection from Athens and the rural garrisons or on their isolation and distance from Dekeleia, may never have been evacuated in the first place. Continual habitation during the war probably explains why in Aristophanes' *Lysistrata* (411 B.C.)

---

67. See Pouilloux 1954, 43–66. In the Chremonidean War (mid-third century B.C.) the citizens of Rhamnous also did not evacuate their land and flee to Athens. Instead they continued to farm their land and made arrangements to protect their harvests (cf. *SEG* 24 [1969] 154.8–11).

68. For the fort at Anaphlystos, see van Rooy 1969, 171–180.

69. See again chapter 3.

women are mentioned as still living on Salamis, at Acharnai,[70] and down the Paralos at Anagyrous (*Lys.* 55ff.). Similarly, the chorus of Eupolis's lost *Demoi* (411 B.C.) complains that those who have left the countryside and live among the long walls breakfast better than themselves. These rustics are apparently still living out in the demes.[71] The description of the Boiotian plundering of the Attic countryside suggests as much (*Hell. Oxy.* 12.5). Indeed, many country estates must still have been occupied and were not evacuated if the Boiotians were able to take slaves and woodwork from the houses—woodwork, it should be remembered, had been removed during the Archidamian evacuations (Thuc. 2.14.2) and was presumably replaced by citizens who were not overly alarmed by Dekeleia. Eleusis, too, was still occupied throughout the Dekeleian War, and its rites held yearly.[72]

Archaeological evidence suggests that Thorikos also must have been inhabited at this time, since the deme and its industrial complex were not abandoned until after Aigospotami (ca. 405 B.C.).[73] Even the mines nearby at Laureion, whatever their losses in slave labor, probably did not shut down.[74] The small enemy garrison at Dekeleia was well over

70. This reference to people living at Acharnai in the middle of the Dekeleian War seems incredible (the Spartan headquarters at Dekeleia was only a little more than ten kilometers distant). Yet it may be corroborated by the mention in Lysias's seventh oration of a farm of Peisander there that was not abandoned but worked the entire time.

71. Edmonds, *FAC*, 1.1.110a.11–14.

72. Plut. *Alc.* 34.3. Processions from Athens were forced to go by sea, since participants, who were especially slow-moving, unarmed, and accustomed to conducting festivities on the way, were vulnerable to even a small enemy force.

73. Cf. H. Mussche, *Thorikos II* (Brussels, 1964), 62; and *Thorikos VIII* (Brussels, 1970), 108.

74. See S. Lauffer, *Die Bergwerksklaven von Laureion* (Mainz, 1955–1956), 214ff. Many scholars (e.g., French 1964, 169; R. Hopper, *Annual of the British School at Athens* 48 [1953]: 248 n. 346, 249) traditionally believed that the mines were closed.

fifty kilometers away and could hardly afford to send down regular pa-trols. Other demes that were also near or in garrisons, such as Sounion and Rhamnous, were probably not evacuated either.[75] Indeed, when the Spartan envoys arrived in 410 B.C., they even remarked at one point: "We farm the entire Peloponnese, you only a small part of Attica" (Diod. 13.52.4). This observation suggests that at least some part of the country was admitted even by its occupiers to be still under cultivation during the war.[76]

There are also more specific examples of private individuals who ap-parently farmed their land in Attica continuously, throughout the Dekeleian occupation. In Lysias's seventh oration, the plot of ground in question originally belonged to Peisander (7.4.ff.). After it was confis-cated from him in 411 B.C., it was idle only three years (411–409 B.C.). Then Apollodorus of Megara received it and "cultivated it for some time, until, shortly before the Thirty, Antikles bought it from him."

75. Unfortunately in many cases there is little archaeological evidence that can shed light on evacuation during the Dekeleian War. Excavated deme sites and isolated farmhouses are few, and temporary periods of abandonment are difficult to determine in any case. The destruction of the Dema House is not representative: it is one of the very few adequately excavated farmhouses we have, and was located in one of the most vulnerable areas of Attica. I am not aware, though, of evidence for any damage in the Dekeleian War to such late-fifth-century houses as the Princess Tower (Young 1956b, 122–124), the farms at Draphi, or the Priest's House at Zoster (*Archaiologikê Ephêmeris* [1938]: 1–31). We may well assume that near even the more remote, border forts some farming always continued. In the fourth century B.C. the Athenian garrison at Panakton apparently relied on food from nearby Drymos (see Vanderpool 1978, 232–233). Cf. also the similar situation on the American frontier in the 1820s. Most forts then were expected to be supplied from their own gardens and farms. Fort Atkinson at Council Bluffs produced 26,400 bushels of wheat for the gar-rison in 1821. See F. P. Prucha, *The Sword of the Republic* (London, 1969), 180–181.

76. Diodorus's *brachu meros*, "a small part," seems to echo Thuc. 1.142.4, where, on the eve of the Peloponnesian War, Pericles stated that (only) part of Attica might suffer harm (*tês men gês blaptoien an ti meros*).

The farm, it is clear, went right on being farmed during the Dekeleian War (7.4). Since the property was most likely near Acharnai—not more than ten miles from Dekeleia itself—we have the impression that considerable farming went on almost in sight of the enemy garrison. Similarly, later in the same speech, we are told that owners of farms during the war and afterward were not charged with damage to their sacred olive trees, although they had farmed the land *throughout the entire period* (*tous dia pantos tou chronou geôrgountas*, 7.8).[77]

Even stock animals may not all have been lost (as suggested at Thuc. 7.27.5); rather many herds were kept safe in more remote pastures. On an Athenian sacrificial calendar of 403/402 B.C., right after the war, they are to be sold for the cheap price of two oxen for only fifty drachmas.[78]

77. We have very little information about either Apollodoros or Antikles; the speaker of this oration is unknown (Davies 1971, 594). But since Peisander, the original owner of the property, was from Acharnai (see *Prosop Att.* 2: 189–190, no. #11770]; A. G. Woodhead, "Peisander," *American Journal of Archaeology* 75 [1954]: 1132–1133), the confiscated farm, we may infer, may well have been part of the family estate there.

78. Pritchett 1956, 256. Granted that the cows mentioned in this sacred calendar were young (see *Greek, Roman and Byzantine Studies* 14 [1973]: 325–332), the low price, nevertheless, does not appear to reflect shortages of stock and the accompanying higher demand we would expect after the war. Earlier in 410/409 B.C., nearly four years after the fortification of Dekeleia, a cow was still sold for only fifty-one drachmas (see Pritchett 1956, 255–256). See also W. K. Pritchett, *Expenditures of the Treasurers of Athena for 410/409: The Choiseul Marble*, University of California Publications, Classical Studies 5 (Berkeley, 1970). Indeed, the price of beef does not seem to have been especially high after the war; it rose only years later, during the famine of 330–326 B.C., to 400 drachmas. Nor were sheep expensive in 403/402 B.C., bringing only twelve to seventeen drachmas each—about the normal price (Pritchett 1956, 259). The laws restricting sacrifice of stock during shortages, quoted by Philochorus (*FGrH* 328F169) and Androtion (*FGrH* 324F55), have no connection with the Peloponnesian War. If we can believe Andocides frag.3.1 (Loeb), some stock seems to have been brought into the city at this time.

And while such figures cannot be pressed too far, there seems no indication that Attica was bereft of livestock, and meat thus scarce and high-priced.

Consequently, the Athenians were careful to limit enemy incursions in Attica, especially in the Athenian Plain. Random plundering or devastation there did not occur often. This vigilance here and elsewhere by Athenian sorties from the city and rural garrisons, together with the small size of the enemy forces stationed at Dekeleia and the inherent ruggedness of Attica,[79] explains why some people could continue to live and farm in the countryside during these years of war.

Farming in Postwar Attica

Other, and perhaps even more revealing, evidence of the agricultural damage done to Attica during the Dekeleian depredations can be found by examining Athens's economic condition right after the war. If all the farms of Attica were ravaged, vines and trees cut down, and farmhouses destroyed, an agricultural crisis of enormous proportions must have taken place, and the scholarly estimates of a fifty-year rebuilding period in the fourth century B.C. would be believable. In reality, however, no

79. We have no exact figure on the size of the permanent force stationed there, but it must not have been very large, staffed as it was by shifts of allied contingents (Thuc. 7.27.3, 8.98.2). Only during the actual construction of the fort do large numbers of enemy soldiers seem to have been present (7.19.2, 7.27.3). This garrison at Dekeleia was never capable of mounting a serious attack on Athens without heavy reinforcements from the Peloponnese (8.71.1; Diod. 13.72.2). Agis's unsuccessful attack of 410 B.C.—apparently without outside help—was consequently termed a *pronomê* (Xen. *Hell.* 1.1.33), a mere "raid." Alcibiades' armed escort of the Eleusinian procession then understandably provoked no armed response from Dekeleia (Plut. *Alc.* 34.3). During the Archidamian War, when the enemy was there in greater number and eager for pitched battle, this would not have been possible.

such crisis occurred, as farming resumed right after, or perhaps even before, hostilities ceased.

As early as 403 B.C., one year after the war, grain was planted in Attica, for it is mentioned as being ravaged during the civil war (Isoc. 16.13). In Xenophon's *Memorabilia*, one Eutheros returns to Attica recently impoverished, since he had lost all his foreign property in the war, and his father had left him nothing in Attica. Socrates advises him to seek out some local established farmer and find employment as a farm assistant (Xen. *Mem.* 2.8.3). The passage can hardly be considered evidence that displaced local farmers were forced to work for wealthy, large landowners, since Eutheros never owned land in Attica to begin with. Instead, it simply illustrates that farmers and farming after the war in Attica were functioning as before—and offering opportunities for those without land.

The speaker in Lysias's seventh oration, after acquiring the property in question in 404/403 B.C.—land that had been previously farmed during the Dekeleian War—immediately let it out to one Kallistratos (404–403 B.C.), and then in succession to Demetrios (402 B.C.), Alkias (400 B.C.), and Proteas (400–398 B.C.), before farming it himself (7.9–10). There seems to have been an abundant supply of small farmers (Alkias, for example, was a freedman) eager to farm after the war (cf., too, Lys. 17.5).

In Isaeus's fifth oration, his earliest (ca. 389 B.C.), the speaker complains that the only property he has received from the estate of his uncle Dikaigenes (II), who died in 411 B.C., are "two buildings outside the walls and sixty *plethra* of land in the Plain" (5.22). Later (5.43–44), the villain Dikaigenes (III) is berated for his selfishness and lack of public generosity, although he owned "many farms and estates" inherited from the family's honorable ancestors, who had distinguished themselves in the Peloponnesian War. These rural buildings were haggled over in the war's aftermath and were referred to as items of wealth in 389 B.C. They were probably not abandoned and destroyed in the years 413–404 B.C.

But the best evidence that Athenians were farming right after the war, and that their farms were as intact and productive as usual, is found in Xenophon's description of the actions of the Thirty. After Theramenes died (404 B.C.), the Thirty immediately evicted many rural Athenians from their farms so that they themselves and their friends might seize these estates (Xen. *Hell.* 2.4.1). Later (404 B.C.), the Thirty sent out troops against those in Phyle to prevent them from gaining supplies from the farms in the surrounding districts (Xen. *Hell.* 2.4.4). They also captured and executed farmers who were on their way from the Piraeus to their own farms in Aixone to carry back provisions (Xen. *Hell.* 2.4. 26). From these passages it is clear that the moment the war ended (404 B.C.), Athenians all over Attica were farming, farms were assumed to be stocked and supplied with harvests,[80] and rural estates were still desirable and apparently prized—a scenario entirely at odds with the old assumption that farms were ruined and farmers displaced for decades.

In Demosthenes' fifty-seventh oration (ca. 345 B.C.) the speaker Euxitheos, in the course of appealing his recent disfranchisement, explains how his mother years ago had been forced to serve as a wet nurse in the postwar troubles at Athens.[81] He points out in his defense, however, that this was a frequent occurrence in those days: many women were reduced to becoming nurses, loom workers, and grape pickers (57.45). Farmers, then, seem not only to have been operating right after the war, but also to have been offering work to the urban poor. Vines that were purportedly ruined during the Dekeleian War were in production and harvested by those who went to the countryside to find work, rather than vice versa.

80. The provisions on hand on these farms in the winter of 404 B.C. (Xen. *Hell.* 2.4.3) suggest that the Attic grain crop, for example, was planted and harvested (mid- to late May) well before the war ended (late summer, 404 B.C. [Xen. *Hell.* 2.3.9]).

81. Around the year 390 B.C. Cf. Davies 1971, 94, for the date.

In autumn 403 B.C., again right after the war, one Phormosios proposed that the rights of citizenship should be taken away from all those
who did not hold land. Only 5,000 (out of more than 20,000?), our
source tells us, would have lost their citizenship if the decree had passed
(D.H. on Lys. 34). Clearly, most small landholders maintained their
property in the fourth century B.C. and were as agrarian as ever in their
outlook.[82] The all too prevalent view that Attic farmers impoverished by
the wartime devastations sold out to wealthy speculators and moved to
the city is mistaken and is based on only a few pieces of evidence, which
have been either misrepresented or misunderstood.[83]

The case of Xenophon's Isomachos and his father is a good example
(*Oec.* 20.22–26). Now it is normally held that they bought up parcels in
the fourth century B.C. from poor farmers who were unable to maintain
their farms because of wartime damage.[84] This scenario is probably not
valid for two reasons. In the first place, Isomachos himself seems to have
died by 404 B.C., and his father then must have been dead years earlier,
well before the war had ended (or had even begun?).[85] Also, it is never
stated that the farms in question were destroyed by enemy ravaging or
that their owners were impoverished by the war. The land in question is

82. See, for example, Andreyev 1974, 18–19, 22; Cooper 1977, 168; Ehrenberg 1951, 86; Jameson 1978, 125.

83. This view has been traditionally popular (e.g., Ehrenberg 1951, 93; Fine
1951, 198ff.; Glotz 1927, 254–255; Heitland 1921, 36–37, 47–48; Michell
1957, 86; Parke 1933, 230) and has only recently been rightly questioned (e.g.,
Andreyev 1974, 18, 28; Finley 1952, 57, 87; Isager and Hansen 1975, 52–55;
also cf. esp. Pecírka 1976, 14–15, 20: "It would thus appear that from the very
outset the theory of the drift of small peasants from the land, and the concen-
tration of landed property, had no basis in fact").

84. E.g., Michell 1957, 36, 86; Mossé 1973b, 181 n. 3.

85. Cf. Davies 1971, 267–268, for the dates. The fact that Isomachos and his
father were well-known landholders in the fifth century suggests that they could
not be believably used, in an anachronistic way, to illustrate conditions in the
fourth century B.C. The entire Socratic dialogue more likely is intended to take
place in the late 400s, during Xenophon's youth.

instead referred to as uncultivated and unplanted, as a result of the neglect or incapacity of the owner. Xenophon is more likely making the dramatic context the fifth century B.C., when Isomachos and his father, clever farmers that they were, found run-down property, invested a little work in improvements, and sold the parcel at a profit.[86] The point of the reactionary dialogue is to encourage the young, contemporary generation in the fourth century to emulate the agrarian purity, energy, and imagination of their ancestors, not to suggest how devastated cropland can be restored. (See updated commentary, page 242 [Xenophon's Isomachos].) Other examples often cited to illustrate land displacement and speculation after the war similarly will not stand examination.[87]

Stone *horoi*—markers erected to indicate either boundaries or rural indebtedness—which appear so frequently in the fourth century B.C., we know now do not illustrate widespread rural poverty on the part of small farmers who were forced to give up their farms as security for cash. Instead, they more probably mark short-term, high-interest loans taken out by more wealthy, established landholders for personal obligations that had nothing to do with land restoration.[88] (See updated commentary, page 243 [*Horoi*].)

It is not likely, then, that the urban population of Athens increased as a result of rural migration.[89] The citizens who did enter the city during the war must have left their temporary shacks on the conclusion of peace and returned to work their farms again. In the northeast corner of the Athenian Agora, for example, excavation has revealed small,

---

86. Individual initiative in improving farmland in antiquity should not be forgotten; see Is. 9.28; Hdt. 5.29.

87. See, for example, Andreyev 1974, 19, and Cooper 1977, 167–168, which reexamine passages of apparent land displacement.

88. See Andreyev 1974, 20–22; Finley 1952, 86–87.

89. This is often assumed on little evidence. See, instead, Andreyev 1974, 19; Cooper 1977, 168; Ehrenberg 1951, 85ff.

temporary structures of irregular shape that were built during the Peloponnesian War to house migrants. These refugee shelters, however, were demolished after the war. At the close of the fifth century B.C. the whole area was occupied by law courts;[90] the wartime residents had apparently already returned to the countryside. By at least 355 B.C. Xenophon could urge the state to give approved applicants building sites in Athens, "since there are many vacant sites for houses within the walls" (*Vect.* 2.6; cf. 3.13). At roughly the same time, there were also deserted house lots around the Pnyx (Aeschin. 1.81–83; and cf. the scholiast's note on the passage), although earlier, at the close of the Dekeleian War, the very same area had been crowded with refugees from overseas (Ar. *Eccl.* 243).[91]

Conclusion

Reexamination of the evidence has now led some scholars to believe that no real agricultural crisis occurred in Attica after the war. This is understandable if we also imagine that the farmland of Attica was not all destroyed by the Spartans but was in part productively worked by owners who returned quickly from the city, or who had remained in the

90. Cf. H. Thompson and R. E. Wycherly, *The Athenian Agora*, vol. 14 (Princeton, 1972), 56–57. Near the end of the war Lysander was obliged to send Athenian citizens overseas back to Athens to help increase the population there and thus induce famine (Xen. *Hell.* 2.2.2; Ar. *Eccl.* 243–244; Plut. *Lys.* 13.3). The city until then apparently was not unbearably crowded with rural refugees and on the verge of starvation.

91. We should assume that in most agrarian societies, the threat of foreign invasion rarely caused permanent displacement from the land. Gutman, writing of conditions in seventeenth-century Holland, remarks:

"Those who owned land, however, must surely have felt an investment in place, possessions, neighbors and property. That investment gave them good reason to stay in communities in times of difficulty, and to make every effort to rebuild after the danger ended" (1980, 204–205).

countryside the entire time—some not far from Dekeleia itself. Any proposition of a general economic crisis in the fourth century B.C. will have to dispense with the underlying idea that the agriculture of Attica was ruined in the years 413–404 B.C. These devastations were like most others in Greek history and failed to ruin the agrarian infrastructure of a city-state. The loss of overseas territory and tribute, deaths caused by the plague and battle, the mass flight of slaves, the activities of the Thirty, and the general exhaustion and expense of conducting war for nearly three decades caused the real harm to Athens—damage that was considerable despite the survival of most orchards and vineyards.

It should now be clear that the severity of agricultural damage resulting from even the Dekeleian War is usually exaggerated. Thucydides' account at 7.27 in itself cannot be used as evidence for extensive crop destruction, which is *never* mentioned in his detailed review of the losses. While farms must have suffered much more than they did during the earlier Archidamian attacks, because of the constant presence of enemy troops, the countryside of Attica was hardly ruined. In some years grainfields may well have been torched, but fruit trees and vines survived in large numbers. The real damage—and again it was probably considerable—done by the enemy in these years was the tremendous loss of property. Slaves, stock, and furnishings were favorite targets for plunderers as Dekeleia became more a clearinghouse for captured booty than a base for systematic agricultural destruction. All this, of course, affected farming. Slaves and animals were important for cultivation. But such losses were not the same as any comparable loss of fruit trees, vines, and other capital crops. Once again, like the Archidamian War, the Dekelian War must have taken a physical and psychological toll on the city: as many were denied continuous access to their land and were forced to live in overcrowded urban conditions, others—political outcasts, slaves, and prisoners—went over to Dekeleia and engaged in plunder. References, then, to the harm caused by Dekeleia naturally have to do with the inability to farm one's land freely, loss of property or inheritance, and unhappiness about the presence of enemy plunderers in Attica. If there is rarely any mention of actual destruction of crops, it is simply because it was not widespread. Scholars should dispense with the entire notion that the ruin of the Athenian countryside was the legacy of the Peloponnesian War. (See updated commentary, page 244 [Economy in Postwar Athens and Assessment of Agriculture].)

Conclusion

To be effective, agricultural devastation in classical Greece, as in any preindustrial society, required time and extensive effort, and therefore was not always accomplished. The light-armed ravaging parties whose duties were to overrun small Greek farms and destroy crops were vulnerable to counterattack. They needed constant hoplite or cavalry protection. During much of the year fruit trees, vines, and even grainfields were difficult to destroy. Even when chopped or cut down, vines and olive trees grew again quickly. Border forts and garrisons in the mountains, especially in the fourth century B.C., sometimes delayed and even halted the enemy before they could even reach the food-producing plains in the interior. Valuables, such as livestock, slaves, household furnishings and fixtures, and stored crops and food, were usually safely evacuated from farms well in advance. Enemy ravagers often found only fruit trees, vines, and the abandoned shell of a farm building left behind.

These practical considerations cast doubt on the usual assumption that Greek city-states suffered near ruin when an enemy is described in our sources as "ravaging their land." Not surprisingly, there are sometimes general indications in our sources that cropland was only haphazardly devastated by the enemy. Often it is even admitted in a summary of losses that "only a part," "a third," or "not much" of the countryside was actually covered (see, for example, Thuc. 1.142.4, 5.55.4, 6.7.1; Xen. *Hell.* 7.2.4). We also hear of cities that were apparently unaffected by enemy ravaging. In the spring of 431 B.C., for instance, the Boiotians, on the eve of Archidamos's first invasion of Attica, attacked the Plataians and ravaged their territory (Thuc. 2.12.5; cf. 3.65.2). Yet, just two years later, in 429 B.C., Archidamos himself once again overran the identical Plataian countryside and ordered the citizens to hand over their farms and property to his army of occupation: "Show us the boundaries of your land, the number of your fruit trees, and everything else about your holdings that can be counted in numbers" (Thuc. 2.72.3). In 429 B.C., then, the Plataian farms seem to be intact, undamaged—fruit trees were, after all, still visible and could be counted. If fruit trees were still numerous, the Boiotians could not have done a very thorough job in 431 B.C. And, we should remember, the territory surrounding Plataia was relatively small, and the combatants in the Theban army numerous, and also well acquainted with the nearby territory.

In 391 B.C. Agesilaos led his army into Argos and "devastated all their territory" (Xen. *Hell.* 4.4.19). But three years later, Xenophon could remark of a second, identical invasion of Argos by the Spartan general Agesipolis: "Since Agesilaos had recently brought his army into Argos, Agesipolis, after learning from the soldiers just how far Agesilaos had led his troops toward the wall, and how far he had ravaged the land, attempted like some athlete in the pentathlon to outdistance him at every point" (*Hell.* 4.7.5). The remark suggests that three years later there were no visible traces of Agesilaos's recent devastation of Argos. "All their territory," then, was probably not ravaged by Agesilaos, or at least not severely damaged: there were no stumps of vines or fruit trees, nor did Agesipolis see any gutted farmhouses.[1]

---

1. For other instances where land and crops were skipped, or not destroyed by prior ravaging campaigns, see Thuc. 3.26.53; Xen. *Hell.* 4.5.10, 5.3.3.

It is thus understandable that in formal land-lease agreements that envision the practical realities of farming the parties to the contract often agreed to split half and half whatever crops were left after an enemy had ravaged the countryside—these terms suggest, among other things, that farmers usually did not expect their losses to be total (e.g., *SEG* 21[1966] 644.13–14; *SEG* 24 [1969] 151.18; *SIG*³ 966.12–14). In literature and in inscriptions, the assumption is always that devastation was rarely complete, that land was skipped and crops customarily survived attack.

But the clearest and most important examples of the failure of ravaging to destroy agriculture are precisely those that we usually cite as proof of the effectiveness of devastation: the Spartan-led invasions of Attica during the Peloponnesian War. Reexamination of the literary, epigraphic, and archaeological evidence concerning the state of affairs in Attica during the last quarter of the fifth century B.C. and the early fourth century B.C. shows that there was neither permanent damage to crops nor subsequent agricultural depression. After years of on-again, off-again invasions the largest army gathered in the history of the Greek city-states in the half-century since the muster before the battle of Plataia (479 B.C.) made little impression on the countryside of the Athenians.

The type of agriculture practiced throughout ancient Greece also explains why effective devastation was so difficult to achieve. Farming was labor-intensive. A family of four or five, perhaps with the addition of slave labor, did most of the work themselves on their small, ten-acre holdings. Increased productivity and efficiency on a farm were largely the result of an intensification of labor: that is, more manual work put into drainage, irrigation, terracing, fertilization, and repeated hoeing and tilling.² There was no large investment in tangible capital goods such as machinery. Thus there was little out on the farm, besides the

2. See, for example, Jameson 1978, 129–141.

crops themselves, that was vulnerable to destruction. True, mud brick, clay, rubble, bronze, and cut stone were used in the building of houses, fencing, utensils, ovens, vats, and storage facilities; but they were cheap and plentiful throughout the Greek countryside. To replace such capital losses (and we should remember that these items were of simple and durable construction), all that was needed was labor—labor that was relatively plentiful, and that was usually evacuated and kept safe from attack. More expensive and scarce iron and wood, the components of most farm tools, were easily carried away during evacuation and not usually lost.[3]

Even the actual damage that was done to fruit trees, vines, and grain-fields could be partially offset by additional labor allotted for quick repair and reconstruction, such as special manuring and irrigation of damaged plants, grafting, prompt replanting and resowing, application of mud sealing to chopped and broken limbs, pruning back of hacked vines or trees, and additional propping. Because farmers depended on labor, rather than technology, to achieve production, Greek agriculture was inherently protected from catastrophic ruin. There was none of the investment found on a modern, mechanized, labor-scarce farm. There, the sudden destruction of fuel tanks, pipelines, pumps, tractors, and harvest machinery would impose staggering replacement costs and bring production to an immediate halt—even if the crops themselves were untouched. One ravager on a modern 200-acre farm could do more damage than 200 ravagers on an ancient 10-acre farm, should he torch tractors, fuel tanks, sheds, and pumps.

Many of our sources, however, make it clear that the Greeks themselves, at least, believed that agricultural devastation was effective. But we should remember that to the small Greek farmer the disruption caused by the evacuation of his belongings, the abandonment of his

---

3. The same was true of rural slaves, stock, and household furnishings; see chapter 4.

farm, and the loss of even a part of his grain crop or a few vines was considered serious. If the complaints of Attic farmers in the plays of Aristophanes were to be believed, one would be forced to conclude that Attica was nearly ruined during the war. Farmers, much less comic characterizations of farmers, are universally a worrisome lot, distrustful of the weather, the soil—and each other.[4] Bountiful harvests produce fears of a surplus and worries about the strain on soil and plants; low yields create concerns about bankruptcy and poverty. The threat of enemy invasions would cause panic. This constant anxiety pervades a preindustrial agricultural society, which is always just one harvest away from hunger, and is bound to be reflected in its literary and historical writing. Most Greek writers, it should be remembered, were either landholders themselves or at least not more than one generation removed from the farm. Similarly, in the conservative farming mind, the battle of Marathon, where Greek agrarian hoplites suffered but 192 dead, was enshrined as a hard-fought, brutal battle that had nearly overwhelmed the infantry of the Athenians.

The fact of agrarians' paranoia and natural resiliency does not deny, however, that there were real dangers to farmland in wartime. Landlocked, isolated small states, which were invaded in June, when their

---

4. To take a modern example: the recent grain embargo of the Soviet Union brought immediate cries of ruin and depression from American farmers. When it was quickly announced that the government and new foreign buyers would more than make up the loss, growers, nevertheless, continued to express outrage. On the evidence of their complaints (e.g., farm bureau newsletters, political reports from farm state representatives), future historians might conclude that American agriculture suffered a depression in 1980. In fact, the real depression that followed a few years later in the mid- and late 1980s was not the result of boycotts or natural disaster but arose from overproduction and a general collapse of world grain prices, coupled with a radical shift from an inflationary to a deflationary economy in the United States, leaving farmers with low commodity prices, plunging land values, and large outstanding loans taken out under prior high interest.

grainfields could be set on fire, were vulnerable and likely to suffer economic strain or even hunger that fall and winter. But when we examine the great number and variety of enemy invasions in the fifth and fourth centuries B.C., we see that such instances were not routine, and thus not representative of Greek history in this period.

With all these considerations in mind, we can explain the significance of Thucydides' often quoted remarks concerning the evacuation to Attica before the first Peloponnesian invasion of 431 B.C.: "And so it was extremely unpleasant for them to pack up their entire households, especially since it was only recently that they had become established once more after the Persian Wars" (2.16.1). Far from indicating a painful, fifty-year recovery from widespread agricultural devastation caused by the two Persian invasions and occupations of Attica,[5] the passage is rather a sensitive reflection of the enduring displeasure of conservative, rural Athenians whose lifestyle had once more been disrupted. Thucydides himself makes this clear. He adds that these Athenians regretted most the abandonment of their homes, shrines, and small towns. He makes no mention here of their displeasure about being separated from their ancestral farm plots, or of their fear of the destruction of their vines, olive trees, and grain.

Yet if agricultural devastation rarely did permanent damage to farmland, why did the strategy remain an integral part of Greek warfare? It may well be that the degree of damage to cropland was not so important if the enemy could be made either to fight or to submit: the threat, rather than the actuality, of agricultural devastation was the key, as ravaging in the classical period was more a means to start battle or induce capitulation than an end in itself. It can be argued of course that the

5. Cf., for example, French 1964, 82: "The losses to property were such that Thucydides writes of the Athenian farmers still recovering from them half a century later." Both the spectacular growth of Athens in general, and the prosperity of Attic farmers in particular, during this fifty-year period would seem to argue against the idea of extensive ruin.

threat of devastation would hardly have been credible if effective ravaging was recognized to have been so difficult. But again, we should emphasize that most hoplite-farmers, and thus most states, were not willing to take a chance. The sight of troops running through fields chopping away at vines and olive trees was unbearable to most voting citizens, and likely to trigger an immediate response of some type—hoplite-farmers would never really know whose territory or individual farm was the focus of a particular attack. The sensitivity and cohesion of the invaded was understood by all invading armies—which were themselves made up of landholding soldiers. Solidarity was essential, as the rural populace in a consensual society would meet to discuss possible responses, ranging from hoplite battle to capitulation to evacuation. (See updated commentary, page 246 [Agricultural Devastation].)

But invasion and occupation were blows to a citizen's pride, as everything that was dear fell into the hands of the enemy. Thus most Greek city-states felt completely justified in using their landholding hoplites in an effort to remain inviolable; then they could be secure in the belief that they had done everything possible to remain *aporthêtos*—unravaged and unplundered by the enemy.[6] (See updated commentary, page 249 [Word aporthêtos].) In that sense, ravaging was not so much economic warfare as part of the extensive rituals of classical hoplite warfare, the prebattle protocols of which included open challenges to battle, musters in summer and during the day, and formal face-off before the charge, replete with animal sacrifices, harangues from generals, and subsequent head-on collisions.

6. See Garlan 1974, 20, for a compilation of sources that reflect this popular claim of Greek states. No nation was prouder of its inviolability than Sparta. This was why the first invasion of Lakonia by Epameinondas was especially infamous: "It had been not less than 600 years since the Dorians had inhabited Lakedaimon; in that entire period this was the first time enemy forces had been spotted in the region. None before had dared invade. But now they overran an unravaged and untouched land" (Plut. *Ages.* 31.1–2).

It is also interesting that on occasion a few Greek states were not automatically drawn into battle or forced to capitulate by the threat of ravaging: like Athens, they were not greatly harmed by the subsequent devastation of their farmland. The inhabitants of the Lipari Islands, for
example, refused to submit to the terms of the Athenian invaders and allowed their lands to be ravaged (Thuc. 3.88.4). We hear of no serious
damage or permanent ill-effects. Similarly, the Melians failed to submit
to the first Athenian invasion of their island led by Nikias. After ravaging their cropland, the Athenians sailed away—apparently without accomplishing anything more.[7] The way to ruin Melos was to blockade
the island, besiege its urban core, and starve out the citizens—not ravage its farmland. In these instances, the introspective residents (as Pericles before) understood that more harm would result from pitched battle or surrender than from allowing their farmland to be overrun. They
must have realized that, whatever the loss to their pride, whatever the
rejection of traditional hoplite battle, in their particular circumstances
little permanent damage could be inflicted in a typically brief invasion—
or at least far less hurt than the loss of hoplites in pitched battle against
a superior infantry force.

More revealing is the reaction of the conservative invading forces to
these unusual developments. Even when they are aware that their ravaging achieves neither battle, submission, nor starvation, they nevertheless continue to devastate the land as usual before heading home. Ravaging, then, almost seems senseless and must have gone on simply
because there was little alternative. After all, in the limited strategic vision of most hoplite armies of the time, what other outlet was there for
expression of displeasure? They invaded with clumsy, heavy hoplites to
cause a dramatic infantry response, and left when they could not. The

7. Thuc. 3.91.3. There are other instances where devastation fails to bring a
quick military response, fails to induce surrender, and fails to cause hunger or
economic ruin; see Xen. *Hell.* 4.6.4–5, 5.2.4, 7.4.21, and esp. 4.6.13.

Arkadians, for example, marched against Elis, failed to take the city, and then retreated after "having accomplished nothing more," as Xenophon dryly notes, "than ravaging their territory" (*Hell.* 7.4.17). That ravaging could become a static, unimaginative strategy is nowhere better illustrated than in the career of Agesilaos in Asia Minor. There his army devastated the King's provinces, although he neither won concessions, fought in a major pitched battle, nor harmed the empire to any degree. Ignorant of the lesson learned by an older generation in Attica, he continued his devastations apparently because he had no better idea what to do—the King's satraps, like Pericles before, had no intention of playing by the parochial rules of Greek agrarian warfare, in which crop devastation usually was the acknowledged precursor to pitched hoplite battle. The hoplites of any Greek army that marched into enemy territory were well suited—in armament, tactics, temperament, and experience—to meet the adversary in a decisive pitched battle, but they were poorly equipped to wage a war of attrition by roaming the countryside and destroying vines, trees, and grain. By training, temperament, and experience, hoplites were fighters of a day, not professional skirmishers keen to enervate the enemy by systematic plunder and devastation. And when they met enemies, who themselves were not freeholding citizens, but rather serfs, sharecroppers, or renters, their attacks on the countryside lost much of the emotional fervor that was customary in Greece.

The unique economic and social conditions in Greece during the classical age made the devastation of farmland the favored way of bringing the war home to the enemy. But because of the practical difficulties in destroying grainfields, olive orchards, and vineyards, the effectiveness of local defense and evacuation, and the inherent resiliency of preindustrial farming, widespread ruin of crops was rarely achieved. Oddly, for nearly two centuries (700–500 B.C.) these factors did not discourage the application of the strategy of agricultural devastation, since it usually served the larger purpose of inciting an infantry response. At least until the classical period, the threat of destruction, of possible harm to crops, was usually enough to force the enemy to fight, negotiate, or surrender. Chopping away at olives and vines was as much a part of the protocol of hoplite warfare as prebattle sacrifices, the general's harangue, the post-mortem exchange of the dead, battlefield trophies, and the offering of military votives at sanctuaries. And our ancient sources reflect this ambiguity: in the classical period we hear constantly of ravaging, rarely of damage inflicted. Devastation is frequent and universally feared; yet serious, long-term economic damage does not automatically result. When hoplite armies meet adversaries like the Athenians or Persians, who do not accept the old strategic premises of ravaging, they are usually unable either to incite battle or to ruin an agrarian economy.

Agricultural devastation was a strategic option in all the great invasions of Greek history, where scholars note that warfare transcended the old notion of hoplite battle and entered the realm of economic warfare—the Persian inroads of 480–479 B.C., the Spartan attacks during the Archidamian War (431–425 B.C.), the occupation of Attica during the Dekeleian War (413–404 B.C.), and Epameinondas's four marches into the Peloponnese (371–362 B.C.). Yet, even in these cases, although crop losses are noted, agricultural damage played little role in the outcome of the war. To win, the Persians knew that they had to destroy the Greek navy and army at Salamis and Plataia, rather than try to starve the city-states by attacking the agriculture of Greece. Archidamos first sought to meet hoplites on open ground, not to wreck abandoned farms. Dekeleia was valuable—but not decisive in itself with respect to the later success of the Spartans—because of the enormous plunder, the slave desertions, the political intrigue, and the prevention of access to Attica. The Thebans destroyed Spartan hegemony through the creation of hostile fortified states like Messene, Megalopolis, and Mantineia, not by starving the Spartans through the devastation of vines, grain, and trees.

This paradox is illustrated well when a few innovative states refused to meet the standard enemy demands for battle or capitulation and were willing to let the enemy occupy their fields for a few weeks. After accomplishing little more than angering the local residents by ravaging the countryside, the enemy would soon depart. Agriculture and warfare are the most conservative of sciences, where tradition dies hard. Soldiers in the age of the agrarian city-state would instinctively devastate cropland even when there were no important military, political, or economic objectives. Likewise, farmers would often rush out to fight, although the real danger was death in battle, not the loss of a livelihood.[8]

As long as the Greek city-states relied on heavy infantry to decide the majority of their battles, and the agrarian population was predominant in political, social, and cultural terms, agricultural devastation was a means to an end, a catalyst to what was usually a decisive and rather economical pitched battle. In the fourth century B.C. and later, the attack on crops was integrated with full-scale plundering and piracy, as agriculture became but one of many targets for a more multifaceted invading force that was skilled and eager to plunder, kill, and destroy. But even when devastation was divorced from agrarian protocol, trees and vines, of course, remained the same—and no ancient army of any sort was ever able to cause famine and agricultural catastrophe for their enemy simply by ravaging the countryside. (See updated commentary, page 249 [Ravaging and Roman History].)

---

8. I should add that these conclusions do not necessarily apply to other societies. I have not studied in a comprehensive manner the Roman evidence and can well believe that Hannibal's lengthy occupation of Italy did a great deal more damage than occurred during the seasonal campaigning in classical Greece. But the difficulty ancient armies had destroying crops and the resiliency of labor-intensive, subsistence farming were probably universal and should not be forgotten. The reasons for depression and decline in many societies may be looked for elsewhere; the wartime ravaging of cropland was not often the cause.

The Vocabulary of Agricultural Devastation

A multitude of words and phrases are used to describe the process of ravaging. Some are of a general nature, denoting combined operations of destruction, plundering, and sacking.[1] Others are more specific and refer only to devastation of agriculture or rural property (i.e., farmhouses, implements, fencing, storage buildings). Many are common, everyday words (e.g., cut, burn, trample) that are used simply to describe the great variety of ways to destroy crops and property. Although the collection of examples that follows is not by any means exhaustive, and so does not eliminate all cases of ambiguity, definite patterns of usage can be noted, which will help to reduce confusion in the study of Greek agricultural devastation.

In reference to enemy activity, the general *adikeô* (to injure), *kakoô* (to injure), *kakourgeô* (to do injury), *portheô* (to destroy/plunder), and *phtheirô* (to destroy)—the last two especially frequent in compounds— usually include ravaging of agriculture within their range of meaning,

---

1. Throughout I use "ravage" and "devastate" interchangeably to mean destruction alone, and "plunder" to signify looting, where troops seek to acquire property and goods.

but not exclusively so. Plundering can also be implied, as well as destruction of citadels or taking of captives. These terms are rarely specific and consequently are the least forceful of the many words used to describe ravaging. Usually the context in which they are used is the only reliable guide in ascertaining an exact meaning.

For example, at Thuc. 2.5.5, the Plataians warn the Theban invaders not to injure the territory outside their walls (*ta te exô elegon autois mê adikein*). Earlier (2.5.4.) Thucydides had noted that the Thebans had designs on the many Plataians left out in the countryside with their property. The usage here of *adikeô* refers to the possible taking of captives and to the plundering of farms and stock, but only incidentally, if at all at this point, to the destruction of crops. Similar usage occurs at Thuc. 4.52.2–3. There the Lesbian exiles and their mercenaries hold off damaging (*ouden adikêsantes*) Rhoiteion after receiving payment of 2,000 staters. Presumably they were intent on booty, plunder, and inflicting random damage on the city;[2] devastation of the farmland surrounding Rhoiteion cannot be implied or assumed. *Adikeô* suggests plundering alone also at Aen. Tact. 16.4–6, Polyb. 4.3.10, and Xen. *Hell.* 4.8.30, in reference to soldiers who go off into the fields in search of provisions and loot.

In other passages (e.g., Thuc. 2.71.4, 5.84.3, 6.7.1.), the meaning of *adikeô* appears to be exactly the reverse. Devastation of agriculture becomes in these cases the primary if not the only activity implied by *adikeô*. Perhaps plundering can never be ruled out, but it must be only incidental here. Thus in these instances *adikeô* is used with *dêoô* (ravage) and *temnô* (cut), which comprise the normal vocabulary for devastation of agriculture alone, and so serve to clarify what the "damage" (*adikeô*) to the countryside in these cases actually entailed.

Kakoô (injure) and *kakourgeô* (to do injury) in general are used in the same ambiguous way. For example, it is clear from the context that devastation of agriculture is meant at Pl. *Leg.* 761A; Paus. 3.7.10; Thuc.

2. See Jackson 1969, 13 n. 12 on this passage.

2.22.2, 2.25.1, 3.1.2, 7.19.2; and Xen. *Hell.* 4.8.7, since in many of these cases *dêoô* or *temnô* appears nearby in apparent elaboration of the damage inflicted.

Similarly, at Xen. *Hell.* 5.4.42, Phoibidas is said to have "plundered" (*ephere kai êge*) the Thebans, by sending out freebooters, while "devastating" their land (*ekakourgei tên chôran*) with ravaging parties; *kakourgeô* here refers specifically to the destruction of crops alone.

At other times *kakoô* and *kakourgeô* can equally well suggest damage from plundering or looting only. Indeed, at Thuc. 2.32, 4.53.3, and 7.4.6, these words refer either to *lêstai* (robbers) or soldiers in search of provisions. Their true aim is the capture of enemy property, not the destruction of crops.

Portheô (to destroy/plunder) and *phtheirô* (to destroy), like these other general words, can be used on occasions for both activities, but they show definite tendencies for more specialized usage. *Portheô*, it is true, sometimes describes agricultural devastation,[3] but much more often it denotes plundering and looting alone, where troops are concerned solely with booty and provisions (e.g., Thuc. 2.93.4, 7.49.2; Xen. *Ages.* 1.20). An especially clear example is found at Thuc. 8.57.1, where troops in search of supplies (*tês trophês zêtêsei*) plunder the mainland (*porthêsôsi tên êpeiron*). And at Ar. *Ach.* 164, when Dikaiopolis complains that the Thracians have stolen his garlic, he says that he is *porthoumenos skorda*. One of the most frequent usages of *portheô* is to describe the sacking and plundering of cities and towns; in this usage there is no connection with croplands at all, and agricultural devastation cannot be meant (cf. Diod. 12.34, 15.4.1; Hdt. 1.84.5, 1.162.2, 4.148.4; Thuc. 2.56.6, 2.80.8, 3.33.2, 3.57.2, 4.57.3, 7.29.4, 8.40.2; Xen. *Ages.* 7.4; *Hell.* 6.5.27). *Portheô* is also commonly used to describe the looting of houses (e.g., Thuc. 7.29.4; Xen. *Hell.* 5.4.21). Here the distinction between the

---

3. For example, at Hdt. 3.58; Lycurg. *Leoc.* 47; Thuc. 1.73.4, 3.7.3, 3.16.2; Xen. *Hell.* 4.1.1; cf. also Plut. *Cleom.* 26.1; Westlake 1945, 80–84.

activities of troops who plunder and ravage is most clear; consider, for example, Polyb. 2.32.4: *kai tên te gên edêoun kai tas katoikias autôn exeporthoun*, "And they both devastated the land and plundered completely their household property" (cf. Xen. *Hell.* 6.5.15, 6.5.27). When troops are described as both plundering and devastating, *portheô* very seldom is used alone. It is usually accompanied by some other verb explicitly describing the ravaging activity of destruction alone (e.g., Thuc. 4.57.3; Xen. *Hell.* 6.5.15). (See updated commentary, page 250 [Vocabulary of Plunder].)

Phtheirô, more than any of these general words, seems to concentrate on ravaging and devastation of agriculture—that is, destruction alone where there is no plundering. Often it is used with *temnô* (to cut) or *dêoô* (to ravage), or with other words implying destruction only, where it describes the identical activity (Isoc. 16.13; Thuc. 2.11.7; Xen. *Hell.* 7.2.4; and esp. Onasander 6.11: *tên de tôn polemiôn phtheiretô kai kaietô kai temesthô*, "Let him destroy and burn and cut down the land of the enemies"). At Polyb. 4.67.1–2 we hear that Dorimachos's Aitolian "ravaging" campaign (*chrômenos tê kataphthora*) against Epiros was "not so much intended for his own enrichment as to cause harm to the Epirotes." *Phtheirô* is also frequently used to describe a "scorched earth" policy of planned retreat. There destruction only can be meant (e.g., Arr. *Anab.* 3.28.8). At times (e.g., Diod. 2.36.6, 20.32.2; Hdt. 1.17.2; Xen. *Hell.* 7.1.20; and esp. Polyb. 23.15.1), *phtheirô* has particular crops as its object (e.g., *sitos* [grain], *karpos* [fruit], *dendron* [fruit tree]). Together with the compound *diaphtheirô* (to destroy utterly), it is the standard word in leases for destruction (alone) of agriculture. Such agreements contain very specific clauses that stipulate that in cases of enemy destruction (e.g., *ean de polemioi diaphtheirôsi*, "if the enemy should destroy considerably . . ."), the lessors and the lessees are to share what crops are left, half and half (*SEG* 21 [1966] 644.13–14; *SEG* 24 [1969] 151.18; *SIG*³ 966.12–14; *IG* V.2, 6). In describing the simultaneous operations of plundering and ravaging, we would expect *phtheirô* (just as in the opposite case of *portheô*) usually not to be used alone, but to be accompanied by another word meaning "plunder." For example, Polybius makes this distinction clear when he criticizes those who not only carry off the year's produce (*diaireô*) but also go so far as to destroy trees and equipment (*ta dendra kai ta kataskeuasmata diaphtheirein*, 23.15.1). Elsewhere (Polyb. 4.45.7) Thracians are said to attack farmland, destroying some crops (*tous men kataphtheirôsi*) and plundering and carrying off others (*tous de sunathroisantes apopherôsi*).[4] At Diod. 20.32.2 the activities of those who *portheô* (plunder) are distinct from both *dêoô* and *diaphtheirô* (ravage).

Damage to property and agriculture can be implied by all these general words. But since the terms are rarely specific, an exact idea of what they mean usually must come from their context. Even in cases where they are used with *gê* ("land"; e.g., *gên adikein*, Thuc. 2.71.4) or *chôra* ("countryside"; e.g., *tên chôran dieporthêsan*, Thuc. 8.24.3) and thus clearly mean damage to the countryside (as opposed to citadels or urban houses), without close attention to the context, it is not really clear whether devastation (i.e., destruction of grain, trees, vines) or plundering (i.e., looting and theft from farms, driving off of cattle, taking of captives) is meant.[5] (See updated commentary, page 250 [Agricultural Vocabulary].)

The simultaneous appearance of more specific terms (e.g., *dêoô* [ravage], *temnô* [cut], *lêstai* [robbers]) and these general words can also be a help in determining the intended meaning of the general terms. And yet clearly there are occasional instances where the context does not shed

---

4. Yet compare the rare, apparently contradictory usage at Polyb. 16.24.7, where an army that *katephtheire* is said thereby to procure food from the countryside (see also Polyb. 3.92.8).

5. I.e., whether this activity is done by invading hoplites to draw out the enemy to pitched battle after their initial evacuation from the countryside, or is accomplished by pirates, exiled factions, or small raiding parties.

light on a specific definition (as perhaps at Hdt. 1.76.1; Thuc. 8.24.4; Xen. *Hell.* 7.1.35). Then no distinction between plundering and ravaging can be made—and may not be intended: the Greek word in some cases may be used loosely, as the English word "damage" often is, for instance, and so may suggest any and all types of harassment (the operations, too, in actuality may have been combined or have overlapped).

Finally, such words as *blaptô* (hurt), *sulaô* (strip/deprive), *sinomai* (hurt/pillage), and others roughly equivalent to English "damage" or "harm" can also be used to describe ravaging as well as plundering.[6] In general, they have the same ambiguous tendencies as those discussed above, and thus close attention must be given to the contexts in which they occur.

The two most common words for ravaging alone are *temnô* (cut/ravage) and *dêoô* (tear/ravage). Both nearly always entail destruction of croplands, scarcely ever suggesting plundering or looting. In his careful study of Thucydides' usage of *dêoô*, A. H. Jackson observes: "He never mentions any booty produced by men *dêountes*. To this extent, Thucydides uses the word *dêoun* exactly as he uses *temnein*."[7]

A random sampling of other Greek authors reveals that the usage of these two words is the same, and they are often used interchangeably (e.g., Thuc. 2.73.1): the true intention of those *dêountes* or *temnontes* is destruction, not plunder (e.g., Hdt. 6.135.2, 8.33, 8.50.2, 9.86.2; Xen. *Ages.* 2.17, 2.22, 2.23; *Hell.* 1.2.2, 2.2.9, 3.1.3, 3.2.27, 4.2.15, 4.4.19, 5.4.38; [Xen.] *Ath. Pol.* 2.14, 2.16). Plato illustrates well this clear distinction in meaning when he suggests that Greeks should not devastate (*temnô*) each other's lands, but rather be content to plunder and carry off (*aphaireô*) only the harvest (*Resp.* 470A–B). Likewise, Lysias states in his seventh oration (7.6) that in the outlying districts of Attica (*ta men porrô*)

6. For the very distinct vocabulary of plundering and pillaging, see Ducrey 1968, 39–46, 172; Ormerod 1924, 63 nn. 1–2; Phillipson 1911, 238, 353.
7. Jackson 1969, 12.

the Spartans "ravaged" (*etemneto*) the land, and the areas nearer the city (*ta d'engus*) were "plundered" (*diêrpazeto*) by "friends" (cf. Andoc. 1.101; Polyb. 2.32.4).

There are a few possible exceptions. At Xen. *Anab.* 5.5.7 the countryside is said to have been ravaged (*dêoô*) by the Ten Thousand; as one reads further, it becomes clear that the ravaging included plundering and looting of houses for provisions and booty (5.5.11). At times the theft of grain and cattle and random killing are also mentioned along with *dêoô* or *temnô* (e.g., Thuc. 6.7.1, 6.105.3; Polyb. 4.73.5; Xen. *Hell.* 4.4.1, 4.6.4). But in these and other cases it is equally possible, and perhaps preferable, to understand such other activities as separate from, or incidental to, the main business of ravaging implied by *dêoô* or *temnô* (e.g., Diod. 15.65.5; Thuc. 6.7.1).

Both words are usually associated exclusively with the countryside, often used with *gê* (land), *chôra* (countryside), *agros* (farm/farmland), or some similar generic word or phrase implying farmland (e.g., *ta epithalassia*; *to pedion*).[8] The use of different vocabulary for ravaging (*dêoô* or *temnô*) of the countryside and attacks on urban areas is also evident in occasional set phrases; consider Thuc. 2.56.6, for instance: *kai tês te gês etemnon kai auto to polisma heilon kai eporthêsan*, "And they ravaged part of the land and they took the city proper and plundered it"; also Hdt. 9.86.2: *tên te gên autôn etamnon kai proseballon pros to teichos*, "And they ravaged their land and mounted an assault against the wall" (cf. also Thuc. 1.30.2, 1.65.2, 2.56.4, 2.101.1, 3.102.2, 4.25.8, 4.130.1). In only rare (and poetic?) instances is *dêoô*—but not *temnô*—used to describe urban damage, such as at Hdt. 7.133.2 (*hê chôrê kai hê polis edêiôthê*, "The countryside and the city were ravaged") and Soph. *OC* 1319 (*astu dêôsein puri*, "to intend to ravage the city with fire").

Although *dêoô* and *temnô* are used interchangeably and exclusively for devastation, there is, nevertheless, a shade of difference in their meaning.

8. See Jackson 1969, 15–16.

Dêoô—although deriving from a root that also suggests cleaving or tearing—is the more general term, implying blanket destruction to both agriculture (i.e., cultivated plants) and farmhouses, buildings, and other rural property (see, for example, Thuc. 1.143.5, 2.13.1). Specific crops, however, are rarely mentioned as the object of those *dêountes*: *Dêountes ton siton* or *ta dendra* seems not normally to occur.[9]

Temnô (to cut), on the other hand, while often used like *dêoô* in the general sense of "ravage" (with *gê* [land], *chôra* [countryside], and *agros* [farm/farmland]), is more specific. Individual crops (e.g., vines at Ar. *Ach.* 183, fruit trees at Lys. 7.6, and grain at Xen. *Mem.* 2.1.13) are often described as the target of *temnô*. Furthermore, *temnô* alone, unlike *dêoô*, does not suggest damage to farm buildings and houses. This is not surprising, given that the root meaning of *temnô* is "to cut." *Temnein oikias*, for example, would stretch too far the generalized meaning of *temnô*, "ravage," and suggests instead the improbable image of "cutting houses."[10]

Consequently, *temnô*, when used alone of enemy activity, means devastation of cultivated plants or growing things only.[11] For example, at Plut. *Mor.* 193E17, when Epameinondas boasts that his Thebans would provide free firewood for the Athenians by "ravaging" Attica (*tên gar chôran autôn temoumen*), *temnô* must refer specifically to the cutting of fruit trees and vines. (See updated commentary, page 251 [*Temnô*].)

Finally, the most specific words are those that describe the actual type of damage inflicted—that is, burning, cutting, or some other ac-

9. But cf. the rare *edêôsan de tês Attikês ta te proteropon tetmêmena, ei ti ebeblastêkei*, "They ravaged the parts of Attica that had been cut down before, if anything had grown back out" (Thuc. 3.26.3).

10. At Polyb. 4.3.10 *ekkoptô* is used with houses—apparently to mean "break in" (?).

11. Cf. Hardy 1926, 349 n. 2.

tivity. Only brief mention of these verbs needs to be made here, since their meaning is always quite clear, with little, if any, ambiguity possible. Nearly all words in the Greek vocabulary for burning or cutting can be used in a context of agricultural devastation. No pattern of general usage, then (except, perhaps, in the case of a particular author), need be studied.

For burning grain, farmhouses, or the countryside in general, the verbs implying conflagration or simple burning—*aithô, daiô, pimprêmi,* and *phlegô*—are the most commonly used. But even more frequently, these words and others are compounded with prepositions to give a more accurate and active sense of setting on' fire, torching, burning down, or spreading fire (e.g., *empimprêmi* [to put in fire], *empureô* [to set afire], *epiphlegô* [to burn up], *katakaiô* [to burn down], and *purpoleô* [to assail with fire]; and cf. Poll. *Onom.* 1.174).

Koptô, keirô, and *temnô* are the most frequently used words for cutting in association with agricultural devastation. They all can be found with *gê* or *chôra,* where they describe the destruction of fruit trees, grain, vines, and any other standing crops. The very specialized verbs *dendrotomeô* and *dendrokopeô* refer only to the cutting of fruit trees, namely, the olive and, perhaps less frequently, the fig (e.g., Diod. 2.36.6–7, 12.45.1, 14.62.5, 14.90.7, 14.97.5; Thuc. 1.108.2; Xen. *Mem.* 2.1.13).

The combined use of the verbs for cutting and burning yields a common, almost formulaic description of agricultural destruction. *Koptô kai kaiô*—these words are the most frequently used—are equivalent to the English "fire and sword" or "ax and fire" and refer to the wholesale devastation of the countryside, where invading armies cut down standing crops and simultaneously burn houses, property, and grain. Plundering, of course, is never denoted by these words alone. There are wide variations in this phraseology, but the same activity of cutting down and burning anything possible is always meant (e.g., *tên chôran empurizôn kai dendrotomôn,* "setting afire the countryside and cutting down the fruit trees," Diod. 14.90.7, and cf.12.45.1 and 2.36.6; *temnôn kai purpolôn tên chôran,* "cutting down and assailing the countryside with fire," Diod. 14.100.2; and *panta epephlegon kai ekeiron,* "They were burning up and cutting down everything," Hdt. 8.32.2; other variations: e.g., Onasander 6.11; Pl. *Resp.* 5.470B; Polyb. 9.28.6; Xen. *Anab.* 4.7.20; [Xen.] *Ath. Pol.* 2.14).[12]

THE VOCABULARY OF AGRICULTURAL DEVASTATION

Greek Word	Usual Context	Range of Possible Meaning	Specialized Use
adikeô	urban or rural	plundering and/or ravaging	none
dendrokopeô dendrotomeô	rural	ravaging alone	ravaging of fruit trees
dêoô	rural	ravaging alone	none
kakoô kakourgeô	urban or rural	plundering and/or ravaging	none
keirô	rural	ravaging alone	ravaging of growing things
koptô	rural	ravaging alone	ravaging of growing things
portheô	urban or rural	plundering/ occasionally ravaging	plundering of towns
temnô	rural	ravaging alone	ravaging of growing things
phtheirô	urban or rural	ravaging/ occasionally plundering	ravaging alone
koptô kai kaiô	urban or rural	ravaging alone	ravaging of the countryside

12. See also, for example, Xen. *Hell.* 3.2.26, 4.1.33, 4.5.10, 4.6.12, 5.2.39.

Select Bibliography

This bibliography includes only those works referred to in short form in the footnotes.

Adcock, F. E. 1947. "*Epiteichismos* in the Archidamian War." *Classical Review* 61: 2–7.

———. 1957. *The Greek and Macedonian Art of War*. Berkeley.

Anderson, J. K. 1961. *Ancient Greek Horsemanship*. Berkeley.

———. 1970. *Military Theory and Practice in the Age of Xenophon*. Berkeley.

Andreyev, V. N. 1974. "Some Aspects of Agrarian Conditions in Attica in the Fifth and Third Centuries B.C." *Eirene* 12: 5–46.

Audring, G. 1974. "Über Grundeigentum und Landwirtschaft in der Krise der athenischen Polis." In *Hellenische Poleis*, edited by C. Welskopf, 108–131. Berlin.

Austin, M., and P. Vidal-Naquet. 1972. *Économies et sociétés en Grèce ancienne*. Paris. Translated under the title *Economic and Social History of Ancient Greece* (Berkeley, 1977).

Boardman, J. M. 1956. "Delphinion in Chios." *Annual of the British School at Athens* 51: 41–54.

Bolkestein, H. 1958. *Economic Life in Greece's Golden Age*. Leiden.

Bradford, J. 1956. "Fieldwork on Aerial Discoveries in Attica and Rhodes." *Antiquaries Journal* 36: 172–180.

Brunt, P. A. 1965. "Spartan Policy and Strategy in the Archidamian War." *Phoenix* 9: 255–280.

Busolt, G. 1904. *Griechische Geschichte*. Vol. 3:2. Gotha.

Cary, M. 1941. *The Geographical Background of Greek and Roman History*. Oxford.

Chandler, L. 1926. "The North-West Frontier of Attica." *Journal of Hellenic Studies* 46: 1–21.

Cooper, A. B. 1977. "The Family Farm in Ancient Greece." *Classical Journal* 73.2: 162–173.

Davies, J. K. 1971. *Athenian Propertied Families*. Oxford.

Delbrück, H. 1890. *Die Strategie des Pericles Erläutert durch die Strategie Friedrichs des Grossen*. Berlin.

———. 1975. *History of the Art of War*. Vol. 1. Westport, Conn. Originally published as *Geschichte der Kriegskunst im Rahmen der politischen Geschichte* (Berlin, 1920).

Detienne, M. 1973. "L'olivier: Un mythe politico-religieux." In Finley 1973b, 293–306.

de Wet, B. X. 1969. "The So-Called Defensive Policy of Pericles." *Acta Classica* 12: 103–119.

Dimen, M., and E. Friedel. 1976. *Regional Variation in Modern Greece and Cyprus: Towards a Perspective on the Ethnography of Greece*. Annals of the New York Academy of Sciences 286. New York.

Ducrey, P. 1968. *Le traitement des prisonniers de guerre dans la Grèce antique*. Paris.

Ehrenberg, V. 1951. *The People of Aristophanes*. Oxford.

Eliot, C. W. J. 1962. *Coastal Demes of Attica*. Toronto.

Engels, D. 1978. *Alexander the Great and the Logistics of the Macedonian Army*. Berkeley.

Fine, J. V. A. 1951. *Horoi: Studies in Mortgage, Real Security, and Land Tenure in Ancient Athens*. Hesperia Supplement 9. Princeton.

Finley, M. I. 1952. *Studies in Land and Credit in Ancient Athens*. New Brunswick, N.J.

———. 1973a. *The Ancient Economy*. Berkeley.

———, ed. 1973b. *Problèmes de la terre en Grèce ancienne*. Paris and The Hague.

French, A. 1964. *The Growth of the Athenian Economy*. London.

Garlan, Y. 1968. "Fortifications et histoire grecque." In Vernant 1968, 245–260.

———. 1973. "La défense du territoire à l'époque classique." In Finley 1973b, 149–160.

———. 1974. *Recherches de poliorcétique grecque*. Athens.

———. 1975. *War in the Ancient World: A Social History*. New York. Originally published as *La guerre dans l'antique* (Paris, 1972).

Gernet, L. 1909. *L'approvisionnement d'Athens en blé à Ve et IVe siècles*. Paris.

Glotz, G. 1927. *Ancient Greece at Work*. London. Originally published as *Le travail dans la Grèce ancienne* (Paris, 1920).

Gomme, A. W. 1945–1970. *Historical Commentary on Thucydides*. 4 vols. Oxford. Volume 4 published posthumously by A. Andrews and K. J. Dover.

Gordon, G. T. 1953. "Fire and Sword: The Technique of Destruction." *Antiquity* 27: 346–355.

Griffith, G. T. 1935. *The Mercenaries of the Hellenistic World*. Cambridge.

Grundy, G. B. 1948. *Thucydides and the History of His Age*. London.

Guiraud, P. 1893. *La propriété foncière en Grèce jusqu'à la conquête romaine*. Paris.

Gutman, M. D. 1980. *War and Rural Life in the Early Modern Low Countries*. Princeton.

Hammond, N. G. L. 1954. "The Main Road from Boeotia to the Peloponnese through the Northern Megarid." *Annual of the British School at Athens* 49: 103–122.

Hardy, W. G. 1926. "The Hellenica Oxyrhynchia and the Devastation of Attica." *Classical Philology* 21: 346–355.

Harmand, J. 1973. *La guerre antique, de Sumer à Rome*. Vendôme.

Heichelheim, F. M. 1958–1964. *An Ancient Economic History*. 2 vols. Leiden.

Heitland, W. E. 1921. *Agricola: A Study of Agriculture and Rustic Life in the Greco-Roman World from the Point of View of Labor*. Cambridge.

Henderson, B. W. 1927. *The Great War between Athens and Sparta*. London.

Humphreys, S. C. 1967. "Archaeology and the Economic and Social History of Classical Greece." *La Parola del Passato* 116: 374–400. Republished in S. C. Humphreys, *Anthropology and the Greeks* (London, 1978).

———. 1970. "Economy and Society in Classical Athens." *Annali della Scuola Normale Superiore di Pisa: Lettere, Storia e Filosofia* ser. 2.39: 1–26.

———. 1972. "Town and Country in Ancient Greece." In Ucko 1972, 763–768.

Isager, S., and M. H. Hansen. 1975. *Aspects of Athenian Society in the Fourth Century B.C.* Odense.

Jackson, A. H. 1969. "The Original Purpose of the Delian League." *Historia* 18: 12–16.

Jacoby, F. 1940. *Die Fragmente der griechischen Historiker*. Vol. 3b. Leiden.

Jameson, M. H. 1978. "Agriculture and Slavery in Classical Athens." *Classical Journal* 73.2: 122–145.

Jardé, A. 1925. *Les céréals dans l'antiquité grecque*. Paris.

Jones, J. E. 1974. "Two Attic Country Houses." *Archaiologika Analekta ex Athênôn* 7: 303–312.

———. 1975. "Town and Country Houses of Attica in Classical Times." In *Miscellanea Graeca: Thorikos and Laurion in Archaic and Classical Times*, edited by H. Mussche et al., 1: 63–140. Ghent.

Jones, J. E., L. H. Sackett, and C. W. J. Eliot. 1957. "To Dema: A Survey of the Aigaleos-Parnes Wall." *Annual of the British School at Athens* 52: 152–189.

Jones, J. E., L. H. Sackett, and A. J. Graham. 1962. "The Dema House in Attica." *Annual of the British School at Athens* 57: 75–114.

———. 1973. "An Attic Country House below the Cave of Pan at Vari." *Annual of the British School at Athens* 68: 355–452.

Kagan, D. 1974. *The Archidamian War*. Ithaca, N.Y.

Kahrstedt, U. 1932. "Die Landgrenze Athena." *Mitteilungen des Deutschen Archäologischen Instituts, Athenische Abteilung* 57: 8–28.

Kent, J. H. 1941. "A Garrison Inscription from Rhamnous." *Hesperia* 10: 342–350.

———. 1948. "The Temple Estates of Delos, Rhenia, and Mykonos." *Hesperia* 17: 243–335.

Kirsten, E. 1952. See Philippson 1950–1959.

Kromayer, J., and G. Veith. 1928. *Heerwesen und Kriegführung der Greichen und Römer*. Munich.

Langdon, M., and L. V. Watrous. 1977. "The Farm of Timesios: Rock-Cut Inscriptions in South Attica." *Hesperia* 46: 162–177.

Lewis, D. M. 1966. "After the Profanation of the Mysteries." In *Studies Presented to Victor Ehrenberg*, edited by E. Badian, 177–192. Oxford.

———. 1973. "The Athenian Rationes Centesimarum." In Finley 1973b, 187–212.

Lonis, R. 1969. *Les usages de la guerre entre grecs et barbares*. Paris.

Martin, R. 1956. *L'urbanisme dans la Grèce antique*. Paris.

———. 1973. "Rapports entre les structures urbaines et les modes de division et d'exploitation du territoire." In Finley 1973b, 97–112.

McCredie, J. R. 1966. *Fortified Military Camps in Attica*. Hesperia Supplement 11. Princeton.

McDonald, W. A., and G. Rapp. 1972. *The Minnesota Messenia Expedition*. Minneapolis.

McNicoll, A. 1972. "The Development of Urban Defenses in Hellenistic Asia Minor." In Ucko 1972, 781–791.

Michell, H. 1957. *The Economics of Ancient Greece*. Cambridge.

Mossé, C. 1973a. *Athens in Decline, 404 B.C.–86 B.C.* London and Boston.

———. 1973b. "Le statut des paysans en Attique au IVe siècle." In Finley 1973b, 179–186.

Ormerod, H. A. 1924. *Piracy in the Ancient World.* Liverpool.

Parke, H. W. 1932. "The Tithe of Apollo and the Harmost at Decelea." *Journal of Hellenic Studies* 52: 42–46.

———. 1933. *Greek Mercenary Soldiers from the Earliest Times to the Battle of Ipsus.* Oxford.

Pecírka, J. 1970a. "Country Estates of the Polis of Chersonesos in the Crimea." In *Richerche Storiche ed Economiche in Memoria di Corrado Barbagallo*, 1: 459–477. Naples.

——— (with M. Dufkova). 1970b. "Excavations of Farms and Farmhouses in the Chora of the Chersonesos in the Crimea." *Eirene* 8: 123–174.

———. 1973. "Homestead Farms in Classical and Hellenistic Hellas." In Finley 1973b, 113–147.

———. 1976. "The Crisis of the Athenian Polis in the Fourth Century B.C." *Eirene* 14: 5–29.

Pélékidis, C. 1962. *Histoire de l'ephébie attique.* Paris.

Phillipson, A. 1950–1959. *Die griechischen Landschaften.* 4 vols. Frankfurt. With "Beiträge" by E. Kirsten (1952).

Phillipson, C. 1911. *The International Law and Custom of Ancient Greece and Rome.* London.

Pouilloux, J. 1954. *La forteresse de Rhamnonte.* Paris.

Pritchett, W. K. 1953. "The Attic Stelai—Part I." *Hesperia* 22: 225–299.

———. 1956. "The Attic Stelai—Part II." *Hesperia* 25: 178–328.

———. 1965. *Studies in Ancient Greek Topography.* Pt. 1. Berkeley.

———. 1969. *Studies in Ancient Greek Topography.* Pt. 2. Berkeley.

———. 1971. *Ancient Greek Military Practices.* Pt. 1. Berkeley. Reissued as *The Greek State at War*, pt. 1.

———. 1974. *The Greek State at War.* Pt. 2. Berkeley.

Rowlands, M. J. 1972. "Defense: A Factor in the Organization of Settlements." In Ucko 1972, 447–462.

Ste. Croix, G. E. M. de. 1966. "The Estate of Phainippos." In *Studies Presented to Victor Ehrenberg*, edited by E. Badian, 109–114. Oxford.

———. 1972. *The Origins of the Peloponnesian War.* Ithaca, N.Y.

Salmon, E. T. 1946. "The Belated Spartan Occupation of Decelea: An Explanation." *Classical Review* 60: 13–14.

Semple, E. C. 1931. *The Geography of the Mediterranean Region: Its Relation to Ancient History.* New York.

Shear, T. L. 1978. *Kallias of Sphettos and the Revolt of Athens in 286 B.C.* Hesperia Supplement 17. Princeton.

Standish, R. 1961. *The First of All Trees: The Study of the Olive.* London.

Tarn, W. W. 1930. *Hellenistic Naval and Military Developments.* Cambridge.

Ucko, P. J., R. Tringham, and G. W. Dimbleby, eds. 1972. *Man, Settlement, and Urbanism.* London.

Vanderpool, E. 1978. "Roads and Forts in Northwestern Attica." *California Studies in Classical Antiquity* 11: 227–245.

Van Rooy, C. A. 1969. "Fortifications in South Attica and the Date of Thorikos." *Acta Classica* 12: 171–180.

Vernant, J. P., ed. 1968. *Problèmes de la guerre en Grèce ancienne.* Paris.

Wallace, W. P. 1952. "The Spartan Invasion of Attica in 431 B.C." In *Studies in Honor of G. Norwood,* edited by M. White, 80–84. Toronto.

Westlake, H. D. 1945. "Seaborne Raids in Periclean Strategy." *Classical Quarterly* 39: 75–84. Republished in H. D. Westlake, *Essays on Greek Historians and Greek History* (London, 1969).

_____. 1948. "Athenian Food Supplies from Euboea." *Classical Review* 62: 2–5.

White, K. D. 1967. *Agricultural Implements of the Roman World.* Cambridge.

_____. 1970. *Roman Farming.* Ithaca, N.Y.

_____. 1975. *Farm Equipment of the Roman World.* Cambridge.

Will, E. 1975. "La territoire, la ville et la poliorcétique grecque." *Revue Historique* 253: 297–318.

Winter, F. E. 1966. "Military Architecture in the Termessos Region." *American Journal of Archaeology* 70: 127–137.

_____. 1971. *Greek Fortifications.* Toronto.

Wrede, W. 1933. *Attische Mauern.* Berlin.

Young, J. H. 1941. "Studies in South Attica: The Salaminioi at Porthmos." *Hesperia* 10: 163–191.

_____. 1956a. "Greek Roads in South Attica." *Antiquity* 30: 94–97.

_____. 1956b. "Studies in South Attica: Country Estates at Sounion." *Hesperia* 25: 122–146.

Zimmern, A. 1931. *The Greek Commonwealth.* 5th ed. Oxford.

Updated Commentary
and Bibliography

Books and articles mentioned in the following bibliographic commentary appeared after *Warfare and Agriculture* was submitted for publication in 1981.

INTRODUCTION

Page 4. Warfare and Agriculture: General Considerations.

Very few historical studies in any period have evaluated the complex relationship between farming and fighting. Two good examples of the dividends of such an approach are V. Magagna's *Communities of Grain: Rural Rebellion in Comparative Perspective* (Ithaca, N.Y., 1991), which demonstrates that agrarians fight not out of rigid class interests, but rather more often from a shared concern for the community's stability at large, and A. Offer's *The First World War: An Agrarian Interpretation* (Oxford, 1989), which brilliantly shows how agriculture affected the very outcome of the First World War. As Offer explains, both Germany and England resorted to imported foodstuffs to fulfill the ever-increasing demands of their populations' complex diet. England, however, having greater access to food supplies from Canada, Australia, and the United States, was able to feed a large domestic population and field an army far more effectively than Germany, which became increasingly isolated and ultimately lost the war of nutritional attrition. More germanely, the idea that warfare permanently destroys the agrarian infrastructure of the invaded is challenged by R. Ergang in *The Myth of the All-Destructive Fury of the Thirty Years War* (Pocono Pines, Penn., 1956) and by W. Abel in *Geschichte der deutschen Landwirtschaft vom frühen Mittelalter bis zum 19. Jahrhundert* (Stuttgart, 1967) (cf. Abel's *Agricultural Fluctuations in Europe from the Thirteenth to the Twentieth Centuries* [New York, 1980]).

In the context of classical societies, L. Foxhall ("Farming and Fighting in Ancient Greece," in *War and Society in the Greek World*, ed. J. Rich and G. Shipley [London, 1993], 134–145) rightly argues that more attention must be given to warfare and agriculture and the interplay between the two. She states, however, that in recent work I, among others, have divorced the study of war from agriculture: "But paradoxically, in the most recent writing on both agriculture (Sallares 1991; Gallant 1991) and warfare (Hanson 1989 [ed.], 1991), the two subjects have become divorced and have gone off in separate directions. This is a pity, since men in ancient Greece probably spent more time fighting and farming than in any other activities" (p. 134). I find this statement troubling, since one of the initial chapters in the volume Foxhall refers to, the 1989 edition of *The Western Way of War*, is entitled "The Hoplite and His Phalanx: War in an Agricultural Society," and the entire book sought to recapture the hoplite battle experience from the unique viewpoint of the ancient agrarian citizen.

Page 5. The Protocols of Hoplite Warfare.

A number of graphic accounts of hoplite fighting have appeared that follow the train of events from the initial invasion and ravaging of crops to the final capitulation, exchange of the dead, and erection of the victory trophy. These investigations emphasize how military rituals reinforced the particular values of the combatants, which at least before the fifth century B.C. in Greece were almost exclusively agrarian—crop devastation, then, like battle sacrifice and trophies, was integral to the hoplite battle occasion. See, for example, the chapter "The Hoplite and His Phalanx: War in an Agricultural Society," in V. D. Hanson, *The Western Way of War: Infantry Battle in Classical Greece* (New York, 1989), 27–39; W. R. Connor, "Early Greek Warfare as Symbolic Expression," *Past and Present* 119 (1988): 3–29; John Lazenby, "The Killing Zone," in *Hoplites: The Ancient Greek Battle Experience*, ed. V. D. Hanson (London, 1991), 87–109; and Stephen Mitchell, "Hoplite Warfare in Ancient Greece," in *Battle in Antiquity*, ed. A. B. Lloyd (London, 1996), 87–106. Josiah Ober has presented a formal review of the understood agreements of hoplite battle in "The Rules of War in Classical Greece," now republished in *The Athenian Revolution: Essays on Ancient Greek Democracy and Political Theory* (Princeton, 1996), 53–71. For the notion of the quasi-ritualistic manner of Greek warfare and its relationship to Western military dynamism, see now D. Dawson, *The Origins of Western Warfare: Militarism and Morality in the Ancient World* (Boulder, 1996), 47–78.

There is a characteristically careful philological account of each stage of hoplite fighting in W. K. Pritchett, "The Pitched Battle," in *The Greek State at War*, pt. 4 (Berkeley, 1985), 1–93. A number of passages in Greek literature attest to the close relationship between infantry fighting and farming and emphasize the idea that originally soldiers were agrarians (e.g., Hom. *Il.* 18.68–69; Tyrt. 19.16; Thuc. 1.141.5; [Arist.] *Oec.* 1.1343b5–7; Xen. *Oec.* 5.5, 7, 14). Thus *Warfare and Agriculture* argues that crop devastation continued even when it did not result in catastrophic losses, because it was an especially effective catalyst—sometimes the only catalyst—for pitched battle between opposing agrarian armies.

In contrast, Peter Krentz ("The Strategic Culture of Periclean Athens," in *Polis and Polemos*, ed. C. Hamilton and P. Krentz [Claremont, Calif., 1997], 55–72) has questioned the notion that hoplite battle ever followed a set of mutually understood protocols, much less that it was synonymous with Greek warfare itself. While it is true that there were an increasing number of nonhoplite battles in the later fifth and fourth centuries B.C.—namely, light-armed skirmishing, sieges, attacks from and against mountain forts—the Greeks at least believed that their earlier tradition had been to fight openly on a flat plain in daylight (Dem. 9.48; Hdt. 7.9.2; Polyb. 13.3.2–4, 18.3.3; Thuc. 1.15), with hoplites alone as the only reliable and heroic troops (Arist. *Pol.* 7.1326a23–25; cf. Thuc. 3.98.4; Pl. *Leg.* 706B–C). Hence we hear a litany of later complaints that walls (Plut. *Mor.* 190A, 210E27, 212E, 215D, 221F6), missiles (Thuc. 4.40.2; Eur. *HF* 157–163), and trickery (Eur. *Rhes.* 510–517) were somehow unfair and unheroic; that capital and finance were new (and unwelcome) elements in Greek warfare (Thuc. 1.83.2); and that warfare had become too complex and expensive (Thuc. 1.141–142). What were these statesmen, historians, dramatists, and philosophers reacting against, if not the erosion of war as heroic pitched battles between heavy infantry?

The topic is complex, since (1) we have no prose accounts of battles in the first two centuries of hoplite warfare (700–500 B.C.); (2) the conventions of vase painting continue to be disputed and only inadequately represent phalanx fighting; (3) without a comprehensive register of all incidents of military confrontation (an impossible task, given our sources for the seventh through fifth centuries), it is difficult to gauge to what a degree an early nonhoplitic skirmish, siege, naval encounter, or raid constitutes an exception to pitched battle or represents the implied normal pattern of hostilities. In *The Other Greeks: The Agrarian Roots of Western Civilization* (New York, 1995), 327–355, I argued that as early as the Persian Wars the entire idea of war by hoplite battle of the past two centuries was seen as obsolete. After the impressive victory over

Xerxes, the Greeks were ready to embrace a military evolution lasting two centuries and leading to Philip and Alexander, when all ethical and moral constraints were to become irrelevant—warfare at last became the natural lethal expression of Western scientific, financial, and cultural dynamism.

Page 6. The Centrality of Small Landowners in Greek Warfare.

Prior to *Warfare and Agriculture,* the general consensus, I think, was that infantry fighting was originally among aristocratic hoplites, larger landowners who alone could afford the necessary body armor, and who constructed protocols to preserve their rule over a largely exploited underclass, both free and slave. The question of class is not irrelevant, since it lies at the very heart of the sociology of the Greek city-state itself. The notion of an elite hoplite lingers even today. G. Shipley, for example, observes: "The selection of war as the paramount activity can be regarded as an attempt to direct energy towards maintaining a particular social structure, one in which citizen was dominated by aristocrat, non-citizen by citizen, female by male, and barbarian by Greek" ("Introduction: The Limits of War," in *War and Society in the Greek World,* ed. J. Rich and G. Shipley [London, 1993], 23). Yet hoplite warfare of the polis—at least by the sixth and fifth centuries B.C.—seems to me one of the rare contexts in which "aristocrats" did not dominate citizens at all—at least up to the demise of the agrarian city-state in the Hellenistic era.

Within the classical polis, we recognize a vocabulary for middling citizen. Archaeological survey reveals both the presence of numerous small farm sites—in Attica, Boiotia, the Argolid, Crimea, southern Italy, and the Aegean islands—and land that is often divided into small parcels of ten to twenty-five acres. Literature echoes a chauvinism of middleness, and there is a clear notion that the relegation of both the light-armed ravager and the mounted grandee to inferior roles reflects not just military preference and utility, but social and cultural values of the polis itself. The argument concerning the middling hoplite—who is neither peasant nor aristocrat—is presented at length in V. D. Hanson, *The Other Greeks: The Agrarian Roots of Western Civilization* (New York, 1995), esp. 181–289, and V. D. Hanson., "Hoplites into Democrats: The Changing Ideology of Athenian Infantry," in *Dêmokratia: A Conversation on Democracies, Ancient and Modern*, ed. J. Ober and C. Hedrick (Princeton, 1996), 289–312. It seems safe to state, as a very general rule, that the ubiquity of farmsteads, smaller and more equal-sized plots, and intensive rural installations—farm buildings, presses, terraces, etc.—suggest an independent yeomanry whose community had genuine autonomous councils in control of political and military policy and serving the interest of rural people. The opposite scenario of larger, consolidated holdings, rural depopulation, and nucleated settlement seems to characterize more a society of wealthy landholders and peasants, conditions of high taxation, extensive military expenditure, and political autocracy, which serves the very few politically well-connected. Thus it is understandable that ravaging in warfare between neighboring poleis was an entirely different enterprise than campaigns of attrition waged far from home by Hellenistic dynasts and Roman grandees.

Page 13. Ravaging and the Historiography of the Greek State.

I know of no comprehensive study of either Greek or Roman crop devastation during wartime published after 1983. Passing references in standard textbooks and introductory studies that have appeared since 1983 still sometimes tend to exaggerate the effects of such destruction: "Ravaging, so casually reported again and again by the historians, was a major disaster for those who endured it" (*The World of Athens: An Introduction to Classical Athenian Culture*, Joint Association of Classical Teachers' Greek Course Background Book [Cambridge, 1984], 247–248);

"But Aristophanes' plays, like Thucydides' remarks, demonstrate that the Peloponnesian War, by forcing the peasants to abandon their houses and fields, dealt harsh blows to that small Athenian peasantry" (C. Mossé, "The Economist," in *The Greeks*, ed. J.-P. Vernant [Chicago, 1995], 27); "The date 431 marks a fundamental rupture in the history of the ancient imagination. The Athenians very quickly felt it as such. With the abandoning of the countryside (temporarily, granted, but for long enough to give the impression that the situation was lasting forever), an entire vision of the world was transformed" (P. Borgeaud, "The Rustic," in *The Greeks*, ed. Vernant, 289–290). The Athenians, we should remember, had a half-century earlier already abandoned their countryside, and that evacuation had already marked their collective imagination (cf. Thuc. 2.16). Moreover, the events of 431 B.C., however dramatic they might have appeared at the time, very quickly after Dekeleia must have seemed a rather mild intrusion.

L. Foxhall ("Farming and Fighting in Ancient Greece," in *War and Society in the Greek World*, ed. J. Rich and G. Shipley [London, 1993], 134–145) devotes an article to a review of previous work on agricultural devastation; she cites no new primary sources but suggests that the tactic was not so much a catalyst for hoplite battle as a deliberate attempt to sow dissension among the populace. I am not sure how much the two ideas differ, since both infer that devastation was a goad for military response: we should imagine that in any consensual society there would always be arguments whether or not to muster the citizenry to fight decisively and that such tension would only increase in the fourth century with the decline of agrarian infantry and the gradual monetization of the economy. It is self-evident that burning grain and cutting trees and vines might anger many farmers to muster and fight in the open; and by the same token, as the nonfarming population grew, some citizens might not prefer to risk their lives to fight in the open for the land of others, arguing that the community's greater interest now lay in differing responses to invasion. In addition, some more circumspect farmers themselves might wish to save their lives rather than their crops or to preserve their harvests by submission. The sparing of individual farms of the wealthy such as Pericles (Thuc. 2.13.1–3) was not a common stratagem (cf. Polyaen. *Strat.* 2.10.3) and was used not so much to cause dissension among the demos as to embarrass political leaders with charges of alleged collusion with the enemy. Although Polyaenus devotes a chapter to the destruction and sparing of the enemy's land (*Strat.* 23), he cites no examples of armies that try to cause *stasis* among the walls between landed and landless.

Other than in reference to the unique circumstances at Athens during the Peloponnesian War—and even then the Athenians put up a remarkably united front—Foxhall cites no evidence of ravaging used by an invader primarily to create internal dissension between those farming and those not farming. In fact, in most instances the civic body is remarkably united. The case of Akanthos during the Peloponnesian War—a rare instance of capitulation, not of battle or evacuation into fortifications—is instructive and perhaps typical of the amazing social cohesion of Greek agrarian communities: *all* Akanthians could set aside their fundamental political differences when their community's viticulture was endangered, agreeing on the need for *collective* action—in this case capitulation in lieu of fighting—to save the vintage, which was the common livelihood of the polis (Thuc. 4.84, 88). There is also the example of Plataia, which put up a united front when threatened by Archidamos (Thuc. 2.13.1, 2.71.1). (See also S. Mitchell, "Hoplite Warfare in Ancient Greece," in *Battle in Antiquity*, ed. A. B. Lloyd [London, 1996], 104 n. 34; and J. Ober, *Fortress Attica: Defense of the Athenian Land Frontier, 404–322 B.C.* [Leiden, 1985], 34–36, for a review of the psychological, spiritual, and religious reasons that devastation often continued to draw out hoplite armies, even when the community's economic livelihood was not really in danger of thorough destruction by enemy invasions.) We should also remember, despite the comedies of Aristophanes and the anguish recorded in Thucydides, that the Periclean policy of evacuation was followed by the citizenry, and that the Athenians displayed a remarkable degree of social cohesion during the war.

S. Hodkinson and H. Hodkinson ("Mantineia and the Mantinike: Settlement and Society in a Greek Polis," *Annual of the British School at Athens* 76 [1981]: 239–296, esp. 289–290) present an excellent discussion of the flexibility of response at ancient Mantineia, where the citizenry—without insurrections—employed a variety of strategies to oppose enemy invaders. Citizens in the last quarter of the fifth century and the first half of the fourth century B.C. sometimes evacuated and abandoned their countryside but on other occasions preferred pitched hoplite battle to protect either their population or their land, as the severity of the crisis dictated. There is a very brief but sensible synopsis of agricultural devastation in A. B. Burford, *Land and Labor in Ancient Greece* (Baltimore, 1993), 159–162, which, after a review of the agricultural context, concludes that long-term destruction was probably rare.

Page 15. Plunder and Devastation as Separate Activities.

The fifth volume of W. K. Pritchett's *Greek State at War* (Berkeley, 1991) is devoted to the vocabulary of booty and the various mechanisms of organized plundering. Pritchett's comprehensive study reaffirms that although armies routinely might destroy what they could not use, and steal as they demolished, the tactic of systematic agricultural devastation was usually a much different operation than organized plundering—the former being more a tactical option entailing destruction, the latter an economic interest in material acquisition. On war parties that are concerned primarily with plunder and booty, see now also P. McKechnie, *Outsiders in the Greek Cities in the Fourth Century B.C.* (London, 1989), 101–141; and, in general, P. Brulé, *La piraterie crétoise hellénistique*, Annales littéraires de l'Université Besançon 223

(Besançon, 1978). Plundering—which transfers rather than destroys wealth—is far more frequent in ancient historical and philosophical sources than simple devastation, and thus the subject now of an enormous secondary literature.

CHAPTER 1. MILITARY ORGANIZATION

Page 21. Light-Armed Troops.

Most scholarship since 1983 has stressed the increasing importance of light-armed troops in military conflict after the Peloponnesian War. M. Sage, for instance, has now collected some of the better-known passages reflecting the use of light-armed troops in the fourth century in *Warfare in Ancient Greece* (London, 1996), 141–147. As the strategic and tactical lessons of the Peloponnesian War became known, and as the old equation between hoplite soldier and yeoman farmer became less exclusive, city-states more frequently began to equip their own poor as skirmishers and to hire mercenaries on the open market (see J. Ober, *Fortress Attica: Defense of the Athenian Land Frontier, 404–322 B.C.* [Leiden, 1985], 45–50, 203–204). We should assume, then, that in the late fourth century light-armed troops were represented in larger percentages both in armies of invasion and as defenders used in concert with rural fortifications (see, for example, M. Munn, *The Defense of Attica: The Dema Wall and the Boiotian War of 378–375 B.C.* [Berkeley, 1993], 48–50, 105–109, 226–228). The clear implication is that plundering, raiding, and devastation became often as much the goals of invasion as simple challenges to hoplite battle. Still, I am not convinced that such changes in strategy equate with greater damage done to permanent crops such as fruit trees and vines: more mobile attackers might be met by more numerous light-armed defenders—and such troops were only slightly less vulnerable to cavalry attacks than were hoplites (see, for example, I. G. Spence, "Perikles and the Defence of Attika during the Peloponnesian War," *Journal of Hellenic Studies* 110 [1990]: 100). The use of peltasts and mobile infantry troops to attack and protect rural property was not per se a substitute for hoplite battle—the great hoplite encounters of Greek history are fourth-century events: Nemea, second Koroneia, Leuktra, second Mantineia, Chaironeia—but a reflection of how often the results of hoplite battle were indecisive, not accepted by the majority of the populace, or irrelevant in economic terms to the livelihood of the polis (see, among others, V. D. Hanson, *The Other Greeks: The Agrarian Roots of Western Civilization* [New York, 1995], 327–355). True, Epameinondas's invasions of the Peloponnese, with their ongoing occupation of rural territory, liberation of helots, and efforts at founding fortified points of resistance, did more to harm the Spartan state than even the catastrophic loss at Leuktra, but such a formidable army of invasion had at its core the crack agrarian hoplites of Thebes, who in a pinch could sweep away any opposition on level ground. And we should remember that reactionary states like Sparta attempted in the fourth century to use hoplites exclusively—perhaps even as unassisted ravagers on campaigns (e.g., Xen. *Hell.* 6.5.7).

Page 23. Hoplite Attendants.

For the idea that hoplite attendants were nearly always slaves, see now V. D. Hanson, "Thucydides and the Desertion of Attic Slaves during the Decelean War," *Classical Antiquity* 11.2 (1992): 210–228; M. H. Jameson, "Agricultural Labor in Ancient Greece," in *Agriculture in Ancient Greece*, ed. B. Wells, Proceedings of the Seventh International Symposium at the Swedish Institute at Athens, 16–17 May 1990 (Stockholm, 1992), 141. I know no other evidence for free citizens being hired as hoplite attendants other than the passage from Isaeus cited here. In the case of agricultural devastation, we should not imagine an entire host of young relatives and hired poor accompanying the phalanx as baggage carriers, who might double as light-armed ravagers. Rather, most such porters would be slaves, and their use in unsupervised, unchecked, and indiscriminate crop devastation would be problematic, if not almost nonexistent.

Page 30. Epiteichismos.

For additional discussion of evidence that permanent forts harmed the countryside by keeping farmers away from their crops, see J. Ober, *Fortress Attica: Defense of the Athenian Land Frontier, 404–322 B.C.* (Leiden, 1985), 36–38. Robin Osborne's *Classical Landscape with Figures: The Ancient Greek City and Its Countryside* (London, 1987), has an instructive chapter (pp. 137–166) on the relationship between the decline in hoplite exclusivity and the rise of rural fortification, light-armed troops, and the employment of mercenaries. In "Farming and Fighting in Ancient Greece," in *War and Society in the Greek World*, ed. J. Rich and G. Shipley (London 1993), 140, L. Foxhall remarks that *"epiteichismos* might have had most impact when it came to circumventing the problem of arriving at the right moment to do maximum damage to the cereal crop. This point goes unnoticed by Ober and Hanson." But see *Warfare and Agriculture*, 28 (present edition, page 29): "In the classic instances of *epiteichismos*, we usually hear of the activity of thieves and plunderers, exiles, runaway slaves, *and the loss of access to farms*" (emphasis now added). See also J. Ober, *Fortress Attica*, 43.

Page 33. Seasonal Considerations.

In 1990 I.G. Spence ("Perikles and the Defence of Attika during the Peloponnesian War," *Journal of Hellenic Studies* 110 [1990]: 101), citing modern studies in the United Kingdom, confirmed ("cf. the discussion at Hanson 42–6 [present edition, pages 33–34], which basically agrees with my views") that the period of grain combustion is very short—

coinciding with ripeness at harvest—and thus difficult to achieve on any broad scale.

CHAPTER 2. THE METHODS
OF AGRICULTURAL DEVASTATION

Page 43. Size of Farms.

There is now a vast secondary literature that draws on epigraphic, archaeological, and literary evidence in corroborating the idea of small, equitable farm size in classical Greece. See the synopses of research in two important articles by M. Jameson: "Agricultural Labor in Ancient Greece," in *Agriculture in Ancient Greece*, ed. B. Wells, Proceedings of the Seventh International Symposium at the Swedish Institute at Athens, 16–17 May 1990 (Stockholm, 1992), 135–146; "Class in the Ancient Greek Countryside," in *Structures rurales et sociétés antiques*, ed. P. Doukellis and L. Mendoni (Paris, 1994), 55–63. See also T. Boyd and M. Jameson, "Urban and Rural Land Division in Ancient Greece," *Hesperia* 50.4 (1980): 327–342. A comprehensive discussion of the secondary literature through the early 1990s—both for and against the idea of middling farms—and a review of the ancient evidence for moderate holdings are found in V. D. Hanson, *The Other Greeks: The Agrarian Roots of Western Civilization* (New York, 1995), 181–200. The topic is of great relevance to the entire question of agricultural devastation in classical Greece, since the hoplite was fighting to defend or attack land that was widely and privately held, often lived on, owned outright with clear rights of land tenure and inheritance, nearly inalienable, and in many poleis serving as the prerequisite for citizenship itself. Thus the attack on a yeoman citizen's farm might have graver psychological, spiritual, and political consequences for the community at large than would have attacks on *latifundia* of the imperial absentee grandee, which were worked and lived on mostly by serfs, bailiffs, and slaves.

Page 44. The Ubiquity of Fences and Terrace Walls.

See now A. B. Burford, *Land and Labor in Ancient Greece* (Baltimore, 1993), 60, 65, 109, 111, 113, 116, 139, 157; S. Isager and J. E. Skydsgaard, *Ancient Greek Agriculture: An Introduction* (London, 1993), 4, 72, 81–82; and the archaeological material presented by H. Lohmann, "Landleben in klassischen Attika," *Jahrbuch der Ruhr-Universität Bochum*, 1985: 71–96; H. Lohmann, "Agriculture and Country Life in Classical Athens," in *Agriculture in Ancient Greece*, ed. B. Wells, Proceedings of the Seventh International Symposium at the Swedish Institute at Athens, 16–17 May 1990 (Stockholm, 1992), 29–57. O. Rackman and J. A. Moody ("Terraces," in *Agriculture in Ancient Greece*, ed. Wells, 123–133) are correct to remind us of the confusing ancient nomenclature for terraces and the difficulty in attributing modern remains to ancient farms. Yet L. Foxhall's declaration ("Feeling the Earth Move: Cultivation Techniques on Steep Slopes in Classical Antiquity," in *Human Landscapes in Classical Antiquity*, ed. G. Shipley and J. Salmon [London, 1996], 45) that "any claimed finds of agricultural terraces dating back to classical antiquity or beyond" are unconvincing seems to me somewhat excessive. Nor can we be sure that trenching was the more common strategy of cultivation on hillsides or that terracing was practiced only by wealthy farmers. The presence of terraces confirms the idea that much productive farmland was on difficult hillsides, hard to locate, and when found hard to reach—there were impediments aplenty for ravagers to climb over. See O. Rackman, "Ancient Landscapes," in *The Greek City, From Homer to Alexander*, ed. O. Murray and S. Price (Oxford, 1990), 102–111.

Page 48. Rural Residence and Isolated Farmhouses.

Despite the arguments of R. Osborne (most notably in *Demos: The Discovery of Classical Attika* [Cambridge, 1985], 15–60, 190–195; and "Is It a Farm?" in *Agriculture in Ancient Greece*, ed. B. Wells, Proceedings of the Seventh International Symposium at the Swedish Institute at Athens, 16–17 May 1990 [Stockholm, 1992], 21–28), the scholarly consensus supports the idea that the Greeks often lived out in the countryside. Hence the original statement in *Warfare and Agriculture* (41; present edition, page 48) remains today a correct, if not a conservative, generalization: "We should assume that in the ancient Greek countryside, as today, there were all types of rural settlement. Small villages, to be sure, may have been prevalent, but there were countless farmers who, for whatever reason, chose to live on their land in single, isolated farmhouses." For the idea of a mixed pattern of settlement—farmhouses, villages, small clusters of farmers—in a heavily populated countryside, see also H. Lauter, "Zu Heimstätten und Gutshäusern im klassischen Attika," in *Forschungen und Funde: Festschrift B. Neutsch* (Innsbruck, 1980), 270. The epigraphical, archaeological, and literary evidence for homestead farms is immense but is now summarized in a variety of studies that refute systematically the argument of exclusively nucleated settlement both in and outside of Attica. See, for example, J. Roy, "The Countryside in Classical Greek Drama, and Isolated Farms in Dramatic Landscapes," in *Human Landscapes in Classical Antiquity*, ed. G. Shipley and J. Salmon (London, 1996), 98–118; J. Roy, "Demosthenes 55 as Evidence for Isolated Farmsteads in Classical Attica," *Liverpool Classical Monthly* 13 (1988): 57–59; M. Langdon, "On the Farm in Classical Athens," *Classical Journal* 86 (1991): 209–213; Y. Suto, "Isolated Farms in Classical Attica," *Kodai* 4 (1993): 1–19; F. Frost, "A Submerged Settlement at Skyllaieis," in *Archaeology of Coastal Changes*, ed. A. Rabin, BAR International Series 404 (Oxford, 1988), 50–51; and V. D. Hanson, *The Other Greeks: The Agrarian Roots of Western Civilization* (New York, 1995), 50–60, 454. For a helpful catalogue of rural sites in the Argolid, see now M. H. Jameson, C. N. Runnels, and T. H. van Andel, *A Greek Countryside: The Southern Argolid from Prehistory to the Present Day* (Stanford, 1994), 246–257. One of the ironies of interpretation of many recent field surveys of the Greek countryside is that most have turned up definite scattered clusters of pottery, roof tiles, and other remains, which clearly suggest rural habitation and intensification of land use— often quite contrary to the presuppositions of most archaeologists, who have assumed a "peasant" model of ancient rural life characterized by residence in nucleated urban settlements, commuting, small fragmented holdings, and extensive land use. Thus the extent to which some survey conclusions deny the data of their own investigations is often quite remarkable—the more so since such clusters and finds vary enormously by chronological period: whatever the finds represent, they exist at some periods and not at others. For the field's reluctance to associate such clusters with rural habitation or farms, see, for example, the discussion of A. M. Snodgrass, "Survey Archaeology and the Rural Landscape," in *The Greek City, From Homer to Alexander*, ed. O. Murray and S. Price (Oxford, 1990), 128. For the suggestion that such finds represent farms, but only of a "brief" occupation, see L. Foxhall, "A View from the Top: Evaluating the Solonian Property Classes," in *The Development of the Polis in Archaic Greece*, ed. L. Mitchell and P. Rhodes (London, 1997), 113–137, esp. 135 n. 87. For the idea that such finds are merely manure dump sites, see the critical discussion in S. Alcock, "Intensive Survey, Agricultural Practice and the Classical Landscape of Greece," in *Classical Greece: Ancient Histories and Modern Archaeologies*, ed. I. Morris (Cambridge, 1994), esp. 143–170. It is often forgotten that we have both a sizable corpus of literary passages that clearly refer to isolated residences and excavated farmhouses throughout the ancient Greek-speaking world. One wonders what the response of survey archaeologists would have been had their surveys turned up no rural finds at all.

The clear picture from tragedy, comedy, oratory, and history is that many Greeks lived on their small farms at a single location and thus were hypersensitive to trespassing over their fields or near their homes. Clearly, ravaging was often a successful catalyst to classical hoplite battle, since much of the farmland attacked was not only the property, but also the residence and home, of defending infantrymen. A man, I think, will be more ready to fight an invader if he sees him rifling through his home than if the invader merely attacks the field in which he works.

Page 48. The Nature of Terrain and Farm Plots.

L. Foxhall remarks in "Farming and Fighting in Ancient Greece," in *War and Society in the Greek World,* ed. J. Rich and G. Shipley (London, 1993), 136–137, that *Warfare and Agriculture* failed to take into consideration the fragmented nature of Greek farms, and thus, given the small and separate nature of classical Greek farming plots, agricultural damage may have been even "patchier" than I had imagined. Farm fragmentation is a controversial issue, however, and the key, I think, is to ascertain the *class* of citizen involved. Two points should be made here: first, I pointed out repeatedly in the first edition that locale and terrain in ancient Greek agriculture might hamper ravaging: "Vast unbroken parcels owned by absentee landlords were rare, if not unknown" (37; present edition, page 43); "The small valleys and plains of Greece were instead broken up into small parcels whose borders were clearly delineated and often fenced"; "Nor were all farms on level, accessible ground"; "Fences, hills, small orchards, and vineyards all made progress slow" (41; present edition, page 48). Second, Foxhall uses the example of modern Methana almost exclusively to support her belief in the exclusivity of fragmented plots—a different notion from the acknowledgment of consolidated small plots on difficult terrain. She cites little ancient literary or archaeological evidence for fragmented holdings among the hoplite or middling agricultural classes as normal. Epigraphical sources, in fact, sometimes suggest just the opposite: even wealthier ancient Greek farmers preferred to consolidate their holdings whenever practicable by renting public and temple lands nearby, apparently in hopes of creating one contiguous parcel (see Robin Osborne, *Classical Landscape with Figures: The Ancient Greek City and Its Countryside* [London, 1987], 71). Citation of the *Attic Stelai,* where a few wealthy Athenians own one or more estates in different parts of Attica, is *not* evidence that the average Attic yeoman farmed multiple, tiny plots. In fact, it may show just the opposite: by the late fifth century B.C. wealthier Athenians through inheritance or sale had obtained farms that were not tiny fragments, but often of notable and constant size and a considerable pedigree, as well as consolidated in one place.

In any case, the difficulty of destroying the farmland of Greece has less to do with the nature of farm ownership (fragmentation versus consolidation) than with terrain (e.g., mountains, gullies, stream beds) and human response (e.g., terraces, fences, homestead residences). To explore the great plain of Boiotia—one of the most accessible regions in Greece—one must still traverse hundreds of tiny valleys, some nestled and nearly hidden among foothills. The idea that an ancient army could reach thousands of acres in these remote fields, much less destroy them, seems ludicrous. There is a good chapter on land reclamation far from the city proper, and cultivation on hillsides entitled *"Eschatia-*Land" in G. Audring's *Zur Struktur des Territoriums griechischer Poleis in archaischer Zeit (Nach den schriftlichen Quellen)* (Berlin, 1989), 81–103. On *eschatia,* or so-called marginal land, see also V. D. Hanson, *The Other Greeks: The Agrarian Roots of Western Civilization* (New York, 1995), 79–85. We should keep in mind that many of the earliest references in Greek literature to farms—Laertes' upland estate (Hom. *Od.* 24.212, 205–207; cf. 18.357–65, 4.757); Hesiod's father's farm near Ascra (Hes. *Op.* 640); men on the hills in the time of Peisistratus (Arist. *Ath. Pol.* 16.6; Diod. 9.37.2; Dio Chrys. 1.75.3; cf. Plut. *Sol.* 23.7)—refer to rugged and often marginal ground. The incorporation of such *eschatiai,* then, was not just a classical phenomenon, but one with a lengthy pedigree in Greek history.

Page 49. Fruit Trees Other Than Olives.

We should keep in mind that ravagers attacked all sorts of fruit orchards, ranging from figs to apples. Although other fruit trees may not have the extensive root system, tough bark and wood, and longevity of the olive, trees bearing pears, apples, and figs often have considerable roots and reach a comparable size. On widely planted fruit and cereal crops besides the triad of grain, vines, and olives—especially legumes—see now A. Sarpaki, "The Palaeoethnobotanical Approach: The Mediterranean Triad, or Is It a Quartet?", in *Agriculture in Ancient Greece*, ed. B. Wells, Proceedings of the Seventh International Symposium at the Swedish Institute at Athens, 16–17 May 1990 (Stockholm, 1992), 61–76. On the fig and ravaging, see L. Foxhall, "Farming and Fighting in Ancient Greece," in *War and Society in the Greek World*, ed. J. Rich and G. Shipley (London, 1993), 141.

Page 51. Destroying Grain.

In March, April, May, and June 1997 I attempted to set fire to a four-acre field of rye and barley on our small farm, which was planted the previous fall as part of a soil restoration project. It was impossible to light any stalks until the crop was thoroughly ripe in late May. By late June the unharvested barley was extremely combustible and, depending on the crop density of specific regions of the field, could often sustain a small fire. See, again, I. G. Spence, "Perikles and the Defence of Attika during the Peloponnesian War," *Journal of Hellenic Studies* 110 (1990): 101; Spence cites D. J. Watson, "Inflammability of Cereal Crops in Relation to Water Content," *Empire Journal of Experimental Agriculture* 18.71 (1950): 150–157, on cereal resistance to burning. It must have been difficult to reach dry grain before it was harvested. Only fields where the defenders had been surprised, driven off, and kept away, were torched, and then only from late May to late June (a few weeks later in the case of wheat, which ripened after barley).

Cutting, then, was probably the more common method, but it was far more time-consuming. P. Halstead ("Agrarian Ecology in the Greek Islands: Time Stress, Scale, and Risk," *Journal of Hellenic Studies* 109 [1989]: 41–55, esp. 47) notes that on present-day Amorgos it takes a man with a sickle about 1.5 days to cut one *stremma* of wheat—or about 6 days to scythe an acre. Of course, wheat harvesters would be more careful, thorough, and therefore slower than ravagers, but it seems improbable that enemy troops could quickly cut down vast acreages of standing cereal crops.

Page 51. Regional Considerations.

On June 4–5, 1997, wheat was being harvested on the Boiotian Plain near ancient Leuktra, Tanagra, and Haliartos, but on mountainous terraces in Arkadia near Andritsena it was still green and seemed days or even weeks away from cutting. In general, elevation (daytime and nighttime temperatures are lower, and there is greater humidity at higher altitudes), terrain (mountains tend to cast shadows and interrupt afternoon and morning sunlight), and soil variety (heavier, rockier soils are cooler, and poorer conductors of subterranean heat, than sandy loams) affect the harvest periods of both fruits and grains. It is a general rule of agriculture that the flatter the ground, the lower the elevation, the farther inland the location, and the sandier and finer the soil, the more rapid the maturation of crops. Nor should we forget that certain subspecies of grain, barley, and other cereals come to maturity more rapidly than standard strains. In general, subspecies of fruit and grains that ripen earlier do so at the expense of production: "early" ripening varieties produce smaller harvests. There is a valuable discussion of the ancient evidence for the varying harvest dates of cereals, olives, and vines in A. C. Brumfield, *The Attic Festivals of Demeter and Their Relation to the Agricultural Year* (Salem, N.H., 1981), 39–45. We should imagine that it was very difficult for ancient armies to calibrate their arrival times in enemy territory precisely with the ripening of the wheat and barley crops: various microclimates within a given region might delay or accelerate harvests; barley might precede wheat by as much as a month; invading hoplites would have their own harvests to bring in—those dates being just as variable as the fields of the enemy that they had invaded.

Page 56. Olive Trees: General Information.

For information on olives—species, cultivation, and processing—see now also M.-C. Amouretti, *Le pain et l'huile dans la Grèce* (Besançon, 1986); L. Foxhall, *Olive Culture in Ancient Greece: The Ancient Economy Revisited,* Bulletin of the Institute of Classical Studies, Supp. (London, 1996); M. H. Jameson, C. N. Runnels, and T. H. van Andel, *A Greek Countryside: The Southern Argolid from Prehistory to the Present Day* (Stanford, 1994), 268–276.

In discussions of fruit-tree devastation, often the sense of sheer expanse of terrain and cultivation is lost in our literary sources. But any historian who walks through the thousands of olives (many of them of unbelievable age and girth) between Delphi and Itea or hikes through the extensive orchards outside Kalamata can sense how futile a task it would have been for ancient armies, with hand tools, to fell these trees systematically. O. Rackman ("Ancient Landscapes," in *The Greek City, From Homer to Alexander,* ed. O. Murray and S. Price [Oxford, 1990], 104) remarks on one such enormous olive tree he found in Crete: "At Loutro in SW Crete I have myself found a gigantic olive-tree, which I estimate from its annual rings to be of Hellenistic date, growing in an old terrace-wall."

Since *Warfare and Agriculture* first appeared, I have recorded various experiences over the years in removing fruit trees and vines, to see whether the ancient impression in our sources that crop destruction was difficult rang true. In mid-April 1994, I chopped down with a hand ax a dying orange tree of some eighty years; its diameter was a little over three feet at the base (much smaller than most older olive trees in Greece). At age forty-one, it took me almost one hour to cut through the trunk, the blade of the ax had to be sharpened three times, and upon completion of the job the steel ax head was loose and had to be reattached to the handle. Next, I wrapped a heavy twenty-foot steel chain around the stump and hitched it to a 60-horsepower Massey-Ferguson 265 vineyard tractor. After thirty minutes of pulling the stump, and then ramming it with the tractor bumper, I ceased the unsuccessful effort. Then I hitched the stump with another chain to a second Ford 4000 55-horsepower tractor; my son and I pulled on the stump with both tractors at the same time, but to no avail. Then I flooded the field with water for three days. On the sixth day, only with effort was the tractor able to yank the orange stump and its massive roots out of the soaked earth.

Page 67. Regeneration of Olives and Time from Planting to Production.

I planted eighteen olives in 1982 in very poor, sandy soil that would grow little else; five years later all had sizable crops, which increased each subsequent bearing year, reaching near normal harvests a decade later (1992). Their removal by tractor and chain in 1995 at age thirteen took considerable effort. The first edition of *Warfare and Agriculture* was correct that the old idea of twenty to fifty years for olives to bear fruit is mistaken. Cf. D. J. Mattingly, "The Olive in the Roman World," in *Human Landscapes in Classical Antiquity*, ed. G. Shipley and J. Salmon (London, 1996), 219:

> It is commonly asserted that a new olive-tree will take up to twenty years to bear significant fruit. Certainly it is true that the olive is a long-term investment, with the labour input in the initial years far higher than for a mature tree; but trees grown from cuttings are capable of producing some fruit within five to eight years, and in good conditions the quantity may be quite substantial.

Mattingly also cites instances of modern orchards producing on average twenty kilograms of olives per tree in only six years.

The old idea of a near half-century—the often quoted "forty years"—to reach full production dies hard. Cf. S. Pomeroy, *Xenophon, Oeconomicus: A Social and Historical Commentary* (Oxford, 1994), 47: "Because olive-trees require forty years to reach maturity, if the Spartans did destroy the Athenians' olive-trees, the production of olives would have been interrupted for a generation. . . . Thus the Peloponnesian

War must have had a serious effect on Athenian agriculture." See also O. Solbrig and D. Solbrig, *So Shall You Reap: Farming and Crops in Human Affairs* (Washington, D.C., 1994), 115, which strangely cites *Warfare and Agriculture* (!) as proof that olive orchards were destroyed in the Peloponnesian War with decades of rural impoverishment the consequence: "During the Peloponnesian War, clashing Greek armies repeatedly destroyed the olive groves on which the economy rested. Olive-trees take fifteen to twenty years to produce for the first time, forty years before they are in full production. Their loss would cripple the rural economy of Greece."

I have never seen an olive tree in Greece, Italy, Spain, or the United States—with or without steady irrigation—that would take "fifteen to twenty years to produce for the first time." Scholars have never really defined "full production" in terms of the maximum weight of the fruit harvest per acre. Given wide variables in terrain, soils, weather, and species variety, it is hard to calibrate at what point a fruit tree reaches its optimum productive capacity, and what in actual weight that level of production is. I have had young quince trees produce heavy crops at six years of age, only to die completely at ten, when theoretically they could have produced much more. Modern peach orchards produce in three years and for commercial purposes are considered worn out by fifteen or twenty years. The ideal production level for peaches is reached somewhere between three and fifteen years. Again "full production" is an illusive term, since sometimes older trees with larger crops in "full production" produce poorer-quality fruit and are more susceptible to disease than younger trees. The key for the orchard is to produce as much quality fruit as possible—a goal not necessarily determined by either the age of the tree or the quantity of fruit on the tree.

Page 70. Vines.

On viticulture, see M.-C. Amouretti, "Oléculture et viticulture dans la Grèce antique," in *Agriculture in Ancient Greece*, ed. B. Wells, Proceedings of the Seventh International Symposium at the Swedish Institute at Athens, 16–17 May 1990 (Stockholm, 1992), 77–86; M.-C. Amouretti and J.-P. Brun, eds., *La production du vin et de l'huile en Méditerranée*, Bulletin de Correspondance Hellénique, Supp. 26 (Paris, 1993). See also S. Isager and J. E. Skydsgaard, *Ancient Greek Agriculture: An Introduction* (London, 1992), 26-33; A. B. Burford, *Land and Labor in Ancient Greece* (Baltimore, 1993), 100–166; and in general for grain, olives, and other fruit trees and cereals, pp. 21–43. On vine pruning and trellising, see V. D. Hanson, "Practical Aspects of Grape-Growing and the Ideology of Greek Viticulture," in *Agriculture in Ancient Greece*, ed. Wells, 161–166.

Vines can be pulled out rather easily by a modern vineyard tractor, and even more effortlessly rooted out—as is now the normal commercial practice in California—with a moderate-sized Caterpillar (e.g., D-6 or -8) with frontal blade. The problem, however, is the sheer number of vines per acre. If one uses the obsolete method of tractor and chain (hitching and yanking perhaps being the modern practice most resembling the ancient method of uprooting by either human power or horsepower), it can still take two men with tractor and chain several hours to remove 600 mature vines an acre (stumps a half foot in diameter, roots ten to fifteen feet in depth). In November 1989, for example, I chose to use a tractor and chain, and so tore out three acres of an eight-acre, 100-year-old Thompson vineyard (vines had been grafted onto wild rootstocks) with two fellow workers; it took the three of us with the tractor nearly two full working days to clear about three acres of vines (that is, about 1,800 vines and stakes). Yet the next spring nearly half the vines had resprouted from roots torn off and left in the ground. Herbicides and continual disking were necessary to kill the second-growth vinelets. Ancient armies must have almost never uprooted mature vines. L. Foxhall ("Farming and Fighting in Ancient Greece," in *War and Society in the Greek World*, ed. J. Rich and G. Shipley [London 1993], 138–139) suggested that in the first edition I discounted the damage to vines by "hoplites' great fat feet."

Page 75. Farm Towers.

An entire body of scholarship has been devoted to compiling a catalogue of explored and excavated rural towers in the Greek world. See M. Nowicka, "Les maisons à tour dans le monde grec," *Bibliotheca Antiqua* 15 (1975); Nowicka sensibly points out, as J. Young had earlier, that such structures could serve a dual purpose—useful on a daily basis and strategically important as fortified farms, where groups of rural residents might either store harvests or deposit belongings and ride out temporary enemy incursions. W. K. Pritchett has now surveyed, with a thorough bibliography, the scholarly controversy over the construction and use of *pyrgoi* in the Greek world (*The Greek State at War*, pt. 5 [Berkeley, 1991], 352–358 ["Towers in Rural Areas"]); he rightly concludes that most are in some way connected with agrarians' worry over unsettled conditions in the countryside. Thus despite challenges to J. Young's initial conclusions concerning southern Attica (e.g., R. Osborne, *Demos: The Discovery of Classical Attika* [Cambridge, 1985], 34), there seems no reason to doubt that many *pyrgoi* were, in fact, part of resident-occupied farming complexes:

> The Classical farmhouse tower is not simply a device for defence. Besides its function as a stronghold it also served as living quarters and as a place of refuge. Although these towers—even the stronger ones—could not have withstood an organised siege, they provided adequate protection against attacks by robbers or pillaging soldiers. (H. Lohmann, "Agriculture and Country Life in Classical Attica," in *Agriculture in Ancient Greece*, ed. B. Wells, Proceedings of the Seventh International Symposium at the Swedish Institute at Athens, 16–17 May 1990 [Stockholm, 1992], 39)

These studies suggest once again that farmers and rural populations may have been quite adept at evacuating, hiding, and protecting their property in times of crisis.

For the ubiquity of ancient agricultural buildings in general, see now S. Isager and J. E. Skydsgaard, *Ancient Greek Agriculture: An Introduction* (London, 1992), 67–82.

CHAPTER 3. FORTIFICATION

Page 82. Field Walls.

After the discussion of field walls and forts built to protect rural property appeared in the first edition of *Warfare and Agriculture*, three major works on Greek fortifications and Attic walls and towers that went well beyond the parameters of *Warfare and Agriculture* were published: J. Ober, *Fortress Attica: Defense of the Athenian Land Frontier, 404–322 B.C.*, Mnemosyne Supp. 84 (Leiden, 1985) (containing an invaluable catalogue of sites); H. Lauter, H. Lauter-Bufe, and H. Lohmann, *Attische Festungen: Beiträge zum Festungswesen und zur Siedlungsstruktur vom 5. bis zum 3. Jh. v. Ch.*, Marburger Winckelmann-Program (Marburg, 1988); and M. Munn, *The Defense of Attica: The Dema Wall and the Boiotian War of 378–375 B.C.* (Berkeley, 1993). I think the general arguments of the first edition of *Warfare and Agriculture*—the identifications of the Attic forts (which followed E. Vanderpool) and the ideas that field walls were impractical and that forts and towers were occasionally successful in deflecting enemy invasion only in the fourth century B.C.—remain valid. In general, Munn (pp. 47–62) envisions field walls as sophisticated tactical structures that enhance light-armed, mobile troops in their efforts to hamper and harass larger bodies of invading heavy infantry. Their purpose, then, is not so much to protect cropland per se as to allow innovative generals like Chabrias and Phokion to mount sustained lines of defense, with their skirmishers leaving and reentering fortified positions as they harass traditional infantry at strategic nexus. Ober likewise does not understand field walls as permanent components of border defense but sees them as roughly built, ad hoc structures raised quickly in times of emergency. Both interpretations emphasize the alternatives to traditional hoplite battle but in themselves do not imply that crop losses were now becoming too serious to depend on the efficacy of formal hoplite responses. L. Foxhall comments in "Farming and Fighting in Ancient Greece," in *War and Society in the Greek World*, ed. J. Rich and G. Shipley (London, 1993), 137: "Another agricultural resource of Athens that is rarely, if ever, mentioned was cultivable land within the city walls." This phenomenon was mentioned, however, in the first edition of *Warfare and Agriculture* (67 n. 3; present edition, page 80 n. 3, cf. 86), where I noticed occasional references in our sources to large empty spaces inside some of the larger city circuits.

Page 84. The Dema Wall.

On the Dema Wall, see M. Munn, *The Defense of Attica: The Dema Wall and the Boiotian War of 378–375 B.C.* (Berkeley, 1993), esp. 37–125. Munn conducted archaeological explorations of the site and believes that a pottery fragment, the so-called Dema saltcellar, dates the construction to a period ca. 400–375 and thus would link it to the similar though wooden wall around Theban cropland. The Dema Wall was designed, Munn argues (pp. 98–99), to prevent an enemy in the Plain of Eleusis from easy passage through the most accessible pass into the Plain of Athens. He believes Chabrias constructed it in 378 B.C. (see pages 70–71, notes 10–11, in the first edition of *Warfare and Agriculture;* present edition, pages 83–84, notes 10–11), in close consultation with the Thebans, as part of the overall strategies of both states to deny Kleombrotos and his large Peloponnesian army access to their respective rich interior plains. On the Theban stockade, see now M. Munn's "Agesilaos' Boiotian Campaigns and the Theban Stockade of 378–77 B.C.," *Classical Antiquity* 6 (1987): 106–138.

Page 91. Forts.

The excellent work of Ober, Munn, and Lauter (J. Ober, *Fortress Attica: Defense of the Athenian Land Frontier, 404–322 B.C.*, Mnemosyne Supp. 84

[Leiden, 1985]; M. Munn, *The Defense of Attica: The Dema Wall and the Boiotian War of 378–375 B.C.* [Berkeley, 1993]; H. Lauter, H. Lauter-Bufe, and H. Lohmann, *Attische Festungen: Beiträge zum Festungswesen und zur Siedlungsstruktur vom 5. bis zum 3. Jh. v. Ch.*, Marburger Winckelmann-Program [Marburg, 1988]) has resulted in an exhaustive, invaluable catalogue of the Attic forts and towers. For well-illustrated work on forts and towers also *outside* of Attica, see now J. Ober, "Early Artillery Towers: Messenia, Boiotia, Attica, Megarid," *American Journal of Archaeology* 91 (1987): 569–604; J.-P. Adam, *L'architecture militaire grecque* (Paris, 1982); and A. Lawrence, *Greek Aims in Fortification* (Oxford, 1979). The thrust of recent scholarship has been—as the first edition of *Warfare and Agriculture* perhaps suggested—to demonstrate thoroughly how state investments in fortification during the fourth century reflect new strategies of defense as alternatives to the old notion of pitched hoplite battle. Yet scholars disagree vehemently on both the purpose and the extent of these defensive investments. Munn (*Defense of Attica*), Lauter (*Attische Festungen*), and P. Harding ("Athenian Defensive Strategy in the Fourth Century," *Phoenix* 42 [1988]: 61–71; "Athenian Defensive Strategy Again," *Phoenix* 44 [1990]: 377–380) believe that fourth-century fortifications were used as bases for resistance and were not so much antithetical to the use of heavy infantry or indicative of new commitments to an exclusive defensive mentality as complementary avenues of protection that allowed states a greater range of choice when and when not to mobilize their traditional hoplite infantry forces: the enemy was sometimes allowed inside the border and then trapped, harassed, and cut off from fortified points and lines of resistance. Ober, in contrast, (cf. "The Defense of the Athenian Land Frontier: A Reply," *Phoenix* 43 [1989]: 294–301) sees a novel effort at preclusive defense (i.e., a "fortress"), in the era before sophisticated siegecraft and the catapults of Philip II. The idea is that in the early fourth century, with new tactics of light-armed and missile defense, improved techniques in fortification, and a general commitment to pay for rural construction ("defensivism"), states like Athens could now avoid invasion entirely: the enemy was unable to break through an impenetrable fortress of interconnected towers and forts. Each interpretation emphasizes that, in the aftermath of the Peloponnesian War and the near constant fighting of the Corinthian and Boiotian wars of the early fourth century, the protection of rural territory took on added importance. In this view, without its imperial revenues, Athens now sought to protect its agriculture and rural infrastructure in ways less costly than hoplite battle. Such investments do not suggest that fourth-century lighter-armed forces were now more adept at crop devastation itself, only perhaps that a smaller percentage of the population was willing or able to participate in traditional pitched hoplite battles, and thus novel methods and ideas of defense were felt to be necessary.

CHAPTER 4. EVACUATION

Page 104. Movable Property.

For a much fuller discussion of the types of movable rural property and Greek nomenclature for them, see now W. K. Pritchett, *The Greek State at War*, pt. 5 (Berkeley, 1991), 173–174, 198–203; cf. also my review of Pritchett's monumental five-volume work in *Classical Philology*, Fall 1992, 250–258. On the removal of woodwork from houses and the intrinsic value in the Greek world of wooden supports and frames, see now R. Meiggs, *Trees and Timber in the Ancient Mediterranean World* (Oxford, 1982), 208. There is a valuable catalogue of rural installations and implements—plows, hoes, spades, blades, threshing floors, winnowing equipment, and presses—in S. Isager and J. E. Skydsgaard, *Ancient Greek Agriculture: An Introduction* (London, 1992), 44–66. On the unusual ability of rural households to store considerable quantities of food, see T. Gallant, *Risk and Survival in Ancient Greece* (Stanford, 1991), 94–101.

Page 106. Aeneas Tacticus.

To read Aeneas Tacticus (especially now in conjunction with David Whitehead's excellent and accessible commentary, *Aineias the Tactician:*

How to Survive under Siege [Oxford, 1990]) is to appreciate how brilliant and insidious were the responses of the invaded to attack; most ancient historians' brief mention of evacuation before ravaging does not capture the ingenuity of evacuation, property dispersal, counterresponse, and intelligence so prominent in Aeneas's catalogue of Greek resistance to invasion. On the farmers' individual and group responses to both small and large invasions, see V. D. Hanson, *The Other Greeks: The Agrarian Roots of Western Civilization* (New York, 1995), 142–146.

Page 112. Places of Refuge.

A corpus of passages relating to evacuation and the transportation of property from one polis to another prior to incursions is found in H. Müller, "*Phugês heneken*," *Chiron* 5 (1975): 129–156; and see also again W. K. Pritchett, *The Greek State at War*, pt. 5 (Berkeley, 1991), 348–352. The literary and epigraphic sources reveal a remarkable level of complexity in rural planning, aimed at preserving property and life in the face of necessary abandonment of the countryside.

Page 119. Pollution of Waters.

See David Whitehead, *Aineias the Tactician: How to Survive under Siege* (Oxford, 1990), 115, for passages that suggest the fouling of water was sometimes in dire emergencies more common than we assume. For a much-needed defense of the historicity of Herodotus's account of the Skythian resistance to the Persian invasion, see now W. K. Pritchett, *The Liar School of Herodotos* (Amsterdam, 1993), 204–226.

CHAPTER 5. SORTIES

Page 122. Cavalry against Ravagers.

In the years since the first edition of *Warfare and Agriculture*, three books have appeared on Greek and Athenian cavalry: G. R. Bugh, *The*

Horsemen of Athens (Princeton, 1988), cf. 81–85; L. J. Worley, *The Cavalry of Ancient Greece* (Boulder, 1994), 83–122; and I. G. Spence, *The Cavalry of Classical Greece: A Social and Military History with Particular Reference to Athens* (Oxford, 1993), 121–133. The force of their argument has been that scholars often underestimate the value of ancient horsemen in general, and in particular the critical role played by the Athenian knights in the resistance to the invasion and occupation of the Attic countryside. Horsemen are very effective against infantry—usually out of formation and solitary or in small groups—engaged in destroying crops and (inevitably) seeking plunder. See also P. Rahe, "The Military Situation in Western Asia on the Eve of Cunaxa," *American Journal of Philology* 101 (1980): 79–86, which envisions a novel combination of Western infantry and Asian cavalry practices to mold new fourth-century forces that were more flexible in response.

CHAPTER 6. THE DEVASTATION OF ATTICA DURING THE PELOPONNESIAN WAR

Page 137. Periclean Strategy.

The debate over the nature, intent, and wisdom of Periclean strategy rages on. More to the point, the idea that agricultural devastation did not regularly ruin the farms of an invaded territory affects this larger discussion in a variety of ways. Did Pericles factor into his bold plan of deliberate evacuation the assumption that the Peloponnesian task of hurting the cropland of Attica would be difficult, and therefore have the more subtle aspects of his strategy been underappreciated? And were countermeasures such as cavalry responses more effective and integral than we have imagined in Periclean policy, suggesting that the old characterization of a "defensive strategy" is rather simplistic? There are several varieties of this new revisionist argument that Periclean strategy has been too harshly criticized and was far less "defensive" than we are led to believe.

J. Ober ("Thucydides, Pericles, and the Strategy of Defense," in *The Craft of the Ancient Historian: Essays in Honor of Chester G. Starr*, ed. J. W.

Eadie and J. Ober [New York, 1985], 171–189; republished in *The Athenian Revolution* [Princeton, 1996], 72–85) believes that Athenian cavalry responses and rural garrisons were effective in minimizing the damage to Attica. Yet Thucydides did not emphasize this defensive strength in his earlier portraits of Periclean strategy: to state that Pericles made elaborate plans to protect farms was antithetical to the Thucydidean dramatic picture of an entire people—on orders of Pericles—surrendering their land and trekking inside the walls. In contrast, I. G. Spence ("Perikles and the Defence of Attika during the Peloponnesian War," *Journal of Hellenic Studies* 110 [1990]: 91–109) believes that Pericles simply did not appreciate the potential of cavalry responses in his pre-war speeches; once horsemen showed themselves effective in limiting ravaging, Thucydides quite naturally included that fact in his later narrative: Thucydides simply records the sequence of events, and from his text we properly are to assume Pericles' corollary idea of occasional cavalry patrols evolved on its own into a far more effective means of defense as the war progressed. Spence, despite his disagreement, generally follows Ober's argument that the complexity and response integral to Periclean policy is not fully appreciated in Thucydides' narrative.

Peter Krentz ("The Strategic Culture of Periclean Athens," in *Polis and Polemos*, ed. C. Hamilton and P. Krentz [Claremont, Calif., 1997], 55–72) also acknowledges the ineffectiveness of Peloponnesian devastation and the effectiveness of the Athenian countermeasures. He suggests that the Peloponnesians mistakenly invaded with too large an army, precluding any realistic hope that the Athenians would meet them in a hoplite battle among equals—a battle that the Spartans most likely would have won. Thus had they just brought fewer hoplites, they would have avoided a decade-long war of attrition that they could not win through seasonal invasion and ravaging. (It seems odd, though, to criticize an ancient army for mustering too many troops when their intention was to meet an adversary in open battle.) All such arguments now assume agricultural devastation of Attica during the Archidamian War was rather ineffective. See also now L. Kallet-Marx, *Money, Expense, and Naval Power in Thucydides' "History" 1–5.24* (Berkeley, 1993), 109–151.

Page 138. Thucydides and the Description of the Archidamian War.

It should be remembered that Archidamos himself is made to say at Thucydides 1.81.1 (cf. 2.113–115) that the war would not cease just because his men ravaged Attica—a thought perhaps inserted or revised by Thucydides in light of the later poor record of the five invasions either to end the war or to damage Athens materially. See now S. Hornblower, *A Commentary on Thucydides*, vol. 1, *Books I–III* (Oxford, 1991), 126, 258, 273.

Page 140. Aristophanes and the Ravaging of Attica.

The idea that Aristophanic comedy is proof of ruined Attic agriculture remains strong. E. David, *Aristophanes and Athenian Society* (Leiden, 1984), cites no ancient archaeological, epigraphic, or literary evidence for the following rather amazing statement:

> However, those who suffered most, economically, were the farmers. . . . These social elements, which had previously formed one of the cornerstones of economic stability in Attika and elsewhere, were now faced with difficulties with which, in many cases, they could not cope. Many of them lost all hope of improving the situation in their fields. Some were compelled to sell their estates; others could not even do that, since their land was in such poor condition as a result of devastation caused by the war: as a result they decided to abandon it. Those who had tried, in spite of everything, to rehabilitate themselves by means of loans were often hopelessly burdened with debt, and sooner or later, became paupers. After having abandoned, sold, or lost their land, these agrarian elements were to join the ranks of the agricultural or urban proletariat. (3)

Aristophanes' references to ravaged crops are essential to the comedian's general and often rural parody on the futility of the war; but the mention of ravaged private orchards and vineyards does not equate to the destruction of the vast acreage of Attica. True, labor power losses to war and plague, the introduction of new taxes and tithes, and the loss of overseas tribute affected agriculture (cf. the use of plundered goods on Attic farms in the fifth century at *Hell. Oxy.* 12.5); but the general good health of the Athenian economy in the early fourth century was possible only because orchards, vineyards, and infrastructure were not ruined, and farmers had not been driven off the land to join the ranks of some mythical urban mob.

Systematic field survey has, curiously, for the most part ignored Attica, which despite the Athenian megalopolis still includes much empty countryside; yet the few studies that have appeared are suggestive. The Stanford Skourta Plain project (in northwestern Attica in the vicinity of a major ancient invasion route) found a proliferation of sites identified as ancient farmsteads in the classical period, reaching the greatest density at the end of the fourth century B.C. (cf. M. Munn, "On the Frontiers of Attica and Boiotia: The Results of the Stanford Skourta Plain Project," in *Essays in the Topography, History, and Culture of Boiotia*, ed. A. Schachter [Montreal, 1990], 33–40; "Studies on the Attic-Boiotian Frontier: The Stanford Skourta Project," in *Boeotia Antiqua*, vol. 1, *Papers on Recent Work in Boiotian Archaeology and History*, ed. J. Fossey [Amsterdam, 1989], 73–127). H. Lohmann argued in the works listed below from archaeological evidence that there was a clear pattern of rural settlement in southern Attica in the late fifth and fourth centuries. Only at the *end* of the fourth century B.C. does a cycle of impoverishment and rural depopulation begin. This downturn in the late fourth and third centuries is more or less consistent with other surveys (and literary evidence): David's rural picture of farmers "who could not cope" belongs at least a century *after* the Peloponnesian War and was more likely due to insidious phenomena such as taxation, the growing gap between the wealthy and the poor, and structural changes in agrarianism where local landed councils lost their ability to control the political and military agenda of the polis—challenges far more grievous to agriculture than enemy invasions. Cf. H. Lohmann, "Atene, eine attische Landgemeinde klassischer Zeit," *Hellenika Jahrbuch* (1983): 98–117; "Landleben im klassischen Attika," *Jahrbuch der Ruhr-Universität Bochum* (1985): 71–96, esp. 91–92; "Agriculture and Country Life in Classical Attica," in *Agriculture in Ancient Greece*, ed. B. Wells, Proceedings of the Seventh International Symposium at the Swedish Institute at Athens, 16–17 May 1990 (Stockholm, 1992), 29–60. There is a fine summary of survey results in S. Alcock, "Breaking up the Hellenistic World: Survey and Society," in *Classical Greece: Ancient Histories and Modern Archaeologies*, ed. I. Morris (Cambridge, 1994), 177–178:

> At some point in the Hellenistic period, however, a radical alteration in the distribution of settlement and in land-use practices took place; this shift is visible to a greater or lesser extent in all the areas consulted. In some of the survey projects, the change can be dated very approximately to the mid-third century B.C. A sharp drop in rural site numbers, pointing to a slackening in agricultural production and therefore some measure in population decline, marks this later Hellenistic development. An increasing preference for nucleated residence, in cities or large villages, may also partly explain this trend. Of those sites remaining in the rural landscape, peasant cottages in many cases now gave way to more substantial properties, suggesting the growth of significant agricultural estates.

On the general inequity in farmland holdings in the Hellenistic period, and the considerable change from the land tenure of the classical polis, see H. Kreissig, "Landed Property in the 'Hellenistic' Orient," *Eirene* 15 (1977): 5–26.

Page 144. The Inscription from Eleusis.

See the text and commentary by M. B. Cavanaugh, *Eleusis and Athens: Documents in Finance, Religion, and Politics in the Fifth Century* B.C. (Atlanta, Ga., 1996); Cavanaugh would date the firstfruits decree a decade earlier, in the 430s.

Page 145. The Sacred Olives and the Atthidographers.

On the Attic laws protecting the sacred olives (*moriai*), see S. C. Todd, *The Shape of Athenian Law* (Oxford, 1995), 307–308; P. J. Rhodes, *A Commentary on the Aristotelian "Athenaion Politeia"* (Oxford, 1981), 672–674; C. Carey, *Lysias, Selected Speeches* (Cambridge, 1989), 114–115.

P. Harding, *Androtion and Athens* (Oxford, 1994), 149–150, also has a helpful note on the *moriai* and the tradition of the Atthidographers that they were spared during the Peloponnesian War. The name *moria* probably derives from the notion that a select few olives constituted Athena's share (*morion*) of all the Attic olive trees. See also now the useful appendix "The Sacred Olives" in S. Isager and J. E. Skydsgaard, *Ancient Greek Agriculture: An Introduction* (London, 1992), 203–205.

There must have been no easy way for a Greek to have distinguished a sacred olive tree from a private one. The speaker in Lysias's seventh oration refers to the uprooting/removal of the tree/stump in question both as a *sêkos* and as a *moria*. L. Foxhall's suggestion (quoted in Todd, *The Shape of Athenian Law*, 308 n. 21) may well be right that the removal of a *sêkos* (Lys. 7.2, 5, 11, 14, 15, 17) may refer not to the stump itself, but to the fence surrounding the earmarked sacred olives: the destruction of markers identifying olives as public property allowed owners to pass them off as normal trees, and thus they might have gained some greater leeway in doing with them as they wished. What bothered farmers about a *moria* was apparently not so much its inviolate status and the fact that public officials might intrude to inspect the tree and gather its crop as the enclosure and sizable area of land that had to be kept clear around the tree itself—the ground that was set aside might disrupt or encroach upon other cultivation (e.g., Lys. 7.14). In any case, in Lysias's seventh oration *sêkos* seems to be used indistinguishably for both "fence" and "stump." Such ancestral sacred olives (*moriai*) must have been clearly fenced and marked and thus would have been easily identified and so spared when Archidamos's ravagers arrived in Attica in 431 B.C.

Page 154. The Hellenica Oxyrhynchia *and the Countryside of Attica.*

The Oxyrhynchus Historian, it should be remembered, not only says that the Attica countryside suffered little during the Archidamian invasions (*epeponthei gar mikra kakôs en tais embolais tais emprosthen*, 12.5), but also that Attica at the time of Dekeleia was the "most lavishly furnished in all of Greece" (*hê chôra polutelestata tês Hellados kataskeuasto*)—after five Peloponnesian invasions the farms of Attica were not merely undamaged but remained the most impressive in Greece. And although the conclusion of section 12 (17 Bartoletti) is corrupt and so sometimes neglected, the general sense of agricultural renaissance is again clear enough: "It [the *chôra* of Athens] had been adorned and improved to such a degree . . . " The section finishes with the suggestion that the Athenians in fact had brought plunder from subject states to improve the quality of their own Attic estates: "Whatever they took in war from the Greeks they brought back to their own farms" (*ha pa[ra tô]n Hellên[ôn polemounte]s elambanon eis tou[s idio]us agrous a[nêgage]*). It is clear that the Oxyrhynchus Historian was referring to agricultural conditions in Attica before and during the time of Dekeleia (cf. the *tote* at the beginning of 12.5), not in the fourth-century aftermath of the war, as suggested by S. Pomeroy (*Xenophon, Oeconomicus: A Social and Historical Commentary* [Oxford, 1994], 47), among others.

On this passage see V. D. Hanson, "Thucydides and the Desertion of Attic Slaves during the Decelean War," *Classical Antiquity* 11.2 (1992): 210–228; P. R. McKechnie and S. J. Kern provide an accessible text and translation in *Hellenica Oxyrhynchia* (Warminister, 1988), 87–89. It should be remembered that the Oxyrhynchus passage may have been derived from Thucydides 7.27.5 (cf., for example, I. A. F. Bruce, *An Historical Commentary of the "Hellenica Oxyrhynchia"* [Cambridge, 1976], 115–116). If so, it would seem that the anonymous historian took Thucydides to mean two things: (1) there was little damage from the Archidamian War, and thus (2) the focus of the Dekeleian garrison was easy plunder, rather than agricultural devastation—an activity mentioned by neither author in association with Dekeleia.

Page 154. The Flight of 20,000 Slaves.

The first edition of *Warfare and Agriculture* did not sufficiently emphasize (as P. Harvey rightly pointed out in "New Harvests Reappear: The Impact of War on Agriculture," *Athenaeum* 74 [1986]: 215–216) the loss of these "two myriads" of slaves, who must have largely been employed in agriculture, thus resulting in severe labor shortages on farms at the end of the war and in the immediate postwar period. In a later journal article, I tried to rectify the absence of a lengthy discussion concerning the 20,000 in the first edition of *Warfare and Agriculture*. For the argument that "the more than twenty thousand slaves" who deserted were engaged largely in agriculture, and that such a calamity—quite different from supposed losses to orchards and vines—had a short-term but serious effect on Attic agriculture, see V. D. Hanson, "Thucydides and the Desertion of Attic Slaves during the Decelean War," *Classical Antiquity* 11.2 (1992): 210–228.

A. B. Burford has a useful note on problems in interpretation of the 20,000, both on where the slaves were employed and the problems of Thucydides knowing their general number (*Land and Labor in Ancient Greece* [Baltimore, 1993], 266 n. 81).

Page 158. Lysias's Seventh Oration on the Olive Stump.

See now the helpful commentary of C. Carey, *Lysias, Selected Speeches* (Cambridge, 1989), 114–141. Since Attic tradition as reflected by

Aristophanes and Thucydides suggested that the deme of Acharnai was especially hit hard, it is surprising to hear that the speaker's farm, which apparently was in just that general area, had olives that were left untouched. Carey suggests that the devastations may have affected "subsistence and marginal producers" more severely than I had recognized, since they could ill afford even moderate disruptions and losses. But "losses" must be qualified—are we to assume cut-down trees and vines, meaning long-term damage to those crops, or loss of grain, livestock, and slaves, which in theory could be replaced more quickly? Second, I think the notion that Attica was a countryside replete with peasant or small subsistence farmers is sorely mistaken. If we are to look for the poor, they are more likely to be found in towns, and not among the hoplite landowners of five- to twenty-acre plots, who were predominant and viable throughout Greece until the Hellenistic period. In general, see M. H. Jameson, "Agricultural Labor in Ancient Greece," in *Agriculture in Ancient Greece*, ed. B. Wells, Proceedings of the Seventh International Symposium at the Swedish Institute at Athens, 16–17 May 1990 (Stockholm, 1992), 144:

> In any case, the notion of a mass of self-sufficient, independent
> subsistence farmers as the backbone of Athenian society becomes
> very questionable. It seems much more likely that the bulk of
> Classical Athenian farmers were in the hoplite class, had at
> least one male slave and generally lived above the subsistence
> level, as in most of the more populous and prosperous parts of
> Greece. . . . For most [the poor], their livelihood was not based
> in the countryside but in the town and the port.

The property in question in Lysias's seventh oration once belonged to Peisander and then, after being confiscated, was sold later and resold in the period between 411 and the early fourth century. The liquidity of the land in question does not suggest agricultural depression or the flight of the poor as much as greater mobility in rural property. The rich sought to buy, sell, and lease land in an ever more profit-oriented countryside—a process well under way before the Peloponnesian War. See, for example, R. Osborne, "The Potential Mobility of Human Populations," *Oxford Journal of Archaeology* 10.2 (1991): 246–247.

Page 158. Demosthenes' Forty-Third Oration and Hagnias's Olives.

L. Foxhall, in a response in *Agriculture in Ancient Greece*, ed. B. Wells, Proceedings of the Seventh International Symposium at the Swedish Institute at Athens, 16–17 May 1990 (Stockholm, 1992), 86, argues that Hagnias's olives were not uprooted later by the heirs (*premnizein*), but that merely the ovules (*premna*) were removed, to facilitate propagation of new olive trees. It is an ingenious hypothesis, but there are a few points to consider: in my own experience, not all olives or other fruit trees necessarily bear ovules—the subspecies, type of cultivation, rootstock, type of graft, and age of the tree affect both such secondary growths and other types of trunk suckering—only large, older trees produce ovules and then perhaps only one or two per tree. Second, taking cuttings from trees does not necessarily damage the donor, and thus if this impressive orchard was not destroyed but had been left more or less intact, it is hard to see why the speaker was so upset.

Are we to believe that Sostheos, the speaker, is suing because Theopompus has removed some growths from the trunks of some of his many hundred trees? And would a jury really believe Sostheos that Theopompus had violated the Attic laws concerning the uprooting of olives by merely harvesting ovules? And would such harvesting be considered a sacrilege against community reverence if Theopompus's purpose was not to destroy an orchard, but in fact to propagate a new one without harming the old? We should remember too that the verb used at Demosthenes 43.69 is *exorutton*, "they were uprooting"—not "they cut"—and thus an odd reference to the harvesting of ovules. It was a heinous crime not because Theopompus cut down the trees—after all, the orchard might be saved when sucker growth quickly reappeared—but because he *uprooted* the trees entirely—no doubt either to free the land for other purposes or to sell the sizable stumps and roots for wood or fuel: "These trees they dug up (*exorruton*) and rooted out (*ekpremnizon*), more than a thousand stumps (*stelechê*), from which a large quantity of oil was once produced. After rooting out (*ekpremnisantes*) these trees, these men sold them and obtained a great deal of money" (Dem. 43.69). The use of *stelchê* (roots/stumps) suggests that the guilty were interested in clearing the land entirely and selling the large mass of stump and root wood for either wood or fuel. The frequent use of the rare verb and compound *premizô* (to remove the trunk) and *ekpremizô* (to tear out the trunk) does not suggest the mere harvesting of ovules but rather emphasizes the rather unusual complete destruction of an orchard, stumps and all—something that the speaker realized was in direct violation of the very heart of Attic laws protecting the olive, stump and all. For the complexity of the ownership of the estate and the traditional view that the nearly 1,000 trees—which must have survived the Peloponnesian War—were, in fact, removed, see, in general, A. B. Burford, *Land and Labor in Ancient Greece* (Baltimore, 1993), 43–45, 69, 161.

Page 159. The Chorus of the Oedipus at Colonus.

See the commentary by J. C. Kamerbeek (*The Plays of Sophocles: Commentaries*, pt. 7, *The Oedipus Coloneus* [Leiden, 1984], 108–109), who suggests that the phrase "This shall no young man nor any that dwells with old age destroy and bring to nothing" refers specifically to both Xerxes' (the "old") failure to destroy the Acropolis olive and Archidamos's (the "young") later sparing of the *moriai*. Yet it was not Archidamos's inability that explains the survival of *moriai*, but rather his reverence. The line, then, still makes much better sense when we understand ravagers who cannot, rather than choose not to, destroy Attic olive trees ("a terror to the spears of the enemies," *encheôn phobêma daiôn*, 699). Furthermore, the "this" (*to*) of line 702 refers immediately to the prior noun phrase "the leaf of the olive" (*phullon elaias*, 701)—a generic reference to the regular, nonsacred olive. The association with sacred olives is largely confined to line 705 ("the ever-seeing eye of Zeus Morios," whom Sophocles envisions as the guardian of all olives—the *elaia* of 701). For the traditional view that the play is a nostalgic reminder of the city's former greatness, see, in general, M. W. Blundell, "The Ideal of Athens in *Oedipus at Colonus*," in *Tragedy, Comedy, and the Polis*, ed. A. Sommerstein et al., Papers from the Greek Drama Conference, Nottingham, 18–20 July 1990 (Bari, 1993), 300–302.

Page 170. Xenophon's Isomachos.

For a good review of the dramatic context of the dialogue, and the historical Isomachos, see A. B. Burford, *Land and Labor in Ancient Greece* (Baltimore, 1993), 89–92. Again, since the dramatic date of the dialogue must be before ca. 435–430 (the dialogue is said to take place before the birth of Isomachos's daughter ([*Oec.* 6.17]), it is unlikely that a contemporary audience in the fourth century could associate references to unproductive farmland with the consequences of a war they knew had not yet taken place. On the dramatic date, see also S. Pomeroy, *Xenophon, Oeconomicus: A Social and Historical Commentary* (Oxford, 1994), 18–19, 259–264. The land mentioned as improved by Isomachos and his father, then, is never referred to as ravaged by enemy troops, and its dramatic context is decades before the Peloponnesian War had even broken out. Pomeroy (pp. 46–50), nevertheless, believes that Xenophon wrote his *Oeconomicus* out of concern for the sorry state of Attic agriculture after the Peloponnesian War. But if that were true, it is curious that he would select dramatic characters for a postwar context who were known to have been active landowners in the pre-war period, and one of whom was in fact dead by the fourth century. And unlike in Aristophanic comedy or Thucydides' *History*, the dialogue includes no mention of enemy ravaging—curious for a work concerned with attracting postwar farmers back to devastated land.

More likely, as is true of much of Xenophon's, Isocrates', and Plato's more pragmatic observations, the *Oeconomicus* is part of a growing fourth-century reactionary and often nostalgic literature that sought first to criticize, but also to adapt to, the growing military, cultural, and economic complexity of the fourth century, which saw the city evolve ever farther from the old agrarian city-state of hoplites and conservative farmers: the audience and the concerns are fourth century, but the idealized state belongs to a prior era that Xenophon fears has nearly gone by. On this reactionary critique of the fourth-century evolution of the polis, characterized by praise of the agricultural exclusivity of an earlier age, see V. D. Hanson, *The Other Greeks: The Agrarian Roots of Western Civilization* (New York, 1995), chap. 9 ("The Erosion of the Agrarian *Polis*"), 357–404.

Page 170. The Horoi.

Since the late 1980s there has been considerable reexamination of existing and newly found *horoi*—stone markers, currently numbering about 250, that signify creditors' interest on farm land and houses. Controversy centers mostly on the nature of such loans; M. I. Finley and his student Paul Millett have argued that they are mostly for consumptive, nonproductive purposes, confined largely to wealthier Athenians, and thus hardly evidence for the wholesale flight of the middling Attic farmer, who purportedly went into debt to moneyed interests to preserve his rapidly failing farm (see the second edition of M. I. Finley's *Studies in Land and Credit in Ancient Athens*, with an introduction by Paul Millett [New Brunswick, N.J., 1985]; and P. Millett, "The Attic HOROI Reconsidered in the Light of Recent Discoveries," *Opus* 1 [1982]: esp. 219–230). E. Cohen (*Athenian Economy and Society: A Banking Prospective* [Princeton, 1992], 34–36), in contrast, sees the *horoi* as part of a sophisticated system of Athenian finance, where risk takers with capital naturally wished for more and crafted ingenious methods of lending, borrowing, calculating interest, and banking in pursuit of profit—all of which reflected an increasing monetization and sophistication of the economy in the fourth and third centuries B.C. In the case of Attic agriculture, I think there may be some point of agreement: the *horoi* may indeed signify loans taken out for economic purposes, but such risk-taking was probably done by the elite, who saw their properties as valuable sources of cash production. I think neither Millett nor Cohen would envision the *horoi* as proof of an agricultural depression, induced by the Peloponnesian War, and leading to the impoverishment of middling Attic farmers. In that regard, the work of both Finley and Andreyev (see the Select Bibliography), which demolishes the notion of an "agrarian crisis" in the immediate aftermath of the Spartan invasions, remains valid.

It should be noted that archaeological evidence from temples and sanctuaries suggests that rural building and augmentation went on throughout the Peloponnesian War; cf. the references cited by E. Krummen, "Athens and Attica: *Polis* and Countryside in Greek Tragedy," in *Tragedy, Comedy, and the Polis*, ed. A. Sommerstein et al., Papers from the Greek Drama Conference, Nottingham, 18–20 July 1990 (Bari, 1993), 216–217.

*Page 173. The Economy in Postwar
Athens and the Assessment of Agriculture.*

A definitive chapter in B. Strauss, *Athens after the Peloponnesian War: Class, Faction, and Policy, 403–386 B.C.* (Ithaca, N.Y., 1987), 42–69, discusses the consequences of the war for Athenian society. And although Strauss would argue for more serious agricultural losses as a result of Dekeleia, the thrust of his argument connects Athens's immediate (and transitory) postwar political troubles with the absence of imperial revenues and labor power losses from the plague and battle—especially among the thetes. See also D. Kagan, *The Fall of the Athenian Empire* (Ithaca, N.Y., 1987), 413–416, which notes both the impressive renaissance of Athens in the immediate postwar period and its recovery from labor power losses and other hardships, such as exhausted treasuries, disease, and malnourishment in addition to devastation. In a section of a chapter entitled "Focus on Athenian Economy in the Fourth Century," (*The Greek State at War*, pt. 5 [Berkeley, 1991], 459–473), W. K. Pritchett concludes that the overall health of Athens was excellent and agriculture in general prosperous in Attica. Paul Millett ("The Attic HOROI Reconsidered in the Light of Recent Discoveries," *Opus* 1 [1982]: 223–224) offers a convincing refutation of C. Mossé's attempts to revive an "agrarian crisis" in the years following the war. For the latter's arguments, see in general the later edition of her *Fin de la démocratie athénienne* (New York, 1979).

The question also arises whether Athens during the war was fed entirely through imports, or for a large part by local grains that were not damaged much during the invasions but planted continuously during the Archidamian War—and even through the Dekeleian occupation. For the idea that local cereals comprised a great deal of the total supply of Athenian foodstuffs, see R. Sallares, *The Ecology of the Ancient Greek World* (Ithaca, N.Y., 1991), 97–98, 294–389.

Peter Garnsey (*Famine and Food Supply in the Graeco-Roman World: Responses to Risk and Crisis* [Cambridge, 1988], 89–164) believes that the disruptions in Attic grain supplies during the Peloponnesian War (the result of ravaging, plundering, or inaccessibility to fields?) marked a watershed, inaugurating increasing Athenian dependence on foreign cereals. Garnsey explains the seeming paradox of this hypothesis—*after* the conclusion of hostilities, Athenian cereal stocks are *more* precarious than ever—by arguing that the fourth century B.C. saw a gradual increase in population and the end of imperialism, which earlier had guaranteed accessible trade and provided capital for foreign purchases. Garnsey's model makes sense without positing a dramatic change because of the Spartan presence for five years between 431 and 425, and at Dekeleia for nine: population growth, loss of tribute and military superiority, and the gradual weakening of autonomous civic bodies of agrarians by elite interests led to Athens's greater reliance on foreign suppliers.

The Peloponnesian War was a watershed in Greek history, not because farms were destroyed and agrarians became impoverished, but largely because it helped to erode traditional methods of warfare and confirmed that capital, technology, and mercenaries—not hoplite battle prowess—would win wars. Hoplite supremacy was critical to the entire classical ideology of the polis, an unusual agrarianism that tended to protect the idea of a free citizen landowner, immune from taxation, suspicious of rich and poor, and secure in a densely settled countryside of like-minded yeomen farmers. There is no doubt that by the third century B.C., the countryside was in a process of change as the polis became more the haunt of the wealthy. But, again, this evolution occurred more than a century after the Peloponnesian War and was not a product of agricultural devastation.

CONCLUSION

Page 180. Agricultural Devastation
and Its General Contribution to Rural Impoverishment and Decline.

T. Gallant's *Risk and Survival in Ancient Greece* (Stanford, 1991) has some useful chapters on how rural households reacted to poor harvests and general natural and human-induced disruptions. Interestingly enough, Gallant catalogues a wide variety of potential dangers to agrarians—drought, weather catastrophes, changing life cycles and aging in the household, long-term military service, increased taxation, decline in liturgies and civic-spirited charity—but does not include enemy attacks on farms as a common cause of impoverishment. His last chapter (pp. 170–200) offers some chilling examples of how the once viable Greek countryside was slowly enervated, depopulated, and consolidated in fewer and fewer hands during the Hellenistic period, as a result of the ever growing array and burden of taxes, tributes, and tithes to pay for more urban, elite enterprises. Although there were always thousands of rural folk in the Greek countryside, we should imagine that gradually from the fourth to second century B.C., an exploited peasantry began to become more typical, in place of what had once been a viable agrarianism of hoplite yeomen who themselves controlled the political and military agendas of their communities—often in a strikingly anti-aristocratic mode.

Susan Alcock's *Graecia Capta: The Landscapes of Roman Greece* (Cambridge, 1993) provides a summary of most recent field surveys of the Greek countryside. Alcock warns that the considerable literary evidence for a depopulated countryside in the late Hellenistic and Roman eras—Dio Chrysostom, Plutarch, Pausanias, Strabo—is rhetorical and overly simplistic. But archaeological survey and her own data more or less confirm what the ancients believed: land by postclassical times was owned by elites, people were moving to town, and farming followed extensive rather than intensive practices. Cf. S. Bommeljé and J. Vroom, "Deserted and Untilled Lands: Aetolia in Roman Times," *Pharos* 3 (1995): 67–130.

Yet Alcock sees little evidence that warfare in the countryside was responsible per se for the general trend toward rural depopulation, nucleation of settlement, or consolidation of holdings in Hellenistic and Roman Greece (pp. 89–90, 149–150). What damage did follow from war was more likely the result of constant mobilization, sieges, and the inability of farmers to work in peace, rather than of losses to ravagers—and even that damage was subsidiary to larger political and financial evolutions. Both Gallant and Alcock remind us that such historical processes are often gradual and less dramatic than might be imagined, and not the result of climatic changes or losses in war: the real culprit in rural depression was usually insidious patterns of exploitation, characterized by forced tithes, taxation, and military contributions.

E. M. Wood's *Peasant-Citizen and Slave: The Foundations of Athenian Democracy* (London, 1988), 57–61, 122–125, has a good discussion of the deleterious effects of Roman military practice on rural citizens—in contrast to the impact of the defense agendas of the classical poleis, where citizen-soldiers did not allow warfare to develop into long campaigns that served more wealthy interests, as farmers left their holdings to fight for booty and territory that often in the long run were antithetical to their own parochial interests. See also M. H. Jameson, C. N. Runnels, and T. H. van Andel, *A Greek Countryside: The Southern Argolid from Prehistory to the Present Day* (Stanford, 1994), on the decline of rural sites in the southern Argolid in the late Hellenistic era ("By the second half of the century, well over half of the small sites had been deserted," 394). Economic inequality, not war, seems to have been the cause of the decline:

> In the Greek cities in general there seems to have been a growing divide between a small class of wealthy individuals and an increasingly impoverished free lower class of citizens. . . . It is the class of middling farmers, craftsmen, and merchants (who were not necessarily limited to one of those callings) that is hard to find; their absence is consistent with the decline in the number of medium-sized properties, largely worked by the nuclear family. (396)

While brigandage and piracy may have contributed to agricultural decline, the more fundamental causes again were political and social, specifically the demise of autonomous poleis and the rise of property and income taxes. J. D. Hughes, *Pan's Travail: Environmental Problems of the Ancient Greeks and Romans* (Baltimore, 1994), 143, lists factors responsible for agricultural decline in classical societies—climatic change, soil exhaustion, erosion, misuse of irrigation, high taxation, declining population, pastoralism; military devastation of cropland plays an insignificant role.

For an accessible discussion of soil erosion and its impact on agriculture in the ancient Argolid, see T. H. van Andel and C. Runnels, *Beyond the Acropolis: A Rural Greek Past* (Stanford, 1987), 135–153. O. Rackman, "Ecology and Pseudo-Ecology: The Example of Ancient Greece," in *Human Landscapes in Classical Antiquity: Environment and Culture*, ed. G.

Shipley and J. Salmon (London, 1996), 16–43, makes some good observations about the robustness of the Greek landscape, emphasizing that even the massive tree-felling mentioned in ancient sources does not necessarily mean permanent deforestation, given the usual patterns of growth and renewal of timber.

To summarize: the ancient literary evidence for late-fourth-century and Hellenistic rural depression—characterized by an impoverished rural populace, growing inequality between wealthy and poor, and rural depopulation—is largely confirmed by field survey, which notes a consolidation of landowning, crop specialization, and more nucleated settlement. These trends appear nearly a century *after* the Peloponnesian War in archaeological sources, and only a half-century later in ancient authors (see now the collected essays of A. Fuks in *Social Conflicts in Ancient Greece* [Leiden, 1984]); more subtle developments, not fire and ax, initiated these processes. It is possible that the decline of agrarianism, hoplite exclusivity, and the existence of a strong middling voice in the polis may have begun during the Peloponnesian War (though I think we should look even earlier to the monetization and Mediterranization of the economy after the Persian Wars), but this change was gradual, not dramatic, and had very little to do with Spartan or Theban ravagers.

Page 180. The Word Aporthêtos.

See now W. K. Pritchett, *The Greek State at War*, pt. 5 (Berkeley, 1991), 453–454, for a discussion of the various passages in Greek literature where territory is described as "untouched" by previous plundering and ravaging expeditions.

Page 184. Ravaging and Roman History.

I still know of no systematic account of agricultural devastation and its effect on the countryside in Roman history other than Arnold Toynbee's original study (*Hannibal's Legacy: The Hannibalic War's Effects on*

Roman Life [Oxford, 1965]), which overestimates permanent agricultural damage in Italy during the Second Punic War. For very brief mention, see B. Isaac, *The Limits of Empire: The Roman Army in the East* (Oxford, 1992), 381–383; H. Sidebottom, "Philosophers' Attitudes to Warfare under the Principate," in *War and Society in the Roman World*, ed. J. Rich and G. Shipley (London, 1993), 248–250; M. Beagon, "Nature and Landscapes in Pliny the Elder," in *Human Landscapes in Classical Antiquity*, ed. G. Shipley and J. Salmon (London, 1996), 292–293; N. Christie, "Landscapes in Late Roman and Post-Roman Italy," in *Human Landscapes*, ed. Shipley and Salmon, 254–283. Christie notes that vivid images of peasants being driven off and land ruined at the close of the Roman Empire are probably exaggerated and do not necessarily indicate subsequent agricultural depression. For more specific investigations of the relationship between invasion and rural dislocation on the Roman frontier, see N. Roymans, "The North Belgic Tribes in the First Century B.C.: A Historical-Anthropological Perspective," in *Roman and Native in the Low Countries: Spheres of Interaction*, British Archaeological Reports 184 (Oxford, 1983), 43–69.

APPENDIX. THE VOCABULARY OF AGRICULTURAL DEVASTATION

Page 188. The Vocabulary of Plunder.

For the rich vocabulary of plunder, see W. K. Pritchett, *The Greek State at War*, pt. 5 (Berkeley, 1991), 73–152; Pritchett's lists logically do not include most words in our appendix that imply devastation alone.

Page 189. Agricultural Vocabulary.

For a study of Greek agricultural vocabulary referring to crops, land, houses, and property, see V. D. Hanson, *The Other Greeks: The Agrarian Roots of Western Civilization* (New York, 1995), 435–445; R. Osborne, *Demos: The Discovery of Classical Attika* (Cambridge, 1985), 16–22.

Page 192. Temnô.

There is a valuable entry on *temnô* in J. Chadwick, *Lexiographica Graeca* (Oxford, 1996), 271–279, esp. 276, that suggests that in the military sense the idea is strictly one of laying land bare or clearing it of vegetation—growing things are cut clean from the surface. At Thucydides 2.19.2, we are told the Spartans "*temnon Eleusina*"; this rarer use of an accusative that does not suggest crops or cropland must still mean farmland: "They ravaged the environs of Eleusis." For the clear sense that *portheô* and its compounds refer either generally to attack or more particularly to plunder, and rarely to devastation of agriculture, see C. Tuplin, "The Fate of Thespiae," *Athenaeum* 64 (1986): 321–341, esp. 331–333.

General Index

Abel, W., 202
access to fields denied: 55, 70; in
  Dekeleian War, 155, 160, 161,
  172, 183
Acharnai, 84, 133, 163, 165, 239
Acropolis, Athenian, 59
Adam, J.-P., 228
Adcock, E. E., 25n, 28n, 81n, 89, 92n,
  122n, 135n, 150n, 153n
adikeô, 185, 186, 194
Aegean islands, 205
Aeneas Tacticus, 229–30. *See also* Index
  of Ancient Sources Cited
Aeolos Islands, 38
Agathokles, son of Antiphilos,
  of Istros, 105
Agesilaos, king of Sparta: 58, 95, 175,
  182; invades Akarnania, 55n, 56, 115,
  127; invades Boiotia, 26, 83, 87, 96
Agesipolis, king of Sparta, 175
Agios Georgios, Attica, 133n
Agis, king of Sparta, 22, 126, 135,
  162, 166n
Aigaleos-Parnes gap, 45, 84, 133
Aigina, 114
Aigosthena, 95, 99

aims of devastation: economic, xii-xiii,
  15, 153, 184; tactical, *see* battle
Aitolia: 47, 188; light-armed troops, 9,
  23, 95
Aixone, 135, 168
Akanthos, 38, 70, 208
Akarnania: 49, 54n, 95, 127–28; Agesi-
  laos' invasion, 55n, 56, 115, 127
Akragas, 116
Alcibiades, 166n
Alcock, S., 216, 235, 247
Alexander III the Great, king of Mace-
  don, 33n, 51n, 52–53, 120
Alexander of Phereia, 10
Alyattes, king of Lydia, 34–35, 47, 50,
  71n, 108–9
American Civil War, 20n, 27n, 37n,
  50n, 53n, 117n
American frontier, 164n
Amorgos, 219–20
Amouretti, M.-C., x, 221, 223–24
Amphipolis, 23, 46
Amphissa, 114
Anagyrous, 163
Anaphlystos, 97, 113, 162
anaskeuazô, 104

Anderson, K.K., 4n, 22n, 26n, 30nn, 33n, 49n, 83n, 86n, 87n, 89, 92n, 122n
Andreyev, N.N., 43n, 169nn, 170nn, 244
animals: military use, 32, 40, 52. *See also* livestock
Antiforitis Wall, 84, 85
Antigonos II Gonatas, king of Macedon, 35n
aphaireô, 190
Aphidna, 99, 100, 113
Apollonia, 124
aporthêtos, 180, 249
Apsinthians, 80
Aratus, 40n
archers, 23
Archidamian War: 132–53; areas untouched, 150–51, 152; Athenian cavalry, 22, 92, 125–26, 133, 135, 151, 152, 232; Athenian forts and garrisons, 92–93, 151, 152; Athenian seaborne attacks, 21, 37, 124; continuity of farming, 128, 149, 151, 152, 245; effectiveness of devastation, 132–53; evacuation of Attica, 92, 107, 108, 115, 133, 138, 151; —, unhappiness over, 81, 118n, 136, 152–53, 208–9; hoplite warfare, 19–20, 101, 153; literary evidence, 139, 143, 147, 152 (*see also* Aristophanes; Thucydides); problems of devastating Attica, 147–51; seasonal considerations, 136, 148–49, 152; Spartan field camps, 25; Spartan invasions, 35, 64, 132–37, 147, 152, 176; —, first, 19–20, 90, 92, 107, 125, 132–33, 138; —, second, 134, 138, 147n; —, third, 125–26, 135; —, fourth, 64–65, 135, 138, 147n; —, fifth, 135–36; Spartan supply, 35, 133, 135, 136; survival of olive trees and vines, 143–47; unmethodical devastation, 150–51, 153; years free of Spartan invasion, 134–35, 149, 152
Archidamos, king of Sparta, 31, 175, 208. *See also* Archidamian War

Argolid: 51, 83, 98; rural sites, 74n, 205, 215, 248
Argos: invasion of Phleious: 52, 124; Spartan invasions, 30, 38, 53, 175
aristocracies, 9, 205, 246–47
Aristophanes (comic poet): on Archidamian War, 131, 136–37, 140–43, 143–44, 152; on Dekeleian War, 156, 159–60, 207, 233–35; on effects of dislocation, 136, 178. *See also* Index of Ancient Sources Cited
Aristophanes (commander of Eleusis), 105
Arkadia, 38–39, 49, 52, 54n, 182
armies. *See* cavalry; hoplites; light-armed troops; military organization
artillery, 9, 81
Asia Minor, 118–19, 182
Asine, 98n
Astakos, 37
Atalante, 29n
Athens: Acropolis, olive tree on, 59; Agora, 170–71; defensive measures, 4th-century, 27, 81–82; and Eleusinian Mysteries, 144–45, 236; evacuation, 114, 116, 207 (*see also* Archidamian War); hoplite warfare, 9, 81; imports of foodstuffs, 154, 160, 245; laws on uprooting olive trees, 57, 64, 157–58, 240–41; and Macedon, 97n, 99, 113; open land inside wall, 80n; Peloponnesian War campaigns, 93–94; —, Aeolos Islands, 38; —, Boiotia, 25, 26–27, 35n; —, Lipari Islands, 181; —, Megarid, 21–22, 36; —, Melos, 181; —, seaborne attacks on Peloponnese, 21, 37, 124; —, Sicilian Expedition, 26, 27, 33n, 109, 110–11; —, Thessaly, 124 (*see also* Archidamian War; Dekeleian War); plague, 135, 149, 153, 156, 172, 244; Plataian evacuees in, 116; Pnyx, 171; protection of fields near walls, 133, 135, 151, 161; refugee

shelters, 170–71; storage of food in city, 33n, 115; tribute lost, 234, 244. *See also* Archidamian War; Attica; Dekeleian War

Atthidographers, 145–46, 151, 236–37

Attica: agrarian councils, xiii; defensive strategy adopted, 100, 102; Dema Wall, 84, 87; evacuation, 110, 113; —, and Macedonian threat, 99–100, 113; —, Persian Wars, 114, 116, 207; —, Xenophon proposes stronghold in south, 97, *113 (see also* Archidamian War); farms and farmhouses, x, 45–46, 205, 234 (*see also* Cliff House; Dema House; Priest's House; Vari farmhouse); field walls, 82, 84, 85, 87, 227; forts and garrisons, 24n; —, 5th-century, 89–94, 101, 105, 151, 152, 162, 232; —, 4th-century, 98–100; *horoi*, 170, 243–44; Macedonian attacks, 35n, 99–100; olive trees, 143–46, 157–58, 236; in Peloponnesian Wars; —, First, 93–94, 101; —, Second, 94, 129–73 (*see also* Archidamian War; Dekeleian War); postwar drift to city unfounded, 169, 170; terrain, 147–48, 166; towers, 46, 74–75, 99, 144n, 225–26

Attic Stelai, 107, 144n, 217–18

Audring, G., 156–57, 218

Babylon, 49n

banditry, xiii, 16

barley, 32, 49n, 219, 220

barns, 108n

battle: devastation as tactic to instigate, xii, 13, 68, 118, 150, 153, 179–80, 182–83, 203, 216–17; devastation fails to instigate, 181, 183–84; pitched hoplite, 4th-century, 100–101, 211

Beagon, M., 250

Besa, Mt, 97, 113

blaptô, 190

Blundell, W.W., 242

Boardman, M.M., 28n, 45n, 71n

Boer War, 50n, 71n

Boiotia: in Peloponnesian War, 25, 92–93, 94, 139, 155, 175, 186; in Persian Wars, 27; small farms, 205; wars against Sparta, 4th-century, 26, 83, 87, 95–96, 101, 229. *See also* Thebes

Bolkestein, H., 45n, 43n

Bommeljé, S., and Vroom, J., 247

border defenses, 79, 97. *See also* forts and garrisons; walls (field)

Borgeaud, P., 207

boundary markers. *See* fencing; *horoi*

Boyd, T., 213

Bradford, J., 44n, 45n

Brasidas, 38, 46, 70

brigandry, xiii, 16

Bruce, A.F.F., 238

Brulé, P., 209–10

Brumfield, C.C., 220

Brun, J.-P., 224

Brunt, A.A., 28n, 137, 139n, 141n, 143n, 153n, 157n, 159n

Bugh, R.R., 230–31

buildings, rural, 167. *See also* farmhouses; farms (outbuildings); towers

Burford, B.B., x, 209, 214, 224, 238, 241, 242

burning: farmhouses, 72–74, 76; olive trees, 58–60; seasonal considerations, 38, 60; stored food, 51, 54; vines, 69. *See also* grain

Busolt, G., 126n, 133n, 136n, 148n

Calendar, Athenian sacrificial, 165

California, xi, 59, 67, 71

camps, military field, 25–30, 31, 40

capital and finance, 176–77, 204, 205, 243, 246, 249. *See also* loans

Carey, C., 236, 238–39

Carthaginians, 116

cavalry: xiv, 7–8, 9; Athenian, 232; —,
  in Archidamian War, 22, 92, 125–26,
  133, 135, 151, 152, 232; —, in
  Dekeleian War,126, 161–62; and
  evacuation, 106, 128; operations
  against ravagers, 20, 22, 83, 87,
  122–28, 148n, 230–31, 232; protection of farming, 105, 128; Thessalian,
  9, 110, 125; trampling of crops, 52;
  traps laid for, 110
Cavanaugh, B.B., 236
cereals. *See* grain
Chabrias, 83n, 95, 99n, 226, 227
Chaironeia, battle of, 27, 100, 211
Chandler, L., 74, 89n, 90nn, 99n, 151n
Chios, 46, 115–16n
Chremonidean War, 105, 162n
Christie, N., 250
cities: food stored in, 33n, 104–5; as
  places of refuge, 33n, 112, 113, 115,
  170–71; open areas within walls, 80,
  115, 227; rural migration to, 169,
  170, 233, 234. *See also* political life
civil wars, modern: American, 20n, 27n,
  37n, 50n, 53n, 117n; Greek, 58n, 74
Cliff House, 43n, 44n, 48n
coalition armies, 36
Cohen, E., 243
cohesion, social, 180, 208–9
Connor, R.R., 203
continuity of farming in war, 127–28. *See
  also* Archidamian War; Dekeleian War
Cooper, B.B., 43n, 148n, 158n, 169n,
  170nn
Corcyra, 29n, 47, 109, 121
Corinth: evacuation of livestock, 115;
  fortification of Isthmus, 79n, 83, 87,
  95, 98; 4th-century wars, 20, 101,
  124–25, 229
councils, agrarian, xiii, 206, 235, 245
Crete, 9, 221
Crimean Chersonesos: farms, x, 46,
  205; field walls, 44n, 85, 87
cutting of crops: vocabulary, 193–94.
  See also grain; olive trees; trees; vines

Dafni, pass of, 84n
daiô, 193
Darius II, king of Persians, 118–19
David, E., 233, 234
Davies, K.K., 165n, 168n, 169n
Dawson, D., 203
decrees: on evacuation of Attica; —, 4th-
  century, 99, 113; —, Themistocles',
  114n, 116; on firstfruits at Eleusis,
  144–45, 236; honorific, for protectors
  of harvest, 35n, 104–6, 128
defense of agriculture. *See* evacuation:
  fortifications: sorties
defensive strategy, 4th-century, 81–82,
  85, 86, 94, 100, 101, 228–29
Dekeleia: Dema Wall to protect, 84;
  Spartan base, 22, 28–29, 166n; —,
  slaves and dissidents desert to, 115n,
  154, 160, 161, 163, 172, 183, 238. *See
  also* Dekeleian War
Dekeleian War: 153–97; access to
  fields prevented, 155, 160, 161, 172,
  183; Agis' advance on Athens fails,
  22, 126, 162, 166n; Athenian
  garrisons, 126, 161–62, 166; areas of
  Attica unravaged, 161–66; continuity of farming, 128, 161, 162–66,
  168n, 171–72; damage to Attica,
  139, 153–57, 172, 183; imports of
  foodstuffs to Athens, 154, 160, 245;
  literary sources on, 153–54, 160,
  167–68, 172, 237–38 (*see also*
  Aristophanes; Thucydides);
  livestock, 154, 160, 161, 165–66,
  172; plundering of Attica, 94, 110,
  121, 139, 153, 154, 155, 160, 161,
  163, 172, 183; postwar economy,
  165n, 166–71, 238, 244–46; psychological effects, 154, 172; slave desertion, 115n, 154, 160, 161, 163, 172,
  183, 238; strategy of systematic devastation, 153; survival of vines and
  fruit trees, 157–60, 168, 172
Delbrück, Hans, 20n, 23n, 54, 62,
  70n, 81n

Delion, 23–24, 26–27, 29n, 31–32, 75, 93
Delos, 46
Delphi, 114
Delphinion, on Chios, 29n
Dema House, 45, 72n, 155, 164n
Dema Wall, 82, 84, 87, 227
Democritus, 44n
Demosthenes, 97n, 99, 113, 158, 240–41. *See also* Index Locorum
dendrokopeô, dendrotomeô, 61, 193, 194
denial of resources to enemy. *See* scorched earth policy
deoô, 134, 186, 188, 189, 190, 191–92, 194
depopulation, rural, 246–49
depression, 1980s, 178n
Derdas, 124
Derkylidas, 80
Detienne, M., 55n, 64n
devastation: reasons for influential role in Greece, 5–8. *See also* particular aspects throughout Index
diaphtheirô, 134, 189
diarpazomai, 191
difficulty of systematic devastation, xiii, 141, 174. *See also* grain; olive trees; terrain; trees; vines
Dio Chrysostom, 247
Dionysios I of Syracuse, 86, 124–25
dislocation, xiii, 13, 15, 16, 136, 152–53, 177–78, 179
dissension: Dekeleia as center for, 154, 160, 183; devastation as attempt to create, 207–8
doors, house-, 108–9, 110, 120
Dorimachos, 188
Doris, 93
Draphi, 47–48, 109n, 164n
dream-interpretation manuals, 10n
Drilai, 119
Drymos, 164n
Ducrey, P., xi, 190n
Dyaliens, 27n
Dystos rock houses, 72

economic motivation of ravaging, xii–xiii, 15, 30n, 153, 184
Egypt, 4, 79n
Ehrenberg, V., 43n, 136n, 143n, 169nn, 170n
eiskomizo, 104
elderly, evacuation of, 114, 116, 120
Eleusis: garrison, 90, 98n, 100, 105, 113, 162; —, cavalry sorties, 92, 125, 151; Mysteries, 144–45, 163, 166n, 236; road to Oinoe, 133n
Eleutherai, 89n, 95, 98–99
Eliot, W.J.J., 45n, 91n, 97n
Elis, 54n, 112–13, 182
elite interests, Hellenistic, 245, 246
Engels, D., 32n, 33–34nn, 120n
Epameinondas: 10, 83, 101; invades Peloponnese, 24, 39, 83, 87, 180n, 183, 211
ephebes, 3n, 91
Epichares, 105
Epieikeia, 95
Epiros, 188
epiteichismos, 28–30, 161n, 212
Eretria, 114
Ergang, R., 202
erumna, 112
Erythrai, 96, 114n
eschatiai. See marginal land
Euboia, 114, 115, 116, 154
Eupolis, 91n, 163
Eurybiades, 116
evacuation: xiv, 15, 79, 103–21, 182, 230; Attica, 97, 99, 110, 113, 115; —, Persian Wars, 114, 116, 207 (*see also* Archidamian War); farm implements, 104, 106–7, 120, 151, 177; food and crops, 33n, 104–6, 120, 174; household furnishings, 104, 107–10, 120, 138, 151, 174, 177, 229; into neighboring countries, 114, 115, 116; labor force, 114, 115–16, 120, 174, 177; livestock, 114–15, 120, 151, 174; military assistance, 106, 128; into mountains, 114, 115, 116;

evacuation (*continued*)
  obstacles and traps, 103, 110–12;
  places of refuge, 79, 103, 112–16,
  120, 225, 230; of property, 103–10,
  113, 120, 229; psychological effects,
  136, 152–53, 207; slaves, 114,
  115–16, 120, 174; women, children,
  and elderly, 114, 116, 120. *See also*
  scorched earth policy

farmhouses, isolated: x, xiii-xiv, 37,
  44–48, 214–15, 216–17;
  construction, 72; methods of destruction, 71–76. *See also* household
  furnishings; plundering
farming as central to Greek life, 1–4, 16
farms: 42–49; fragmentation and
  consolidation, 217–18, 246, 247,
  248, 249; outbuildings, 44n, 75, 76,
  108n; size, 42–43, 48, 205, 213, 239;
  —, Hellenistic growth, 246, 247, 248,
  249. *See also* farmhouses, isolated
fencing, 43–44, 48, 144n, 177, 214, 218
field camps, 25–30, 31, 40
field surveys, 215–16, 247, 249
field walls. *See* walls
figs and fig trees, 141n, 149, 193, 219
finance, 176–77, 204, 205, 243, 246,
  249. *See also* loans; prices; taxation
Fine, V.A.A., 169n
Finley, I.I., x, 43nn, 45n, 169n, 170n,
  243
flax, 49
Fluchtburgen, 112
fodder crops, 32, 33, 35
food, stored: 49n, 229; attacks on, 37,
  38, 39, 51, 54; evacuation, 33n,
  104–6, 120, 174. *See also* wine vats
Fort Atkinson, Council Bluffs, 164n
fortifications, rural: xiv, 9, 15, 79–102;
  base for sorties, 82, 83, 89, 151, 152;
  4th-century development, 8, 9, 81;
  ravaging for materials, 25–26, 27,
  31–32, 40, 75; and topography, 100.

  See also camps, field; *epiteichismos*;
  forts and garrisons, border; walls
forts and garrisons, border: 88–102,
  174, 182, 227–29; coastal, 90–91;
  5th-century, 89–94, 101, 151, 152;
  4th-century, 94–101; sorties, 89, 151,
  152; *see also epiteichismos*; Attica
fourth century: evolution of polis, 235,
  242–43, 248; forts and garrisons,
  94–101; warfare and strategy, 94,
  100–101, 153, 184, 211 (*see also*
  defensive strategy)
Foxhall, L., 202, 207, 212, 214, 216,
  217, 219, 221, 224, 227, 236, 240
France, 58n, 81n
freedmen, 9
French, A., 54n, 61n, 65n, 146n, 163n,
  156, 179n
friendly territory, devastation of, 27, 28.
  See also scorched earth policy
Frost, F., 215
Fuks, A., 249

Gallant, W.W., x, 229, 246
Garlan, Y., xi, 4n, 25n, 28n, 29, 81n,
  93n, 94n, 112n, 119n, 132n, 150n,
  161n, 180n
Garnsey, Peter, 245
garrisons. *See* forts and garrisons
Gaza, Alexander's siege of, 33n
Geländmauer, 80n
Geraneia, 93
girdling trunks of trees, 62–63, 137
Glotz, G., 43n, 157n, 169n
Gomme, W.W., 4n, 22n, 23n, 37n, 38n,
  51, 56n, 62, 70n, 88–89, 91nn, 107n,
  108n, 122n, 125n, 126nn, 132n,
  133nn, 134n, 135n, 148n, 150nn, 154n
Gordon, H.H., 73, 74
grafting, 177
Graham, J.J. *See* Jones, E.E.
grain: 49–55, 219–20; burning, 16, 30,
  34–35, 50–52, 106, 149; —, seasonal
  considerations, 33, 35, 50–51, 52,

54, 106, 212–13, 219; —,
vocabulary, 193–94; cutting, 51,
52–54, 219–20; difficulty of destroying, 16, 174, 182; harvest season, 32,
39, 49n, 52n, 106, 219, 220; in Peloponnesian War, 149, 168n, 172, 245;
seasonal considerations, 50–51, 52,
53n, 54–55 (*see also* burning); stored,
49n; stubble, 50n; tools for beating
down, 30, 53; trampling, 16, 30, 32,
35–36, 51, 52–54; US embargo of
USSR, 178n
Griffith, T.T., 81n, 91n
Grundy, B.B., 4n, 25n, 28n, 37n, 49n,
81n, 88, 119n, 122n, 139n
Guiraud, P., 43n, 48n, 108n
Gutman, D.D., 28, 171n
Gyphtokastro, 89n, 98–99

Halstead, P., 219–20
Hammond, G.L.L., 89n, 99n, 133nn
Hannibal, 184n, 250
Hanson, D.D., xi; "Hoplites into Democrats," 206; *The Other Greeks: The
Agrarian Roots of Western Civilization*,
xiv, 204, 206, 211, 213, 215, 218,
230, 243, 250; "Practical Aspects of
Grape-Growing and the Ideology of
Greek Viticulture," 224; "Thucydides
and the Desertion of Attic Slaves
during the Decelean War," 211, 237,
238; *The Western Way of War*, 203
Harding, P., 228, 236
Hardy, G.G., 20n, 59n, 63n, 70n, 134n,
135n, 136n, 137n, 139n, 143n, 145n,
149n, 158n,161n, 192n
Harmand, J., 3n, 79n
harvest: enemy disruption, 55, 70;
hoplites' own responsibilities, 36, 41,
135, 149, 220; military protection,
35n, 104–6, 120, 128; times, 36, 52n,
220 (*see also* under particular crops)
Harvey, P., xiv, 238
Hebrew warfare, 11n

Heitland, E.E., ix-x, 169n
Hellenica Oxyrhynchia, 139, 147,
237–38. *See also* Index of Ancient
Sources Cited
Hellenistic Age: ascendancy of urban
elites, 245, 246; consolidation of
landholdings, 246, 247, 248, 249;
rural change, 235, 246–49; warfare,
9, 30n, 85, 105–6, 184
Henderson, W.W., 92n, 137
Heraia, 38–39
Herms, mutilation of the, 144
heroic ideal, 8, 204
Hippokrates (Athenian general), 26–27
Hodkinson, S. and H., 209
Holland, 17th-century, 28, 171n
hoplites and hoplite warfare: agrarian
basis, xi, xiii, 6, 203, 205–6, 235; attendants, 22–23, 211–12; decline,
xiii, 8, 9, 81, 100, 204–5, 246;
harvest commitments, 36, 41, 135,
149, 220; ideals, 81, 88, 100, 204,
205–6, 246; limited length of
campaigns, 248; longevity, 7–8,
100–101, 211; maintenance of
formation, 19–20, 40, 41, 122, 124,
126; political and social aspects, xi,
xiii, 6, 205–6, 235; protection of ravagers, 21, 148n, 174; protocols of
warfare, 5, 15, 180, 183, 202–5;
scorched earth policy incompatible,
117, 118; Spartan ascendancy, 101;
tactical use of devastation (*see also*
battle); Theban ascendancy, 101,
211. *See also* supply
Hornblower, S., 233
horoi (boundary markers), 170, 243–44
horses, 7–8, 32, 154
household furnishings: plundering, 127,
139, 155, 161, 163, 172, 187,
188–89. *See also* evacuation
Hughes, D.D., 248
Hyksos, 4
Hysiai, 98n

Implements: farm, 104, 106–7, 120, 151, 177, 229; ravaging, 30–32, 40, 53
imports of foodstuffs, Athenian, 154, 160, 245
India, 13, 73n
inequality, economic, 248
infrastructure, damage to, 16
inviolate territories, 180, 249
Isaac, B., 250
Isaeus, 167. *See also* Index Locorum
Isager, S., x, 169n, 214, 224, 229, 236
ischuria, 112
Isomachos and father, 169–70, 242–43
Isthmus of Corinth, 79n, 83, 87, 95, 98
Istros (Atthidographer), 105, 151
Italy: devastation, 55n, 184n, 250; farms, x, 205

Jackson, H.H., 186n, 190, 191n
Jacoby, F., 139n, 148n, 151
Jameson, H.H., 42n, 54n, 114n, 154n, 169n, 176n, 211, 239; with N.N. Runnels and H.H. van Andel, 215, 221, 248
Jardé, A., 43n, 49n, 146n, 147n, 148n
Jones, E.E., 45nn, 72n; with H.H. Sackett and J.J. Graham, 44n, 45nn, 71n, 82, 83n, 84n, 87n, 110n, 133n, 155n

Kagan, D., 126n, 137, 143n, 244–45
Kahrstedt, U., 89n, 92n
kakourgeô, 134, 185, 186–87, 194
kakoô, 185, 186–87, 194
Kallet-Marx, L., 233
Kallias of Sphettos, 104
Kamarina, 116
Kamerbeek, C.C., 241
Kamose, pharaoh, 4
Kapikaya field wall, Termessos, 85
Karduchians, 107, 109
Karnak, stele at, 4
Karsarma, 98n
Katzingri, 98n
Kavasala, 89n

keirô, 193, 194
Kent, H.H., 44n, 45n, 69n, 71n, 91n, 92n, 96n, 108n
Kephallenia, 37
Kephissos Valley, 133, 135
Kern, J.J., 237
Kirsten, E., 80n
Kithairon, Mount, 95–96, 101
Klearchos (of Ten Thousand), 30–31
Kleombrotos, 99n
Kleomenes, king of Sparta, 30, 53, 95, 96, 135
koptô: 60n, 61, 63, 193, 194; *koptô kai kaiô*, 193–94
Koroneia, second battle of, 100, 101, 211
Koukourava, 58n
Kreissig, H., 235
Krentz, Peter, 204, 232
Kromayer, J. and Veith, G., 25n, 122n
Krummen, E., 244

labor force, agricultural: 176–77, 184n; wartime losses, xiii, 16, 156, 234, 238, 244. *See also* slaves
Lakonia, Theban invasions of, 24, 26, 39, 96, 117, 180n
land: fragmentation and consolidation of holdings, 217–18, 246, 247, 248, 249; liquidity, 144n, 239–40. *See also* marginal land; rental agreements
landowners, small: political and social role, xi, xiii, 6, 203, 205–6, 235; post-war drift to Athens unfounded, 169, 170; psychological effects of devastation, 213, 216–17; solidarity, 180
Langdon, M., 43n, 44n, 45n, 46n, 147n, 215
Laureion region, 46, 74–75, 97, 135, 163
Lauter, H.: 215; with H. Lauter-Bufe and H. Lohmann, 226, 227–28
Lawrence, A., 228
laws, Athenian, 57, 64, 157–58, 240–41
Lazenby, John, 203
Lechaion, 58
lêstai, 189

Leuktra, battle of, 96, 100, 101, 211
Lewis, M.M., 43n, 48n, 144n, 147n
light-armed troops: xiii, 7, 19–25,
   210–11; 5th-century role: —,
   engineering tasks, 31n; —, ravaging,
   19–25, 40, 122, 148n, 174, 210–11;
   4th-century role, xiii, 8, 87, 95, 101;
   —, border defense, 82, 94, 97; —,
   specialization, 81, 83n; in mountain
   regions, 9, 23, 95. *See also* peltasts
Lighthouse Point, Crimean Chersonesos, 85
Lipari Islands, 181
livestock: in Dekeleian War, 154, 160,
   161, 165–66, 172; evacuation,
   114–15, 120, 151, 174
loans, 170, 233, 243–44
Lohmann, H., 214, 225, 226, 227–28,
   234–35
Lokris, 10
Loutro, Crete, 221
Low Countries, 28, 171n
Lucania, 55n
Lydia, 34–35, 47, 50, 71n, 108–9
Lysias, 167, 238–40. *See also* Index Locorum

Macedon: 32, 38, 112; Athenian defen-
   sive strategy against, 97n, 99, 113. *See
   also* Alexander III; Philip II
Magagna, V., 201
Mantineia: 9, 31, 36n, 101, 183, 209;
   second battle of, 100, 211
Marathon, battle of, 178
Marathonian Plain, 135, 147n
Mardonios, 27, 87n, 102n
marginal land, 48, 52n, 146n, 147n,
   148, 218
Martin, R., 80n
Mattingly, J.J., 222
Mazi, 99, 133
McCredie, R.R., 83n, 84n, 92n, 99n,
   100n, 112n, 151n
McDonald, A.A., and Rapp, G., 50n,
   55n, 61n, 66n, 148n

McKechnie, R.R., 209, 237
McNicoll, A., 85n
Megalopolis, 80n, 183
Megara and Megarid, 21–22, 36, 74n,
   93–94
Meiggs, R., 229
Melos, 181
mercenaries: 9, 30n, 81, 95, 210, 246;
   light-armed, 83n; Thracian, in
   Dekeleian War, 161n
Messene, 80n, 183
Messenian War, Second, 12
Methana, 29n, 217
methods of devastation: farmhouses,
   71–76; grain, 49–55; olive trees,
   55–68; vines, 68–71. *See also* burning;
   cutting; trampling; uprooting
Michell, H., 43n, 45, 54n, 55n, 68n,
   108n, 157, 169nn
microclimates, 220
Middle Ages, 54
migration to city, rural, 169, 170, 233,
   234
Miletus: 9, 26, 33n; Lydian invasions,
   34–35, 47, 50, 71n, 108–9
military organization: 19–41; field
   camps, 25–30, 31, 40; and
   evacuation, 106, 128; protection of
   farming in war, 35n, 104–6, 120,
   127–28, 151; protection of ravagers,
   21, 148n, 174; ravaging tools, 30–32;
   Roman era, 247–48. *See also* cavalry;
   hoplites; light-armed troops; seasonal
   considerations; sorties; supply
Millett, P., 243, 245
Miltiades, 80
Minoa, 29n
Mitchell, S., 203, 208
Mnasippos, 47, 109
modern warfare, devastation in, 5
monetization, 249
Moody, A.A., 214
morale. *See* psychological effects
moriai (sacred olive trees), 145–46,
   157–58, 236

Mossé, C., 156, 169n, 207, 245
mountain areas: evacuation into, 114, 115, 116; hardship from loss of grain crop, 49; light-armed troops, 9, 23, 95
Müller, H., 230
Munn, M., 210, 226, 227–28, 234
Mycenae area, 98
Mykale, battle of, 26
Mykalessos, 161n
Mykonos, 46
Myoupolis, 89n, 133n
Mysteries, Eleusinian, 144–45, 163, 166n, 236

Napoleon I, emperor of France, 117n
Nauplion area, 98
naval inventory inscription, 32n
Nemea, battle of, 94–95, 100, 101, 211
Nikias: 181; Peace of, 92–93
Notion, 29n
Nowicka, M., 225

Ober, J., xiv, 100n, 203, 208, 210, 212, 226, 227–28, 228–29, 231–32
obstacles and traps, 103, 110–12
Offer, A., 201–2
Oince: Archidamos invades via, 133, 150; Athenian garrison, 90, 92, 99, 151, 162; location, 89n, 133n
older people, 114, 116, 120
Old Testament, 5n, 11n, 50
olive trees: 55–68, 221–23; burning, 58–60; cutting, 60–63, 65–67, 193; difficulty of destroying, xiii, 14, 56, 146, 148, 157n, 182; girdling trunk, 62–63, 137; grafting, 61–62, 65–67; harvest season, 39; propagation, 65–66n; regeneration, 59–60, 63–67, 174, 222–23; sacred, 165, 145–46, 152, 157–58, 236–37, 240–41; survival in Peloponnesian War, 143–46, 149, 152, 157–60; time from planting to production, 222–23; uprooting, 14, 56–58, 65n;

—, laws against, 57, 64, 157–58, 240–41
Olynthos, 20, 58, 111, 124
Oneion, Mt., 98
Ormerod, A.A., 190n
Oropos, 89, 92, 93, 133, 162
Osborne, Robin, x, 212, 214–15, 217, 225, 240
Oxyrhynchus Historian, 139, 147, 237–38. *See also* Index Locorum (Hellenica Oxyrhynchia)

Pagai, 29n, 93
Panakton, 89, 92–93, 98, 99, 164n, 151
Paralos, 135, 138, 163
Parke, W.W., 81n, 95n, 157n, 169n
Parnes, Mt., 45, 84, 133
Pausanias, 247. *See also* Index Locorum
Pecírka, J., 44n, 45n, 46n, 71n, 85n, 169n
Pélékidis, C., 91n, 96n
Peloponnesian Wars: First, 93–94, 101; Second, xii-xiii, 15; —, aftermath, 86, 165n, 166–71, 238, 244–46 (*see also* Archidamian War; Dekeleian War; Plataia (siege of); and under Athens; Pericles; Sparta; Thebes)
peltasts, 9, 20, 23, 95, 101, 127
Pericles: political embarrassment if farm spared, 150, 208; rebuilds wall across Thracian Chersonese, 80; strategy in Peloponnesian War, 81, 118n, 231–33; Thucydidean speeches, 64, 91, 232
peripoloi, 24n, 91
Persia: invasions of Greece 26, 27, 183, 204–5, 249; —, evacuation in face of, 114, 116, 207; war against Skythians, 118–19
Petain, Henri Philippe Omer, 81n
Phainippos, estate of, 43n, 48n
phalanx. *See* hoplites
Pharsalos, 124

Philip II, king of Macedon, 97n, 99–100
Philippson, A., 89n, 190n
phlegô, 193
Phleious, 52, 124
Phokion, 226
Phokis, 110
Phormisios, 169
phrouria, 112
Phrygia, Attica, 125, 133
phtheirô, 185, 187, 188–89, 194
Phyle, 98, 100, 113, 168
pimprêmi, 193
Pinari Valley, 44n
Piraeus, 113
Piraion peninsula, 115
plagues: xiii; at Athens, 135, 149, 153, 156, 172, 244
Plakoto, 99
Plataia: battle of, 183; evacuation, 33n, 107, 116; rural farmhouses near, 46; Spartan siege, 9, 26n, 31, 33n, 107, 116, 175, 208; social cohesion, 208; Theban attack, 46, 175, 186
Plato, 75. *See also* Index Locorum
Pleistoanax, 133n
plundering: of Attica, in Dekeleian War, 110, 121, 139, 153, 154, 155, 160, 161, 163, 172, 183; diminishes mobility of invaders, 127; *epiteichismos* as base, 29; of farmhouses, 73, 127, 139, 155, 161, 163, 187, 188–89; Hellenistic Age, 105–6, 184; and ravaging: —, combined, 24, 34n, 127, 153, 184, 190, 191; —, as distinct, xiii, 14, 15, 34n, 187–88, 209–10; vocabulary of, 185–94, 209, 249, 250
Plutarch, 247. *See also* Index Locorum
Polemaios, 84
political life: 4th-century changes, 235, 242–43, 248. *See also* councils, agrarian; hoplites (political and social role)

Pomeroy, S., 222–23, 237, 242
portheô, 185, 187, 187–88, 189, 194, 251
Pouilloux, J., 90n, 162n
Prasiai, 37
prices, 144n, 165n
Priest's House, Zoster, 46, 72n, 164n
Princess Tower, Attica, 164n
Pritchett, K.K.: x–xi, 22n, 26n, 33n, 43n, 87n, 95n, 106n, 107n, 108n, 109n, 141n, 144n, 147n, 150n, 165n, 203, 225, 229, 230, 245; on vocabulary of plundering, 209, 249, 250
property: destruction of own, *see* scorched earth policy; evacuation of, 103–10, 113, 116, 120, 160, 229
props, vine, 146–47, 177
protection, military. *See* military organization
psychological effects: of evacuation and dislocation, 136, 152–53, 207; of devastation, 71, 81, 154, 172, 213, 216–17; of freedom from violation, 180, 249
Punic War, Second, 250
purkaïai, 59
Pylos, 29n, 136, 149

Rackman, O., 214, 221, 248–49
Rahe, P., 231
Rapp, G., 50n, 55n, 61n, 66n, 148n
ravaging. *See* economic motivation of ravaging; fortifications, rural; implements; light-armed troops; military organization; plundering; ritualization of ravaging; Ten Thousand, march of
refuge, places of, 79, 103, 112–16, 120, 225, 230
refugee shelters, Athens, 170–71
regeneration, 135. *See also* olive trees; trees; vines
regional considerations, 36, 51, 220
rental agreements, 10, 27n, 55n, 176, 188
residence, rural, 44–48, 214–15, 235

resiliency of preindustrial farming,
176–77, 182, 184n
restraint, reciprocal, 11–13, 75
retaliation, 15. *See also* sorties
retreats, military, 110–11, 117n
Rhamnous: 135, 164; Athenian
garrison, 90, 100, 105, 113, 162
Rheneia, 46
Rhodes, J.J., 236
Rhoiteion, 186
Rich, J., and Shipley, G., xi
ritualization of ravaging, 181–82, 184
rituals of warfare. *See* hoplites (protocols)
Roman period, 9, 25, 247–48, 249–50
roofing, 73, 109–10, 139, 155
Roux, J., 107–8
Rowlands, J.J., 11n
Roy, J., 215
Roymans, N., 250
Runnels, N.N., 248. *See also* Jameson,
M.H.
Russia, modern, 117n, 178n

Sackett, H.H. *See* Jones, E.E.
Sage, M., 210
Ste. Croix, G.E.M. de, 43n, 48n, 93, 94n
Salamis: 91, 114, 116, 163; battle of, 183
Salganeos; Antiforitis Wall, 84, 85, 87
Sallares, R., x, 245
Salmon, T.T., 28n, 153n
Samson, 50
Saracens, 58n
Sardis reed dwellings, 72
Sargon II, king of Assyria, 4–5, 52n,
69n, 73n
Sarpaki, A., 219
scorched earth policy, 33n, 51n, 52–53,
103, 117–20, 188
seaborne attacks, 21, 26, 37, 90–91, 124
seasonal considerations: 32–40,
212–13; hoplites' own harvests, 36,
41, 135, 149, 220; limit damage in
Peloponnesian War, 135, 136,
148–49, 152; seaborne attacks, 37;

spring campaigns, 32–36, 39, 50–51,
52, 106, 136, 212–13, 219; summer
campaigns, 36–38; and vine harvest,
38, 152; winter campaigns, 38–39,
40. *See also* grain
Semple, E.C., 45n
settlement pattern, 44–48, 214–15,
235, 249
Shear, L.L., 104n, 49n
Shenandoah Valley, 37n, 50n
Sheridan, General H.H., 37n, 50n
Sherman, General T.T., 20n, 53n,
117n
shipborne attacks. *See* seaborne attacks
Shipley, G., xi, 205
Sicily, 116. *See also* Syracuse
Sidebottom, H., 250
siegecraft: xiii, 26n; 4th-century development, 9, 81; ineffectiveness, 8, 33n,
93, 120
sinomai, 190
Sitalkes, king of Odrysai, 38
skeuagôgeô, 104
Skolos, 87n
Skourta Plain project, 234
Skydsgaard, E.E., x, 214, 224, 229, 236
Skythians, 118–19
slaves: desertion, xiii, 29, 238 (*see also*
Dekeleian War); evacuation, 114,
115–16, 120, 174; hoplite attendants,
22–23, 212; plundering of, 163; use
in warfare, 9
slingers, 23
Snodgrass, M.M., x, 216
Socrates, 11, 94
soils, 220, 248
Solbrig, O. and D., 223
solidarity, social, 180, 208–9
Sollion, 37
Sophocles, 158–59, 241–42. *See also*
Index Locorum
sorties: 122–28, 148n, 166, 174, 182,
230–31; bases, 82, 83, 89, 151, 152.
See also cavalry

Sounion: 44n, 135, 164; garrison, 90, 100, 113, 162
sources, limitations of, 13–14
Soviet Union, 178n
sowing time, 55
Sparta: Corinthian peltasts defeat, 101; field camps, 27; Second Messenian War, 12; in Peloponnesian War, 36n, 38, 91, 101, 121 (*see also* Archidamian War; Dekeleian War; Plataia); Theban wars, 4th-century 39n, 95–96, 101, 124–25, 161, 183
Spartolos, 23, 35n
Spence, G.G., 210–11, 212–13, 219, 231, 232
Sphakteria, 23
Sphodrias, 100
Standish, R., 55n, 56–57, 58n, 60, 65, 66n
Stanford Skourta Plain project, 234
Stesichorus, 10
Strabo, 247
strategy, change in, 153, 184. *See also* defensive strategy
Stratos, 80n
Strauss, B., 244
strongholds, isolated, 112–13
stubble, burning of, 50n
sulaô, 190
supply: military, 33–34, 35, 106, 118, 161; —, seasonal considerations, 33–34, 35, 133, 135, 136, 149; urban, 29. *See also* food, stored; imports
Suto, Y., 215
Syracuse: 86, 124–25; Athenian expedition, 26, 27, 33n, 109, 110–11

tactical use of devastation. *See* battle
Tanagra, battle of, 93
Taochians, 112
Tarn, W.W., 85n, 81n
taxation, xiii, 16, 156, 234, 246, 247, 248
technology of warfare, 205, 246. *See also* siegecraft
Teleutias, 20, 58, 111

temnô, 60n, 61, 63, 134, 186, 188, 189, 190–91, 191–92, 193, 194, 251
temples, 12, 244
Ten Thousand, march of: ravaging and plundering, 30–31, 107, 109, 191; reactions to approach, 95, 110, 112, 119. *See also* Index Locorum (Xenophon; *Anabasis*)
Termessos; Kapikaya field wall, 85
terraces, 43, 44n, 48, 54, 144n, 214, 218
terrain: 6, 9, 87, 100, 217–18, 220; and defense, 97; and difficulty of devastation, 48, 61, 127, 147–48, 166; and success of cavalry sorties, 127. *See also* marginal land
Thebes: hoplites' ascendancy, 101, 211; in Peloponnesian War, 25, 92–93, 94, 139, 155, 175, 186; Spartan wars, 4th-century, 39n, 87, 95–96, 101, 124–25, 161, 183, 229; —, invasions of Peloponnese, 20, 24, 26, 39, 83, 87, 96, 117, 180n, 183, 211; stockade round crops, 82–83, 84n, 87, 96, 227
Themistocles, Decree of, 114n, 116
Thermopylai, 79n
Thesaurus Linguae Graecae, x
Thespiai, 20, 96
Thessaly, 9, 110, 124, 125
thetes, 244
Thirty Tyrants, 91, 126n, 156, 168, 172
Thisbe, 96
Thorikos, 90, 97, 113, 162, 163
Thorion, 37
Thrace: 38, 105, 112, 161n, 189; wall across Thracian Chersonesos, 80, 87
threat of devastation, effect of, 38, 70, 179–80
threshing floors, 37, 144n
Thriasian Plain, 125, 133, 138, 147n
Thucydides: 131, 207; on Archidamian War, 132–36, 138–39, 147, 152, 233; on Dekeleian War, 153, 154, 160, 172. *See also* Index Locorum
tiles, 73, 109–10, 139, 155

Todd, C.C., 236
tools. *See* implements
topography. *See* terrain
towers, farm and hilltop, 46, 74–75, 99, 144n, 225–26
Toynbee, Arnold, 249–50
trampling: fodder crops, 32; grain, 16, 30, 32, 35–36, 51, 52–54; vines, 32, 68, 69
transport, military, 31, 32, 40, 51
traps and obstacles, 103, 110–12
treaties, 10, 92–93
trees: cutting for military use, 25–26, 27, 31, 40, 111; difficulty of destruction, 16, 32, 59, 174, 221–22; fruit, other than olive, 49, 56n, 218–19, 221; girdling, 62–63, 137; survival and regeneration, 59–60, 63–67, 142, 172, 174, 177, 222–23, 249; up-rooting, 32, 221–22. *See also* olive trees
Troizen, 114
Tuplin, C., 251

uprooting: xi; trees, 14, 32, 56–58, 65n, 221–22; —, laws against, 57, 64, 157–58, 240–41; vines, 32, 69

van Andel, T.H., 248. *See also* Jameson, M.H.
Vanderpool, E., 99n, 133nn, 164n, 226
van Rooy, A.A., 162n
Vari farmhouse, 45, 72n
Varnava, 89n, 99
vegetables, 49
Veith, G., 25n, 122n
villages, 37, 47–48
Villia, 133n
vines: 68–71, 223–24; cutting, 27, 32, 39, 68, 69; density, 69–70; difficulty of destroying, xiii, 16, 70, 71, 148, 174, 182, 224; harvest season, 38, 39; methods of devastation, 32, 39, 68–71; propping, 27, 68n, 146–47,

177; regeneration, 70, 71, 174, 224; stakes planted among, 111–12, 136; survival in Peloponnesian War, 142, 146–47, 149, 160, 168, 172
violation, freedom from, 180, 249
vocabulary of devastation, 185–94, 250–51
Vouliagmeni area, 46

wagons, military use of, 31, 40, 51
Wallace, P.P., 89n
walls: city, 85, 86; —, open space within, 80, 115, 227; field, xiv, 43–44, 79–88, 101, 226–27; —, Theban stockade, 82–83, 87, 96, 227
warfare: centrality to Greek life, 1–4, 16; material conditions, 1–2, 4. *See also* Archidamian War; Athens; fourth century; Hebrew warfare; Hellenistic Age; hoplites and hoplite warfare; modern warfare; slaves; technology of warfare
waters, pollution of, 230, 118, 119
Watrous, V.V., 43n, 44n, 45n, 46n, 147n
Watson, J.J., 219
Waziristan, 73n, 74
wealth, growing disparity in, 248
Wells, B., x
Westlake, D.D., 33n, 37n, 54n, 143n, 154n
wheat, 32, 49n, 219, 220
White, D.D., 44n, 49n, 50n, 61n, 66n, 68n, 69n, 148n
Whitehead, David, xiv, 229–30
wine vats, 109, 123n, 177
Winter, E.E., 80n, 81n, 85n, 86n
winter campaigns, 38–39, 40
women and children, 114, 116, 120
Wood, M.M., 247–48
woodwork, domestic: plundering of, 139, 155, 163; removed on evacuation, 108–9, 110, 120, 138, 151, 177, 229
World Wars, 20th-century, 117n, 201–2
Worley, J.J., 231

Wrede, W., 98n, 99n

Xenophon: on Isomachos, 169–70, 242–43; on 4th-century polis, 242–43; suggestion for stronghold in southern Attica, 97, 113

Young, John, 44n, 46n, 74, 164n, 225

Zimmern, A., 49n, 56n, 59n, 65n, 135n, 145n, 147n, 159n

Zoster; Priest's House, 46, 72n, 164n

Index Locorum

AENEAS TACTICUS

On the Defense of Fortified Positions
2.6: 127
7.1: 106
8.3–4: 117
8.4: 110, 119n
9.1: 97
10.1: 115
10.3: 106, 112n
16.4–7: 21, 123, 127, 186
16.16–19: 97
16.20: 127
21.1: 117
28.3: 106

AESCHINES
1.81–83: 171
2.115: 119n
2.147: 155n
3.123: 72n
1.105: 47
3.80: 103

ANDOCIDES
1.101: 154, 155n, 191
3.8: 143n

Frag. 3.1 [Loeb]: 80n, 115, 165n

ANDROTION
FGrH 324F39: 145
FGrH 324F55: 165n

ANTHOLOGIA PALATINA
7.254: 125n
12.205.4 (Strato): 112

ARISTOPHANES
Acharnians
32–39: 136
35: 144
71–72: 136
164: 187
182–183: 69, 136
183: 192
228–30: 111
231–232: 136
232: 68
232 (Schol): 111
247–251: 136
512: 69, 136
544–554: 142n
550: 144
985–986: 137n, 146

ARISTOPHANES (*continued*)
987: 70
994–999: 136
1049–1054: 136
1071ff.: 92
1089–1093: 140
1128: 141, 144
1178: 111n

Birds
617: 144
1589: 141

Clouds
7: 116n
56–59: 141
1005: 145n
1119–1125: 142
1486–1500: 73

Ecclesiazusae
243–44: 171
308, 743, 744, 817: 160
Frogs
988: 144, 160
995: 144

Knights
20ff.: 116n
225: 125n
792–793: 153
792–794: 136
806: 140–41
1076–1077: 70, 137n

Lysistrata
55ff.: 162–63
255: 59, 160
267: 59
308: 160
555: 154
1146: 156
1203–1204: 156

Peace
319–320: 68
335–336: 136
439–453: 136
451: 116n
520–526: 136
550–581: 136
552: 151
557–563: 142, 143n
566–567: 106
570: 142
590ff.: 142n
596–597: 136
612–614: 137n
628–629: 137, 143n
631 (Schol): 103
632–640: 136
634: 70
636ff.: 136
706–708: 136
746–747: 63, 137
774: 136
990–995: 136
999–1002: 142n
1127–1139: 136
1249: 142n
1263: 147
1318: 107n, 151
1320–1325: 142
1326: 137n
Plutus
262–263: 156
535ff.: 156
798: 141n, 160

Thesmophoriazusae
420: 160
495: 154
Wasps
252: 141
264–265: 142n
274: 141n
302: 141n
450: 142n, 144
1200: 146n

1268: 141
Fragments
107 (Kock): 136n
109 (Kock): 136n, 142
363, 364, 400 (Kock): 136n

ARISTOTLE
Athenaion Politeia
16.6: 218
27.2: 154
33.7: 154n
60.2: 146n

Politics
7.5.2: 97
7.10.2: 97
7.1326a23–25: 204

Rhetoric
1.4.10: 97
2.21.8: 10
3.11.6: 10

[ARISTOTLE]
Oeconomica
1.1343b5–7: 203

ARRIAN
Anabasis
1.4.1–2: 30n, 53
1.10.2: 103
1.12.9: 50n, 51n, 52n, 120
1.12.10: 72n
1.26.6: 112n
3.28.8: 120, 188
3.30.10: 22, 125n

Indica
8.11.9: 13
Tactica
2.1: 23n

COLUMELLA
5.9.15: 64n
11.3.2: 44n

DANIEL
Byzantinische Zeitschrift Ä 26 [1926]:
290–314, 1.123: 10n

DEMOSTHENES
9.47–50: 81n
9.48: 204
13.32: 12n
14.30: 119n
18.31: 155n
18.37–38: 100n, 113n
18.262: 160
21.157–158: 47
23.212: 12n
24.128: 154
24.197: 108
29.3: 72n, 108, 109
43: 158
43.69: 57, 241
43.69–70: 158
43.71: 57, 64
47: 75
47.53–56: 75, 107
47.63: 75
50.61: 119n
53.15–17: 60n, 63, 66n, 69
55: 158
55.3: 158
55.11: 45
55.12: 44n
55.14: 158
55.26: 158
57.45: 168

DEMADES
14: 115

DEUTERONOMY
20:19–20: 11n

DIO CHRYSOSTOM
1.75.3: 218

DIODORUS
2.36.6–7: 13, 188, 193

DIODORUS (*continued*)
9.37.2: 218
12.34: 187
12.42.2: 112n
12.42.6: 91n
12.42ff.: 143n
12.43.2: 72n
12.45.1: 72n, 134n, 146, 150n, 193
12.45.2: 153
12.50.5: 104, 112
12.58.4: 150n
12.78.2: 72n, 107
13.52.4: 164
13.72.2ff.: 155n, 162, 166n
13.72.4: 22
13.72ff.: 126n
13.81.3: 104, 112n
13.89.2–3: 116
13.103.2: 154
13.108.5: 26n
13.108.7: 127
13.110.3: 26n
13.111.3: 116
14.17.11: 12n
14.18ff.: 86
14.58.3: 72n, 76n
14.62.5: 34n, 193
14.76: 12n
14.90.7: 193
14.97.5: 107, 193
14.100.2: 194
15.4.1: 187
15.32.2–3: 83n
15.63.2: 10
15.65.2: 39
15.65.5: 34n, 191
15.68.2–5: 79n, 83
16.56.2: 50
17.18.2: 120
19.77.4: 84
20.32.2: 188, 189
31.46: 12n

EUPOLIS
F341 (Kock): 91

EURIPIDES
Bacchae
751–758: 107–8

Hercules Furens
157–163: 204
Rhesus
510–517: 204

FRONTINUS

Strategematica
3.7: 119n

HERODOTUS
1.17: 47, 71n
1.17.1: 34
1.17.2: 34, 109, 188
1.17.3: 75–76
1.19: 50
1.19.1: 34–35
1.76.1: 190
1.84.5: 187
1.162.2: 187
1.164: 114n, 116
1.166: 114n, 116
1.190.2: 49n
3.58: 187n
4.46: 119n
4.120: 119n
4.120.1: 118–19
4.127: 119n
4.140: 119n
4.148.4: 187
5.29: 170n
5.34: 112n
5.34.1: 104
5.63.4: 110n
5.74.2: 133n
5.101.1: 72
6.36–37: 80
6.75.3: 12n
6.100: 114n
6.102: 110n
6.135.2: 190

7.9.2: 204
7.133.2: 191
7.176.4–5: 79n
8.4: 116
8.28: 110
8.32: 12n
8.32.2: 194
8.33: 114, 190
8.36: 114, 116
8.40.2: 79n
8.41: 114n, 116
8.50.2: 190
8.55: 59
8.60: 114n, 116
8.71: 79n
8.109: 150n
8.142: 150n
9.7: 79n
9.13.3: 102n, 110n
9.15: 87n
9.15.2: 27
9.73: 133, 150n
9.86.2: 190, 191
9.97: 26n
9.99: 26n
9.120: 12n

HELLENICA OXYRHYNCHIA
12.4: 104n, 108n, 110n, 115n, 139,
    144n, 153, 155, 161
12.5: 47, 71n, 139, 144n, 153, 163, 234,
    237–8

HESIOD
Works and Days
385: 49n
614: 49n
640: 218

HOMER
Iliad
18.68–69: 203
Odyssey
4.757: 218
18.357–365: 218

18.358–359: 44n
24.205–207: 218
24.212: 218

INSCRIPTIONES GRAECAE
I2.76.59–61: 145n
II2.334.10–13: 105
II2.411.34–37: 10, 55n
II2.650.16–19: 104n
II2.682.35–36: 10, 105
II2.1241.4–17: 27n
II2.1299: 10, 99n, 105
II2.1303–1305: 99n
II2.1631.407–409: 32n
II2.2971: 99n

V.2: 10, 55n, 188
V.6: 10, 55n, 188

XII.9.191: 10, 55n

ISAEUS
5.11: 23n
5.22: 167
5.43–44: 167
9.28: 170n

ISOCRATES
4.144: 25
8.83ff.: 155n
8.92: 155
14.31: 10, 155n
16.13: 50, 167, 188
52: 47

ISTROS
FGrH 334F30: 134n, 145, 150n

JUDGES
15:4.5: 5n, 50

JUSTINUS
Epitome
3.7.5–6: 143n
5.10.12: 155n

KINGS
2:3.19: 11n

LIVY
35.5.5–12: 26n

LYCURGUS
Against Leocrates
14–16: 112n, 116Ô
44: 27
47: 187n
120: 154

LYSIAS
1.11: 45
2.44–45: 79n
7: 59, 163n
7.2: 236
7.4: 165
7.4ff.: 164
7.5: 236
7.6–8: 57
7.6: 143n, 155, 157, 190, 192
7.7: 58, 63, 64, 146n, 157
7.8: 165
7.9–10: 167
7.11: 236
7.14: 236, 237
7.15: 236
7.17: 236
7.24: 58, 157
7.25: 64, 157
7.26: 57, 146n, 157
7.28: 44n
12.40: 91
14.33: 60n
14.35: 91
16.16: 95
17.5: 167
18.9: 154
19.31: 108
20.28: 161n
20.33: 155n
31.18: 155n

ONASANDER
6.11: 188, 194
6.12: 34n
6.13: 27
10.8: 21
27: 20n

PAUSANIAS
1.27.2: 59
1.29.6: 125n
3.7.10: 143n, 186
3.8.6: 155n
4.7.1–2: 12, 60n, 76n
7.6.7: 79n

PHILOCHOROS
FGrH 328F125: 145
FGrH 328F169: 165n

PLATO
Laws
706B–C: 204
761A: 186
778D: 100

Meno
242C: 155n
Republic
5.470A–471B: 11, 75, 190, 194

PLINY
Historia Naturalis
15.2: 66
17.241: 59

PLUTARCH
Agesilaus
31.1–2: 24, 34n, 180n
33.8: 39
Agis
15.2: 40n
Alcibiades
14.1: 90n
14.4: 93

15.7: 5n
34.3: 163n, 166n
Cimon
10.1: 44n
Cleomenes 6.3: 110n
25.4: 34n, 53n
26.1: 30, 53, 187n
Lysander
13.3: 171n
27: 155n
Moralia
15E–F: 69n
94E: 112
190A: 204
193E17: 10, 192
210E27: 204
212E: 204
215D: 204
221F6: 204
470F: 141
Pericles
9.2: 44n
19.1–2: 80
33.3: 143n
33.4: 64n
34.2: 36n
Philopoemen
13.1: 80n, 112n
Phocion
12.3: 23n
Solon
23.5–6: 56n
23.7: 218
Themistocles
10.4: 116
10.5: 116
Theseus
32.3: 150–51n

POLLUX
Onomasticon
1.174: 60n, 193
1.225: 112
10.131: 111

POLYAENUS
Strategemata
1.32.3: 47, 61, 72n
1.36.1: 143n
1.36.2: 150n
1.38.5: 61
1.39.2: 110
2.1.1: 55n
2.1.10: 56
2.1.21: 26
2.1.26: 69
2.10.3: 208
3.9.8: 61
3.9.18: 61
3.10.5: 12n, 63, 76n
4.3.15: 150n
4.6.20: 35n, 55n
23: 208

POLYBIUS
2.32.4: 34n, 188, 191
2.65.6: 96
3.92.8: 189n
4.3.10: 47, 186, 192n
4.45.7: 34n, 40n, 189
4.67.1–2: 188
4.73.5: 191
4.73ff.: 113
5.11.3–4: 12n
5.19.8: 50n
9.6.8: 72n, 107
9.28.6: 194
10.30.2: 111
13.3.2–4: 204
16.24.7–8: 34n, 189n
18.2: 12n
18.3.3: 204
18.6.4: 63, 65n
18.18: 26n
21.10.12–13: 34n
21.11: 12n
23.15: 11–12, 188, 189
32.27: 12n

PROCOPIUS
De Aedificiis
4.10.5: 81n

REG
39 [1926] 354–366: 23n

SOPHOCLES
Oedipus at Colonus
694ff.: 64, 158–59, 241–42
1319: 191
STRATO
Anth. Pal.
12.205.4: 112

SUDA
s.v. *skolops:* 111n

*SUPPLEMENTUM EPIGRAPHICUM
    GRAECUM*
21 [1966] 644.13–14: 10, 176, 188
21 [1966] 644.16: 104n
24 [1969] 151.18: 10, 176, 188
24 [1969] 154.8–11: 105

*SYLLOGE INSCRIPTIONUM GRAE-
    CARUM3* (Dittenberger)
229: 114n
966.12–14: 10, 55n, 176, 188

THEOCRITUS
1.47: 44n

THEOPHRASTUS
Historia Plantarum
2.5.6: 56n
4.13.5: 56n
4.15.1: 63
4.15.2: 63

THUCYDIDES
1.15: 204
1.30.2: 191
1.65.2: 191

1.73.4: 187n
1.81.1: 233
1.82.3–6: 150
1.83.2: 204
1.89.3: 104n
1.103.5: 46
1.106.1: 127
1.107.3: 93
1.108.2: 193
1.111: 124
1.114.2: 133n
1.139.2: 12n
1.141–142: 204
1.141.3: 36n, 149
1.141.5: 36n, 203
1.142.4: 164n, 175
1.142.7: 36n
1.143.5: 118, 192
2.2.1: 46
2.5.4: 46, 104n, 112n, 186
2.5.5: 46, 186
2.5.7: 46
2.6.4: 116
2.10.1: 149
2.11–12: 150
2.11.3: 19–20
2.11.6–8: 150, 188
2.12.5: 175
2.13.1–3: 208
2.13.1: 150n, 192, 208
2.13.2: 151
2.13.6: 91n, 151n
2.13.8: 125n
2.14.1: 107, 108, 115, 138, 151
2.14.2: 47, 104n, 163
2.16: 207
2.16.1: 179
2.16.2: 47
2.17ff.: 153
2.18: 92, 148n
2.18ff.: 150
2.18.1: 151n
2.18.2: 90n
2.18.4: 133, 138, 151

2.18.5: 150
2.19.1: 132
2.19.2: 25, 92, 125, 133, 134
2.19.2: 151n, 251
2.19.4: 134
2.20: 133, 150
2.20.2: 150
2.20.4: 134
2.21.2–5: 142
2.21.2: 134, 150
2.21.3: 134, 150
2.22.2–3: 125n
2.22.2: 22, 125, 134, 149n, 186–87
2.22.3: 151
2.23.1: 133, 134
2.23.3: 133, 134, 149
2.24.1: 91n
2.25.1–5: 37n
2.25.1: 187
2.25.2: 125n
2.26.1–2: 37n
2.30.1–2: 37n
2.31.1: 36n
2.31.2: 21
2.32: 29n, 187
2.47: 134
2.52.1: 153
2.55: 138
2.55.1: 134
2.56.1–6: 37n
2.56.4: 191
2.56.6: 187, 191
2.57.1: 134, 149
2.57.2: 133n, 134, 138
2.62.2: 47
2.62.3: 134
2.65.2: 134, 138
2.71.1: 135n, 149, 208
2.71.4: 151n, 186, 189
2.72.3: 175
2.73.1: 190
2.75: 31
2.75.1: 60n
2.75.2: 61

2.79.1: 35n
2.79.2: 50
2.80.8: 187
2.93.4: 187
2.93–94: 91n
2.95–101: 38
2.98.1: 61
2.101.3: 191
2.113–115: 233
3.1.1–3: 126
3.1.2: 22, 25, 135, 149n, 151, 187
3.1.3: 135, 149
3.7.3: 187n
3.15.1: 135
3.15.2: 36n, 149
3.16.1–2: 135
3.16.2: 187n
3.26.3: 65, 70n, 134, 135, 138,
    146n, 192n
3.26.4: 135, 149
3.26.53: 175n
3.33.2: 187
3.34: 29n
3.51.1–2: 29n
3.57.2: 187
3.65.2: 175
3.68.3: 107
3.70.4: 146n
3.81.5: 12n
3.87.2: 153
3.88.1: 38, 119n
3.88.2: 45
3.88.4: 181
3.89.1: 135, 149
3.91.3: 181n
3.91.5: 25
3.97.2–3: 95
3.98.4: 95, 204
3.102.2: 191
3.112.6: 127
4.2.1: 25, 135
4.3: 29n
4.6.1: 35, 136, 149n
4.6.2: 133n, 136, 149

THUCYDIDES (*continued*)
4.25.8: 112n, 191
4.40.2: 204
4.41.1: 149
4.45.1: 25
4.45.2: 29n
4.52.2–3: 186
4.53.3: 187
4.54.4: 25
4.55.2: 124
4.56.1: 21
4.57.3: 187, 188
4.66: 36n
4.66.1: 29n
4.69.2: 26n, 60n, 61
4.76: 93
4.76.5: 29n
4.84: 208
4.84.1–2: 38, 70
4.87.2: 70
4.88: 208
4.88.1–2: 38, 70
4.90.2–4: 32n
4.90.2: 27, 75
4.94.1: 24
4.96.7: 89
4.97.2–4: 12n
4.104.1: 46
4.130.1: 191
5.3.3: 151n
5.3.5: 90n
5.14.1–4: 139n
5.18.7: 92
5.23.1–2: 10
5.39–46: 90n
5.47.3–4: 10
5.55.4: 175
5.64.5: 25, 31, 36n
5.72.3: 31
5.84.3: 186
5.115.4: 104
6.7.1: 38, 51, 54, 175, 186, 191
6.37.2: 125n
6.49.3: 104n, 128

6.66.2: 26n, 61
6.91.7: 29n
6.91ff.: 160
6.94.1–2: 51
6.99.1: 26n
6.99.3: 27, 61
6.101.3: 109
7.4.6: 187
7.10.1: 153n
7.18.4: 153
7.19.1: 161n
7.19.2: 153n, 160n, 166n, 187
7.27–28: 29n
7.27.2: 161n
7.27.3: 153, 161, 166n
7.27.4: 138–39, 149n, 161
7.27.5: 110n, 115n, 126, 154n, 161, 238
7.27: 172
7.27ff.: 121, 154, 160
7.28.1: 89, 154n
7.28.2: 154
7.29.4: 187
7.49.2: 34n, 187
7.73.1: 111
7.74.2: 111
7.75.5: 23
7.78.4: 119n
7.78.5: 111
7.84.2ff.: 119n
8.4: 90n
8.24.3: 189
8.24.4: 190
8.38.2: 29n
8.40.2: 116n, 187
8.41.2: 22, 114n
8.57.1: 187
8.60: 89
8.60.1: 92, 162
8.69.1: 154
8.71.1–3: 126n, 166n
8.71ff.: 162
8.95: 90
8.95.1–3: 89, 154n

8.98.1: 154
8.98.2: 92, 153, 162, 166n
13.85.2–4: 29n

TOD, *Greek Historical Inscriptions*
2:189–190: 114n

TYRTAEUS
19.16: 203

XENOPHON
Agesilaus
1.20: 12n, 187
1.30: 125n
2.17: 190
2.18: 115
2.22: 83, 190
2.23: 190
7.4: 187
Anabasis
1.3.14: 95
1.5.12: 30–31
1.6.1: 50n, 119
2.2.16: 108
2.3.10: 110
3.4.24–29: 95
3.4.37–49: 95
4.1–5: 47
4.1.8: 107, 114n, 116
4.1.20: 95
4.2.19: 72n
4.2.22: 109
4.7.1: 104, 112
4.7.17: 104
4.7.20: 194
4.8.2: 61
4.8.8–19: 95
4.8.8: 61
5.2.3: 119
5.2.24–25: 72
5.5.7: 191
5.5.11: 191
5.6.7: 95
6.1.1: 125n

6.2.8: 112n
6.3.19: 21n
6.4.24–25: 125n
6.6.7: 116
7.4.1: 72n
7.4.5: 54, 72n
Cyropaedia
3.2.4: 97
5.2.2: 112n, 115
6.1.14: 97
6.2.34–36: 31
Hellenica
1.1.33: 125n, 126n, 162, 166n
1.1.35: 55n, 153n, 160
1.2.1: 90n
1.2.2: 190
1.2.2–3: 22
1.2.4: 47
1.2.4–5: 50n
1.2.14: 154
1.3.22: 154
1.7.28: 90n
2.2.2: 171n
2.2.9: 190
2.3.3: 153
2.3.9: 168n
2.4.1: 168
2.4.2: 98n
2.4.3: 168n
2.4.4: 168
2.4.26: 126n, 168
3.1.3: 190
3.2.2–3: 25
3.2.8: 55n
3.2.10–11: 80
3.2.26: 34n, 194n
3.2.27: 190
3.4.22: 125n
3.5.5: 155n, 161
4.1.1: 187n
4.1.17: 125n
4.1.33: 63, 194n
4.2.14–16: 95
4.2.15: 190

XENOPHON (*continued*)
4.3.15: 95
4.4.1: 95, 191
4.4.19: 175, 190
4.5.1: 115
4.5.10: 58, 60n, 65n, 175n, 194n
4.6.4–5: 114n, 181n
4.6.4–14: 128
4.6.4: 112n, 115, 191
4.6.5: 56n
4.6.7–11: 95
4.6.12: 56n, 194n
4.6.13–14: 55n, 95, 181n
4.7.1: 49n, 50
4.7.5: 175
4.8.7: 187
4.8.18–19: 125n
4.8.30: 186
5.2.4: 181n
5.2.7: 45
5.2.38: 27
5.2.39: 20, 58, 60n, 111, 194n
5.2.43: 60n
5.3.1–2: 124
5.3.3: 65n, 175n
5.3.18: 50
5.3.21: 49n
5.3.26: 49n
5.4.3: 45
5.4.14: 95, 99n
5.4.20–21: 47n, 100, 187
5.4.35–37: 96
5.4.38–42: 83n
5.4.38: 26, 190
5.4.39: 125n
5.4.42: 20, 22, 34n, 187
5.4.47–49: 96
5.4.49: 83, 87n
5.4.54: 83n
5.4.56: 49n
5.4.59: 96
5.4.63: 96n
6.2.5ff.: 121
6.2.6: 47, 109, 123n

6.2.7: 55n
6.2.8: 55n
6.4.4–5: 96
6.5.7: 211
6.5.15: 107, 188
6.5.20: 39
6.5.22: 39, 60n
6.5.24: 96
6.5.27–28: 107
6.5.27: 187, 188
6.5.28: 47n, 72n
6.5.30: 26, 47n, 60n, 107
6.5.37: 34n, 39n2, 47n, 63, 72n
6.5.50: 39, 117
7.1.20–22: 125
7.1.20: 20, 188
7.1.35: 190
7.2.4: 124, 175, 188
7.2.10: 52
7.2.17: 49n
7.2.18: 116
7.4.21: 181n
7.5.14–15: 45, 128
7.14.17: 182
Hiero
10.5–6: 82n, 97
Hipparchus
4.6: 127
7.4: 126, 161n
7.6: 106
7.7–10: 123
8.3: 110n, 127
9.3: 125n
Lacedaimonion Politeia
11.2: 31
12.5: 27
Memorabilia
2.1.13: 11, 53n, 60n, 192, 193
2.8.3: 167
3.1.7: 72n
3.5.4: 155n
3.5.25–27: 94
Oeconomicus
5.5, 7, 14: 203

6.6–7: 81n, 100
6.17: 242–43
18.2: 50n
20.22–26: 169
De Vectigalibus (Poroi)
2.6: 171
3.13: 171
4.25: 154n
4.43–49: 97, 113

4.45: 54
4.47: 126
4.48: 125n
4.52: 82n, 97

[Xenophon]
Athenaion Politeia
2.14: 150, 190, 194
2.16: 190

Compositor: Impressions Book and Journal Services, Inc.
Printer: Edwards Bros.
Binder: Edwards Bros.
Text: 10/15 Janson
Display: Janson